BETWEEN

NATION

AND

STATE

Pitt Series in Russian and East European Studies

Jonathan Harris, Editor

BETWEEN
NATION
AND
STATE

Serbian Politics in Croatia
Before the First World War

Nicholas J. Miller

UNIVERSITY OF PITTSBURGH PRESS

Published by the University of Pittsburgh Press, Pittsburgh, Pa. 15261

Library of Congress Cataloging-in-Publication Data
Miller, Nicholas John, 1963–
    Between nation and state : Serbian politics in Croatia before the
  First World War / Nicholas J. Miller.
        p.   cm. — (Pitt Series in Russian and East European studies)
    Includes bibliographical references and index.
    ISBN 0-8229-3989-4 (cloth : acid-free paper)
    1. Serbs—Croatia—Politics and government. 2. Croatia—Politics
  and government—1800–1918. I. Title. II. Series.
  DR1524.S47M55 1997
  320.94972'009'041—dc21   97-4821

A CIP catalog record for this book is available from the British Library.

To my parents, William N. and the late Elizabeth A. Miller

CONTENTS

PREFACE

The Yugoslavia that I knew when I began research for this book no longer exists. Instead there are new states on its soil: Croatia, Slovenia, Macedonia, Bosnia-Hercegovina, and, strangely, Yugoslavia, which doubles as one of two new Serbian states (with the Republika Srpska, in the former Yugoslav republic of Bosnia-Hercegovina). Any study of the history of the interaction of Serbs and Croats must inevitably contribute to our understanding of the issues that underlie the wars that ended the second Yugoslavia. I hope that my book does so. It reflects the belief that political behavior that presumes the supremacy of the collective nation over the individual is bound to fail in lands so ethnically intermixed as those of the former Yugoslavia, or more broadly the Balkan peninsula. The study before you examines a small corner of that canvas: Serbian political behavior in Croatia before the First World War. In its broadest thematic context, this book concerns the interrelationship of nationhood and sovereignty. It is about political behavior in a culturally mixed region under the stress of the challenges of political modernity: the transformation of political actors from subjects to citizens, and the nature of that transformation.

The period from 1903 to 1914 was one of opportunity for Serbs and Croats in the Habsburg monarchy, a period when they nearly conquered their collective mutual suspicions, which they inherited from their forebears. Their failure to do so in this crucial period of opportunity contributed mightily to their inability to establish a civic/democratic tradition in interwar Yugoslavia. This study traces the ideologies and interaction of the two leading Serbian political parties in Croatia (the Serbian Independent party and the Serbian Radical party) as well as their relationship with the major actors in Croatian politics before the First World War. Its focus is on the Serbian parties and their constituency, the Serbian community of Croatia. The study does not provide a political history of Croatia—instead, it offers an examination of the political strategies of Serbian parties in the Croatian context.

In the period covered here, from 1903 to 1914, the Croato-Serbian Coalition dominated Croatian politics. That Coalition was formed in 1905; its raison d'être was the implementation of a political policy known as the "New Course." The New Course was formulated by Dalmatian and Croatian politicians to bring together all potential opposition in Croatia to Austro-Hungarian dualism, which divided Croatian territories and thus allegedly sapped the strength of the Croatian state and people. Thus one (but only one) of the foundations of the New Course was Croato-Serbian reconciliation and cooperation. The usefulness of the New Course ended in 1907, but the Croato-Serbian Coalition lived on until 1918 and provided the stage from which the Serbian Independent party could dominate the politics of the Serbian community of Croatia and perhaps even of Croatia as a whole. The Serbian Radical party, which left the Coalition in 1907, would remain in brisk competition with the Independents for the hearts of Serbian voters in Croatia.

The fundamental goal of each party was to defend the integrity of the Serbian nation as they defined it. But they had different definitions and chose radically different political strategies in the pursuit of those policies. I analyze their competition by using the major concepts and definitions that have been developed by students of nationalism in the twentieth century. Scholars and other commentators have long detailed, and for the most part accepted, a dichotomy between *civic* (or *political*) and *ethnic* (or *cultural*) nationalisms. The first asserts the primacy of political ideals in the composition of a national identity; the second posits the ethnic group as the fundamental basis of nationhood. The Independent party, under the leadership of Svetozar Pribićević, strove to establish a civic model in Serbian nationalist politics, by which the Serbian community of Croatia and Croatia's dominant Croatian population could coexist on the basis of constitutional government and political participation. The Radical party, with Jaša Tomić at the head, preferred to look to an ethnic model of political action, by which the collective Serbian nation would strive to isolate itself from its non-Serbian neighbors, only then to establish government on a foundation of national homogeneity.

Different peoples call the regions described in this book by different names. When there were options (almost always), I utilized a vaguely consistent system. Generally, I chose to use the name that was used by the legal rulers of the place in question. Thus, Temesvár (Hungarian) instead of Temišvar (Serbian/Croatian) or Timișoara (Romanian). But I used Srijem (Croatian) instead of Srem (Serbian), demonstrating that I considered Croatia and Slavonia to have been legally governed as a Croatian (and not a Hungarian) territory. I also broke my own rules when I used Croatian forms for Dalmatian cities, Serbo-Croatian names for Bosnian cities and regions, and by utilizing Novi Sad instead of Ujvidék, among others.

ACKNOWLEDGMENTS

In preparing this study, I have accumulated many debts of gratitude. My graduate school advisors at Indiana University, Charles Jelavich and Barbara Jelavich, helped me in different ways: Charles Jelavich is an enthusiastic mentor who has always shown confidence in my work; Barbara Jelavich's firmness always kept me working. Dimitrije Djordjević of the University of California, Santa Barbara, first kindled my interest in the region and has been a wonderful influence as a scholar and as a person. The Jelaviches, Henry Cooper, and Jim Diehl of Indiana University read the manuscript as a disssertation; Gale Stokes and John Lampe offered advice as I prepared this book as a dissertation; Langdon Healy also read and critiqued the manuscript at an early stage. All of my colleagues at Boise State University encouraged me; special thanks go to Todd Shallat and to the chair of my department, Errol Jones, who supported requests for release time and money. Three institutions also helped. Research for this book was supported in 1988–89 in part by a grant from the International Research and Exchanges Board (IREX), with funds provided by the National Endowment for the Humanities, the United States Information Agency, and the U.S. Department of State, which administers the Russian, Eurasian, and East European Research Program (Title VIII). The Andrew Mellon Foundation, by way of the Russian and East European Institute at Indiana University, helped with a dissertation write-up grant. To the Office of Research Administration at Boise State University, I owe a debt of gratitude for release time in spring 1995. I benefitted from the aid of several scholars in former Yugoslavia: in Zagreb, I was aided greatly by Dr. Ivan Čizmić, and in Belgrade I would not have survived without the assistance of Vojislav Pavlović and Momčilo Pavlović. To Meggan Laxalt, my appreciation for preparing the maps. Thank you also to Langdon Healy, Sarah Kent, Melissa Bokovoy, and Carol Lilly for their friendship and encouragement. My father and mother, William N. and the late Elizabeth A. Miller, my sister Erin Miller, and my grandmother Hazel Miller all taught me to love to read and write, if not necessarily history. Above all, Lynn Lubamersky gets my most profound and loving thanks for everything.

BETWEEN
NATION
AND
STATE

1

THE CROATIAN
BACKGROUND

Croatian Lands and Their Peoples

WHERE IS CROATIA? The term has meant different things to different people across time. In the eighth and ninth centuries, two Croatian states emerged in the zone on the fringes of the Byzantine and Frankish empires: one in Dalmatia, the other to the north, known as Pannonian Croatia.[1] These two Croatias drew their name from a non-Slavic tribe that had previously been assimilated by its Slavic hosts; it is doubtful that the Croatianness of these people meant anything more than that they lived in a certain place. Dalmatian and Pannonian Croatia were first united by King Tomislav, the leader of the Dalmatian state, in the tenth century. At that point, Croatia most likely consisted of today's Croatia, Slavonia, Dalmatia from Rijeka to the Cetina river, and northern and western Bosnia.[2] In 1102, the Hungarian king, Koloman, annexed a weakened Croatia under circumstances that are still debated. This Croatia consisted of most of Tomislav's state. Its union with Hungary was personal, as the Croatian nobility retained the right to elect its own monarch. The agreement by which the two states were joined was called the Pacta Conventa. Here too, though, the general population of this state was not Croatian in any modern sense; its peasants and soldiers did not possess a national consciousness. The state's nobility, on the other hand, certainly believed itself to be different from the nobility of Hungary, Serbia, or any other neighboring state, but that was a distinction based on feudal notions of obligation and personal privilege, not ethnicity.

Croatia became a muddled concept in succeeding centuries. In 1526, after the death of King Louis II in battle with the Ottoman Empire, Croatia and its aristocracy followed neighboring, sovereign Hungary into the domains of the Habsburg monarch, Ferdinand I. Royal (or Habsburg) Hungary included a very small slice of modern northwestern Croatia; the rest became part of Ottoman Hungary and spent most of the next two centuries as a battleground. The definition of Croatia grew more unclear when Ferdinand I established the Military Frontier (or Border; *Militärgrenze* in German, *Vojna krajina* in Serbo-Croatian) in 1522 in Croatia and Hungary, along the monarchy's southern border. As the Habsburgs reconquered Hungary and Croatia, some of this territory was added to the Military Frontier, so the physical outlines of Croatia became ever less certain. By the eighteenth century, the Military Frontier cut a variable swath across southern Croatia and Hungary, placing much of the reconquered portions of those states in a separate jurisdiction, out of the hands of the Hungarian and Croatian nobility. Furthermore, Dalmatia and Istria had been absorbed by Venice and then, following the Napoleonic wars, by the Austrian monarchy. Croatia and Hungary became less geopolitical facts than fantasies of their literate orders until the eighteenth century. The Ausgleich of 1867 formalized a division between Austria and Hungary that left Croatia, Dalmatia and Istria, and the Military Frontier in different jurisdictions (Croatia in Hungary, Dalmatia and Istria in Austria, and the Military Frontier still its own entity). Thus it was that by the nineteenth century, military necessity, dynastic whim, and political expediency had grafted new divisions upon other, only relatively new, divisions, leaving the definition of what was Croatia open to interpretation.

What was the condition of these lands as they entered the Habsburg monarchy once again in the seventeenth and eighteenth centuries? As the eighteenth century began, Ottoman Hungary, Transylvania, Croatia, Slavonia, and even Habsburg (Royal) Hungary and (Civil) Croatia had been made wastelands by two centuries of war. The seventeenth century had been one of almost nonstop warfare as the Ottomans and their Transylvanian allies fought the forces of the Habsburg Empire for control of the Hungarian plain.[3] Although the ghosts of the two states were Habsburg possessions after 1526, one cannot govern what one does not control, and it was not before Prince Eugene of Savoy settled the Hungarian inheritance militarily in the late 1690s that Hungary and Croatia became fully Habsburg. From 1699, when the Austro-Ottoman Treaty of Karlowitz (modern-day Srijemski Karlovci) between the Habsburg monarchy and the Ottoman Empire was signed, Habsburg armies held the upper hand for good in the ongoing duel with the Ottoman Turks. Famine and disease accompanied the warfare, further decimating the population. The once fertile land had returned to nature. The revival of Hungary, including Croatia, in the eighteenth century resulted in part from conscious policies of resettlement ("populationism") by the Habsburg monarchs and those Hungarian nobles who worked with them. Following the Treaty of Karlowitz, Habsburg authorities, via the Commissio Neo Acquistica (Commission for Newly Acquired Lands), parceled out and attempted to revive desolate Pannonia. Hungary and Croatia were repopulated with migrants from northern Hungary (Slovaks), from Central Europe (Germans), and from the Ottoman domains to the south (Orthodox Christian Serbs). By the time of the French Revolution in 1789, Hungary's demographic miracle was in full swing. It had a population of over nine million, more than either Bohemia or the Austrian crownlands. Between 1700 and 1787, Hungarian towns tripled in size. Hungary had six cities of over twenty thousand inhabitants in 1787, but of its nine millions, 95 percent were rural.[4] The greatest boost to population growth came from immigration, but it was also the result of lowered infant mortality and the decline of disease and famine associated with war.

What was the nature of the populations of these lands? The population of Croatia, Bosnia, Serbia, Dalmatia, and Macedonia has always been mixed, regardless of the categories employed. The Slavs who came to the Balkan peninsula in the seventh century A.D. were undifferentiated. Into that mass, which proved to be sedentary and not particularly warlike, were mixed other, non-Slavic tribes, which were by and large assimilated by the existing Slavic populations over the next three centuries. The Bulgars, for instance, came from the Caucasus in the seventh century and conquered the inhabitants of the southeastern section of the Balkan peninsula militarily, but were themselves conquered civilizationally by the existing Slavs, who today have only the Bulgarian name as a reminder of that conquest. The original Croats and Serbs were not Slavic either, although they gave their names to groups of Slavs already present on the peninsula in the seventh century. Over time, though, the names came to denote two different civilizations, thanks to the division of the Balkan peninsula between the Roman and Byzantine Christian churches. With the much earlier division of the Roman Empire in 395 A.D. and the establishment of the two competing variants of Christianity on the Balkan peninsula by the tenth century, faith became the main determinant of a population's identity. Religious categories were plastered over original tribal ones. The process by which the Croats were catholicized ended in the tenth century. As for the Serbs, their conversion to Orthodoxy occurred in the early thirteenth century, under the influence of Stefan Nemanja, Serbia's king, and his son Rastko, the future St. Sava. Thus by the late medieval period, a Croat was of the western church, a Serb most definitely of the eastern.[5] With the Ottoman incursion, which began in the fourteenth century, Islam joined the field. Jews also lived in the Balkans by the seventh century, but in such small numbers as to make a minor impact on the political and cultural history of the region. Until the modern era the treatment of peoples by states depended on their religion.

Had the original dividing line between Roman and Byzantine civilizations solidified and remained impenetrable, today we might not be reading this book because conflict might have been avoided. Alas, between the fourteenth and nineteenth centuries, populations moved. The primary cause of these movements was the continuous if variable Ottoman penetration of the Balkan peninsula and Central Europe. Before the Turks fled mainly Orthodox Christian populations, thus pushing the border between Rome and the east northward, but not uniformly. Left in the wake were not mere population pockets but completely intermingled groups of Orthodox and Catholic Christians, not to mention newly converted Muslims. The mixing was dangerous enough through the early modern period, but in the modern nationalistic era, when faith could come to denote nationhood (especially in the Serbian case), which in turn often emphasized particular territories in its definition, the protoethnic weave was a time bomb.

The Origins of Orthodox Settlements in Croatia

Orthodox Christians first came to Croatian lands after the Ottoman conquest of medieval Serbia in the fourteenth and fifteenth centuries.[6] The character of that population has always been a provocative topic, if not a particularly fruitful source of scholarly debate. The people who came to the Habsburg monarchy from the south, Orthodox Christians for the most part, today almost universally consider themselves to be Serbs. But the sources on those migrant populations often, if not always, refer to them as *Vlasi* (Vlachs). Many of these Vlachs were Orthodox Christian herders who indeed spoke a language of their own, were seminomadic, and quite different from the Orthodox Christian speakers of Serbian who also came north. Nonetheless, Habsburg and Ottoman authorities called *all* of them Vlachs: thus, as just one example, the Statuta Valachorum, a seventeenth-century decree applied to Orthodox Christians, was so-named because it applied to "Vlachs"; its contents were actually directed at Orthodox Christians. By the nineteenth century, any true Vlachs, speaking Vlach, had been assimilated by their host populations, which left their Orthodoxy as the only point differentiating them from their Catholic or Muslim neighbors. Thus they could be considered Serbs when such a distinction became socially valuable, or considered *not* to be Serbs equally easily. Today, however, the question of the original "Vlachness" or "Serbianness" of the Orthodox population of Croatia and Vojvodina is a critical one for historians who believe that past distinctions have some bearing on modern national identities. Thus, for instance, on the question of whether a given group of people was once Vlach or Serbian hinges its right to claim to be Serbian today. In a Croatia in which Serbs were separatists in the 1990s, and among Croats who certainly honor the principle of nationality, a descendant of Vlachs is not the same thing as a Serb—and the term Vlach becomes a weapon in the war to devalue Serbian claims to territory and history in Croatia.[7] At this point, the insistence of any historian on calling the Orthodox Christians of Croatia Vlachs is tendentious and purposefully provocative. At best, it constitutes an attempt to refute the equally tendentious attempts of Serbian historians to claim certain rights in Croatia, now or in the past, as a result of privileges granted by Habsburg emperors to them (or to Vlachs). The distinction was valid for an earlier era, but is now irrelevant.

Orthodox Christians were concentrated to the south of Croatia at the time of the Ottoman conquest. Medieval Serbia was firmly Orthodox Christian at the point when the Ottomans overthrew the Serbian state (1389–1459). Bosnia was the northernmost region with an Orthodox presence before the fifteenth century, although that presence was not notable.[8] As the Ottoman Empire extended its control to medieval Serbia and Bosnia, Croatia's religious character was certainly Catholic. The Ottoman threat to Croatia and

Hungary was obvious after the Battle of Smederevo in 1459, after which Serbia definitively fell, and the fall of Bosnia in the summer of 1463. In 1526, the death of Louis II left Hungary and Croatia without a king. After a period of contention for the inheritance between János Zápolyai of Transylvania and Ferdinand I of Habsburg, the Habsburg claimant was able by 1528 to extend his control of northern Croatia and what remained of Slavonia. The border area between the lands of the House of Habsburg and that of Osman became a zone of mixing, as border raids and migrations contributed to a constant ebb and flow. On each side of that border, the empires established a frontier zone that would serve as a first line of defense and a buffer. The Austrian zone was the Military Frontier.[9]

Waves of migration brought hundreds of thousands of Orthodox Christians to Croatia and Hungary. Each wave was distinct: different populations, provoked by different causes, made their way to new homes. The first groups of settlers were pushed northward by the Ottoman conquests of Serbia after the Battle of Smederevo in 1459 and the fall of Bosnia in 1463. Orthodox Christians moved into Srijem thereafter. By 1483, perhaps two hundred thousand had moved into central Slavonia and Srijem.[10] The Turkish conquest of Bosnia also pushed refugees and migrants into western Croatia, for two reasons. First, many fled before the Turks, moving north of the new border; others were forcibly settled in Lika-Krbava, which the Ottomans captured in 1528, in order to defend the border against Austrian incursions.[11] The Turks preferred to have Orthodox Christian border populations, rightly believing that they were likely to defend themselves against the advances of a Catholic state. So both emperors saw the value of placing Orthodox Christians along their borders. In the early sixteenth century, Orthodox settlements in free Croatia were established for the first time around Ogulin, Otok, and Modruša. Their safety and certain freedoms were assured by a decree of Habsburg Emperor Ferdinand I in May 1540.[12]

Another major movement of settlers provoked by the Ottoman conquest of Bosnia was one which took a large group of Uskoci from the region of Glamoč northward into Žumberak (today in northern Croatia and southern Slovenia).[13] This move occurred in three waves, in 1526, 1531, and 1538. The final one came under the protection of decrees issued by Ferdinand I in 1535 and 1538 allowing free movement for these Orthodox Christians into abandoned villages in Croatia. This population, the first to be organized and brought into the Habsburg domains under the protection of a previous agreement with the Habsburg emperor, was almost completely catholicized by the eighteenth century.[14] The agreement that brought them to the region gave them certain rights that would be replicated for other migrant Orthodox populations: they were relieved of taxation for twenty years, were allowed to retain their plunder in raids on Turkish outposts, and enjoyed the status of soldiers rather than serfs. These conditions remained in force for them until the reorganization of the frontier in 1746.

Another migration following the fall of Serbia and Bosnia brought Orthodox Christians to the north-central regions of Croatia, which would become the Varaždin Frontier. Then the collapse of Hungarian control of Slavonia in the 1540s resulted in two demographic movements of note: earlier Orthodox populations moved northward toward Bjelovar and Križevci, while new Orthodox settlers moved in (taking their place) at the urgings of their Turkish overlords, who wished to have their border with Catholic Austria lined with Orthodox settlements. Many moved to the Križevci region from Žumberak in 1542, from Pakrac following the Ottoman conquest of the Slavonian plain in the 1580s, and from Bosnia between 1600 and 1610, during and after the Long War (1593–1606).[15] Western Croatia also gained more Orthodox settlers after 1600: movements into Srpska Moravica, Vrbovsko, and Gomirje began in the late 1590s, lasting until the 1630s when the last group entered from Cazin. Others wound up in Karlovac, Ogulin, Plaški, and Otočac, arriving by the 1660s.[16] Emperor Leopold I's decree of July 1659 allowed this wave to enter Habsburg territories under favorable conditions.[17]

Normally, the Orthodox settlers were treated with reserve by their local Catholic hosts. The Orthodox who came to the lands of the Habsburgs did so under the patronage of the emperors and their militaries, not of local notables. Their settlements were allowed in return for service along the Military Frontier; their faith was overlooked, except when their freedoms had to be guaranteed against the violations of the Hungarian and Croatian aristocracy. Thus, for instance, when local authorities in Croatia or the Croatian Sabor (diet) refused to recognize concessions granted by Ferdinand II to Orthodox immigrants in the Varaždin Frontier region, he was forced to confirm his own decree with the so-called Statuta Valachorum in 1630.[18] Leopold I did the same in 1666.[19] These and other decrees like them, issued on an ad hoc basis over the centuries, constituted the basis for the autonomous cultural existence of Serbs in Croatia and Hungary. Together they are known in Serbian historiography as the Serbian Privileges.[20] The most important of them accompanied the most important of the migrations: that of 1690, the so-called *Velika seoba srba* (the Great Migration of Serbs) in which up to forty thousand Orthodox Serbs followed their patriarch, Arsenije III Crnojevic, from Kosovo to today's Vojvodina, contributing to the transformation of the demographic structure of that region of southern Hungary just as Hungary was reentering the Habsburg domains after a century of warfare.

This Great Migration came as the result of negotiations between representatives of Arsenije and Emperor Leopold I. Orthodox Serbs had been actively supporting Austrian armies in their recent wars with the Turks, in which the Austrians gained Turkish territory but then withdrew, leaving the Serbs in a precarious position. Leopold agreed to allow them to move north from Kosovo. This decision was issued in a patent of August 1690; it was confirmed many times over the following century. As a result of these agreements, Arsenije's flock fled to southern Hungary and Srijem with a guarantee of religious autonomy and of some degree of self-administration. Amid all the migrations and privileges, those pertaining to this movement would prove to be the most important from the Serbian perspective later, when the position of this autonomous Orthodox community began to have heady implications for the development of Croatian and Hungarian statehood in the nineteenth century.

Serbian Life in Croatia and Hungary

The Orthodox Christians who came to the Habsburg domains saw their lives dominated by two separate institutions. One was the Military Frontier, the other was the Orthodox church, which nourished the idea that its flock was not just made up of Orthodox Christians, but of Serbs. These two institutions each served to separate Orthodox Serbs from their neighbors: the Military Frontier physically, the Orthodox metropolitanate of Srijemski Karlovci spiritually. Eventually, the two independent notions of space and spirit would merge, as the Orthodox community of Croatia expressed its spiritual individuality through its desire for physical separation from its Catholic neighbors. A further critical difference between the two institutions is that the Military Frontier was not a Serbian, or even an Orthodox, institution: it included people of all faiths and orders in Croatia and Hungary. Its logic was not to separate peoples, but to collect them in such a way as to defend the Habsburg monarchy's long border with the Ottoman Empire. The Orthodox metropolitanate, on the other hand, was obviously an Orthodox Christian institution with a limited potential flock. Even it, however, included many Romanian Orthodox until the mid-nineteenth century.

The Habsburgs established the Military Frontier in fits and starts. In the 1520s, Ferdinand I first set up rudimentary defenses along his threatened border with the Ottoman Empire. By 1568, the frontier in Croatia was divided into two sections: one known as the Croatian frontier *(Hrvatska krajina)*, the other the Slavonian *(Slavonska krajina)*. After 1592, a third section of the frontier was established in Croatia, the Banija frontier *(Banska krajina)*, which occupied a position between the other two. Its importance grew after 1688, when the region between the Kupa and the Una Rivers was retaken from the Turks and added to it. Karlovac was the seat of the Croatian frontier, while the Slavonian frontier was centered in Varaždin until the nineteenth century (they eventually took the names Karlovac Generalcy and Varaždin Generalcy, for their respective headquarters). The single most important change in the administration of the Military Frontier came with the expulsion of the Ottoman Empire from Hungary and Croatia with the Treaty of Karlowitz in 1699. Although the Treaty of Passarowitz (Požarevac, in modern Serbia) of 1718 would briefly extend the Habsburg borders into northern Serbia, they were quickly pushed back by the Treaty of Belgrade in 1739.

The eighteenth century was one of great change for the occupants of the frontier, especially those of the Orthodox faith. The Military Frontier shifted as the fortunes of the Austro-Turkish war shifted. Originally, it bisected Hungary and Croatia; as the line dividing them from the Ottoman Empire moved south and east, the frontier moved with it. Its inhabitants were Christian (mainly Orthodox) refugees from the Ottoman Empire, serfs fleeing their obligations to the north, mercenaries, and bandits. These warrior/farmers were organized militarily and socially in territorial units; their freedoms were guaranteed by their willingness to defend the border. Safety, opportunity, and personal freedom drew large populations from the Ottoman territories northward from the fifteenth century on. They received much in return for their service: land to work, schools in which to be educated, freedom from the bonds of serfdom, and freedom to practice their religion. The zone of Serbian settlement in Croatia and Vojvodina today is virtually identical to the geographical extent of the Military Frontier. It became a zone apart in a socioeconomic as well as a political and military sense. It was governed directly by Vienna, although its distinct local districts were administered by military commanders who doubled as governors.

The privileges of the frontiersmen were unique and have always been the source of historians' interest. Until the reconquest of Hungary and Croatia, the Military Frontier served a crucial purpose for the Habsburg monarchy. Thus conditions therein were unique for its inhabitants. I have already mentioned some of the special grants to settlers from the south in Žumberak and the Varaždin Generalcy, as well as those associated with the Great Migration. Generally, those conditions held for all the immigrants who were willing to fight in the service of Austria for the duration of whichever war was inevitably in process. Thus, immigrants could count on paying no taxes for up to twenty years; serving as soldiers in time of war and free farmers in time of peace; and keeping much of the spoils of their border raiding. However, decrees issued by various emperors regarding certain populations of immigrants differed according to conditions. One constant was the tension that reigned among the settlers, the crown, the army, and the local nobility, whether Hungarian or Croatian. The crown often had to come to the defense of frontiersmen whose privileged position was threatened by local landowners. The Habsburgs readily did so as long as the threat of war with the Ottoman Empire was palpable.

The best example of this sort of care was the Statuta Valachorum. It was issued in 1630 by Emperor Ferdinand II, necessitated by the fact that the Croatian nobility of the Varaždin Generalcy (between the Sava and the Drava Rivers, the Slavonian *krajina*) had not respected the right of the *Grenzer* to be free of certain types of taxation and had taken to physically abusing them. The issue showed the potential for conflict between the feudal nobility and the crown in Austria and highlighted the fact that the local aristocracies were not pleased with having their traditional authority over peasants usurped by the Habsburg military. The emperor sided with his military against the local Hungarian and Croatian nobility, however, and the statute of 1630 was the result. The Statuta Valachorum removed these frontiersmen from the judicial authority of the Croatian Sabor, placing them under imperial jurisdiction. Internal organization of the *krajina* would be based on local autonomy, with courts for each of three *kapitanije* (subunits of the Varaždin Generalcy) elected for year-long terms by the elders of each district. This civil government and the courts that accompanied it would be in charge of all civil penalties; military courts were limited to corporal punishment and that only of those who were part of the military. The statute also elaborated military requirements: a minimum of six thousand were required to gather within three hours of any alarm. They were free from the obligation to pay the various land and protection taxes required of others.[21]

The nature (shape and administration) of the Military Frontier changed greatly after the Treaty of Karlowitz in 1699, when the border between Habsburg and Ottoman lands shifted to the south and east. Lika-Krbava in the west and Slavonia and Srijem in the east were joined to the lands of the Habsburgs; both now became integral to the Croatian Military Frontier. Lika-Krbava joined the Karlovac Generalcy in 1712, and Slavonia and Srijem were placed in a new district of the frontier (along the Sava River basin) after 1702. The eighteenth century brought far-reaching reforms in the administration and duties of the frontiersmen. Initially, these reforms emphasized the goal of governing the frontier in a unified fashion. The *Grenzer* in any given region would receive the same treatment as those in others. One of their new tasks would be to serve as monitors of cross-border trade, a sort of customs control. Ultimately, especially under Maria Theresa, the most critical goal was to make them into a capable and unified fighting force, a part of the regular Habsburg military controlled by imperial authorities in Vienna rather than by the Austrian nobility or local authorities in Croatia and Hungary. This goal of uniformity brought Habsburg authorities into conflict with frontiersmen who could claim privileges unique to their own communities. Attempts to codify the conditions of the frontiersmen of the Varaždin Generalcy began in the 1730s. Those attempts, as it happened, limited the freedoms and the pay of the regular soldier in the military district. The result was violent disorder through the 1730s, which brought about the need for a new statute in 1737. Reorganization followed in the Karlovac Generalcy, in the newer, smaller Slavonian districts, and in Banija in the 1750s. By 1754, the Varaždin and Karlovac Generalcies were given unified orders by which Vienna took over all aspects of the administration of the districts, ending the traditional self-governance of the oldest sections of the frontier.[22] After a long series of violent uprisings that culminated in that of 1755, further centralization of the frontier followed by the 1780s.

Outside the frontier, Croatia and Slavonia had civil administrations (thus they were known as Civil Croatia and Civil Slavonia), which were divided into *županije* (counties). As the Military Frontier shrank and shifted, Civil Croatia and Slavonia shifted and grew. In 1785, the *županije* included Severin, Varaždin, and Križevci in Civil Croatia, and Požega, Virovitica, and Srijem in Civil Slavonia. By the early twentieth century, there were eight *županije*

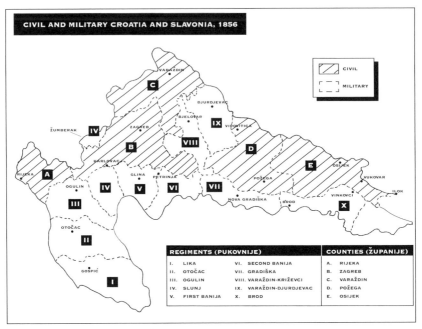

Civil and Military Croatia and Slavonia, 1856.

and four free cities in Croatia. Until 1881, however, the frontier remained, and from the 1850s, it was divided into 11 *pukovnije* (regiments), which reflected the shrinkage of the frontier as a whole and its parcelization: the eleven were the Lika, the Otočac, the Ogulin, the Slunj, the First and Second Banija, the Gradiška, the Križevci, the Djurdjevac, the Brod, and the Petrovaradin Regiments. By the time it was closed down in 1881, the Military Frontier was no longer a functioning defensive buffer; rather it served solely as a cordon against unwanted trade, disease, and refugees from the south.[23] The reduced, reordered Military Frontier had become little other than a new, separate jurisdiction within the Habsburg monarchy, and its fate was the subject of great debate within the governing elites of the monarchy.

The Military Frontier was not a Serbian entity, and it was not an Orthodox Christian entity. The fact that it was dominated by Serbs was purely fortuitous: the frontier would have existed regardless of who populated it. On the other hand, Serbian, or Orthodox Christian, life in the Habsburg monarchy did find some more distinct order in the Orthodox Church. By the grace of the Austrian emperor, Serbs gained an autonomous church as one among the many concessions to this population that would defend his southern border. If the frontier drew the Orthodox populations northward and provided them with an existence, the church gave them a separate cultural life. Eventually, as identity became less a function of status and faith and more of ethnicity and culture, this autonomous cultural existence would provide the basis for a thriving Serbian community in the southern reaches of the monarchy, lulling those who lived there into believing that they deserved not only an autonomous culture but political self-determination.

The Orthodox church was represented in Croatia as early as the 1560s with the installation of a "Serbo-Slavonian" bishop (in a metropolitanate of Požega) centered in the monastery of Remeta.[24] Later, in the seventeenth century, a bishopric *(episkopija)* was founded at the monastery of Marča, in the Croatian krajina. Both of these entities were subordinate to the Serbian Orthodox Patriarchate of Peč (in Kosovo), which had been reestablished in 1557 and lasted under Ottoman governance until 1766. Other dioceses *(eparhije)* were founded, although their approval by Habsburg authorities probably hinged on the belief that they would facilitate the union of these Orthodox Christians with the Catholic church. In fact, many, including some bishops of the Orthodox church, did unify with Rome.[25]

The glorious (and ultimately contentious) years of the Serbian church in the Habsburg monarchy began with the Great Migration, the flight of Patriarch Arsenije III Crnojević in 1690 from Peč to Hungary. With his arrival, the balance of authority in the Serbian church shifted from Kosovo to southern Hungary. From that point, the cultural center of Serbdom was removed from its old domain to an entirely new one. If some Orthodox Serbs had arrived earlier, those of the Great Migration brought the soul of the future nation to the lands of the Habsburgs. It has been asserted that the Serbs who migrated earlier were an ethnic mass; those who came in the Great Migration were *politically* (nationally) Serbs.[26] The difference lies in the timing of this migration as well as its constitution: it brought with it the single definitive indicator of Serbianness, the faith, and the leader of that faith, the patriarch. And more than that, for the first time the emperor (here, Leopold I) guaranteed the right of the Serbian church to minister to its flock throughout Austria with his four decrees of 1690–1695. Many interpreters believe that Leopold also guaranteed self-governance to the Serbs. It was only a matter of time before those migrants, led by their church, were indeed made into Serbs in the national sense. Serbia had completed its northward migration.

The organization of the church varied over time. Leopold's final decree, of 1695, mentions bishoprics in Temesvár, Upper Karlovac, Szeged, Buda, Mohács, Verscz (Vršac), and Várad.[27] Arsenije III came as patriarch and remained in that position until his death in 1706, after which the relationship of the new Serbian Orthodox community to Peč and the Habsburg monarchy came into question. At the monastery of Krušedol in 1708, Arsenije's successor was elected and Krušedol itself was named the seat of the new Krušedol-Karlovci metropolitanate; it was moved to Srijemski Karlovci in 1716, where it remained, known thereafter as the metropolitanate of Srijemski Karlovci. From 1784 to 1863, the Orthodox Romanians of Transylvania and Hungary were also subordinate to the metropolitanate.[28] The metropolitanate included the bishoprics of Upper Karlovac (Plaška), Pakrac, and Srijemski Karlovci in Croatia, with Versecz, Buda, Bacska, and Temesvár in Hungary. By the late nineteenth century, there were other metropolitanates in Dalmatia, Bosnia, Hercegovina, Macedonia, Serbia, and Montenegro, each including several bishoprics and/or metropolitans. Until the Ottomans ended the existence of the Peč patriarchate in 1766, the metropolitanate of Srijemski Karlovci remained subordinate to it. Thereafter, it became the main center of Serbian Orthodoxy, inheriting all of the spiritual authority of its predecessor.

The Orthodox Serbs of the Habsburg lands felt threatened from the beginning of their settlements there, because Habsburg authorities, religious and otherwise, never hid their intention to convert the Orthodox of the frontier when their military utility declined. In fact, one entire community of Orthodox migrants had become Uniate by the eighteenth century: that of Žumberak, one of the first regions to be settled with Orthodox under the emperor's protection. The wave of proselytization that followed the Treaty of Karlowitz in 1699 ended within several years as a result of the nobles' rebellion in Hungary led by Ferenc II Rákóczi, during which Vienna wished to be certain of Serbian neutrality. Following that, Maria Theresa was willing in times of weakness to confirm the privileges, and Joseph II's toleration decrees included the Orthodox of the Habsburg lands. Ultimately, in spite of the always-impending pressure to convert, the Orthodox church and its organization were able to persevere into the nineteenth century with their privileges and their strong role among the Serbian flock intact.

Until this point, Hungary and Croatia have been treated as one place, legally and administratively, with the Military Frontier existing in something of a nether zone between Vienna and the local Hungarian and Croatian nobilities. In fact, Hungary and Croatia were, until the modern, national, era, united under one elective king by virtue of a feudal relationship that began with the Pacta Conventa of 1102. In the reintegration of the *neoac-*

quistica, Hungary and Croatia were treated more or less as a single unit. Through the eighteenth century, the burning question remained whether the Military Frontier would be handed over to the nobilities. The Josephine reforms, however, placed the question in a new context, as they aspired to the complete centralization of the monarchy. Hungary, and then Croatia, responded to Joseph II's centralizing measures by emphasizing certain liberties (the right to use the vernacular language, either Hungarian or Croatian) that ultimately spurred the growth of Hungarian and Croatian nationalism. While the provincial border between Hungary and Croatia/Slavonia was not contested, the place of Croatia within the Hungarian state would be, and violently so. As this debate grew over the course of the nineteenth century, the Serbian populations of the two lands became actively involved. In fact, as Croatia attempted to assure itself some independence vis-à-vis Hungary, the Serbs of the regions would attempt to do the same at the expense of both Hungary and Croatia. The contentious nature of the national question as it grew in the nineteenth century gave the Habsburg authorities advantages in times of crisis: they could play one nationality against the other. This practice became commonplace with regard to Croats and Serbs by late in the century. One important effect of this type of manipulative politics was that borders and loyalties were continually adjusted and readjusted as part of a cycle of rewards and punishments for service to Vienna. It did little to insti!l modern political values—instead training peoples to be loyal to the emperor and dependent on royal patronage.

The borders of Hungary and Croatia were revised on several occasions in the nineteenth century. The first occurred during and after the revolutions of 1848, which of course had a deep effect on Hungarian, Croatian, and Serbian societies. In the fall of 1848, the Serbs of the metropolitanate of Srijemski Karlovci, under the leadership of Metropolitan Josip Rajačić, allied themselves with Vienna against the Hungarian revolutionaries of Lajos Kossuth. As a result, Emperor Franz Joseph issued a patent organizing a Serbian Vojvodina consisting of much of the Banat, Bacska, and Srijem minus the Military Frontier. This unit was considered a reward for Serbian services to the monarchy, but the reality did not satisfy Serbs, who hoped for more: territorial autonomy on the basis of previously granted privileges. From 1849 to 1860, the Serbian Vojvodina was little more than an administrative district in an absolutist Habsburg monarchy; it had no Serbian character at all. In 1860, following the loss of Lombardy-Venetia in the Italian war of unification, and fearing another Hungarian attempt at independence, the emperor handed the Vojvodina over to Hungary. This transfer served as a prelude to negotiations for what became the Ausgleich of 1867, by which Hungary attained much autonomy within the Habsburg domains. By this agreement, Hungary and Austria were bound by their monarch (the emperor of Austria, but the king of Hungary), their budget, their ministry of foreign affairs, and their defense ministry. Austria became Austria-Hungary, the Dual Monarchy. This momentous agreement settled the general organization of the monarchy until 1918. Hungary was charged with organizing and governing the lands to the east of the Leitha River, including Civil Croatia and Slavonia (but not yet the Military Frontier). The Ausgleich of 1867 was followed by the Hungaro-Croatian Nagodba of 1868.[29] The Nagodba regulated Croatia's political and economic relationship to Hungary until 1918. Although the agreement allowed Croatia to have some autonomy, opposition to the Nagodba grew as it became evident that Hungary did not view it as a guarantee of Croatian existence as a state, but rather as the first step in the transformation of Croatia into a province of Hungary.

Serbian Life in Croatia and Hungary

By the middle of the nineteenth century, Serbian populations of the Habsburg monarchy were scattered across southern Hungary as well as Dalmatia, Civil Croatia and Slavonia, and the Military Frontier. They were parts of unique legal and administrative systems. The Serbian Orthodox population of the Habsburg monarchy had accumulated in regions to which it had fled in previous centuries, predictably most concentrated in the Military Frontier. The figures in table 1 indicate the relative size of the Catholic (Croatian) and Orthodox (Serbian) populations of the Military Frontier and Civil Croatia/Slavonia (after 1881 these territories would be united). In both frontier regions, Orthodox Serbs made up about half the population, whereas in Civil Croatia/Slavonia, not including the frontier, Serbs made up a considerably smaller minority. Table 2 further delineates the locations of Orthodox Serbs in Civil Croatia/Slavonia, where they constituted a significant portion of the population only in Civil Slavonia (about 43 percent). In Civil Croatia, there were almost no Serbs. Within the Military Frontier, there were three regiments with absolute Serbian majorities in the 1850s: the Lika regiment, in

Table 1. Croatian and Serbian Population of the Military Frontier and
Croatia in 1840 (in real numbers by region)

	Croatian Frontier	Slavonian Frontier	Civil Croatia/ Slavonia	Total
Croats	258,454 (51.8%)	127,326 (49.44%)	689,847	1,075,627 (66.99%)
Serbs	240,493 (48.2%)	122,853 (47.7%)	140,833	504,179 (31.41%)
Total	498,947 (100 %)	250,179 (97.14%)	830,680(+?)	1,579,806 (98.4%)

Source: Roksandić, *Srbi u hrvatskoj od 15,* 77–78.

Table 2. Population by Religion in Civil Croatia-Slavonia, 1840 (in percentage)

County	Catholic	Uniate	Protestant	Orthodox	Jewish
Croatia					
Zagreb	99.48	0.007	0.6	0.347	0.111
Varaždin	99.52	0.002	0.006	0.117	0.361
Križevci	97.08	0.011	0.183	2.517	0.206
Subtotal	99.14	0.006	0.062	0.6	0.193
Slavonia					
Požega	56.44	–	3	43.26	0.299
Virovitica	69.02	1.445	0.111	29.097	0.323
Srijem	33.74	2.096	1.212	62.87	0.08
Subtotal	55.06	1.314	0.43	42.96	0.24
Total	81.55	0.53	0.21	17.5	0.21

Source: Kessler, *Politik, Kultur, und Gesellschaft,* 129.

which Serbs were about 67 percent of the population; the First Banija regiment, in which they provided about the same proportion; and the Second Banija regiment, in which they comprised about 63 percent of the population.[30] In addition, in the Otočac, Ogulin, and Slunj Regiments, Serbs made up nearly 50 percent of the population.[31] Only in western Slavonia (Gradiška regiment) and northern Croatia (Djurdjevac and Križevci Regiments) were Serbs significantly outnumbered.

The final major change in the status of the Croatian/Hungarian lands came in 1881, as Croatia/Slavonia and its portions of the frontier were united. The incorporation of the Military Frontier into Croatia in 1881 meant the inclusion of lands populated by large numbers of Serbs, which drastically altered Croatia's demographic profile. The functional transfer of governing responsibility from the emperor to the *ban* (viceroy or governor, appointed by the Hungarian minister-president and the emperor) took place on September 1, 1881.[32] With the new lands, Croatia added 61 percent more territory and 663,000 more people, of which 55 percent were Serbs.[33] This simple transfer of land and people from one jurisdiction to another upset the equilibrium of Croatian politics by inserting a non-Croatian element into what had been a largely Croatian land. The final pre-1914 geopolitical status of the lands of Croatia and Slavonia was settled by the unification of the Military Frontier with Croatia. By 1910, Orthodox Serbs made up approximately 25 percent of Croatia's population.[34]

The Orthodox church in Croatia/Slavonia served people who were poorer than their Catholic neighbors, and it did so from a position of weakness. The Catholic church was the church of the Habsburg monarchy: others were not even legally tolerated until in 1791 the Hungarian Parliament passed a law legalizing the Orthodox and Protestant churches in Hungary. Orthodox church leaders rightly objected to the fact that authorities referred to their church as the Greek-Nonunified *(grčko-nesjedinjena)* church, which clearly implied the inevitability of union with the Catholic church. After 1868, Croatia and Slavonia had three Orthodox bishoprics: that of Srijemski Karlovci, which included the seat of the metropolitanate and the monasteries of the Fruška Gora, and those of Pakrac and (Upper) Karlovac, which were substantially poorer. In fact, the Orthodox church was poorer in general in Croatia/Slavonia than it was in Hungary, in spite of the fact that the metropolitanate and many of the monasteries were in Srijem. The reason was that at the parish level the Orthodox church depended on the contributions of its parishioners, and parishioners in Croatia/Slavonia were much poorer than those in southern Hungary. Thus there was a wide disparity in the education, wealth, and general competence of priests in parishes of the Orthodox church. Whereas the high clergy of the church would generally be well-educated, literate, and prosperous, the parish clergyman might well be illiterate and poorer than some of his peasant parishioners.

The single uncontested right of the Orthodox Serbs of the metropolitanate of Srijemski Karlovci was the election of their metropolitan (after 1848, patriarch), which occurred at meetings of the National-Church Congress as needed. The Church Congress met for other purposes also, but only on the approval of the emperor. Between 1744 and 1790, it met seven times; thereafter, it met to elect metropolitans and on extraordinary occasions (such as during revolutions or when drastic restructurings of the monarchy were being considered). The more momentous ones were in 1790 (the Temišvarski Sabor), when Emperor Leopold II wished to annul his brother Joseph's radical legislation; in 1848, when the Serbs of Hungary sided with Austria during the Hungarian revolution; and in 1861 (the Blagoveštenski Sabor) which was most concerned with the fate of Serbs as the monarchy was once again reformed from above. The Church Congress never had the character of a representative body for the Serbs of the Habsburg monarchy, just as those same Serbs were never considered by the authorities in Vienna to be anything more than a corporate mass of citizens of a certain faith with certain guarantees. But there was always tension between the political aspirations of the Serbs of the Habsburg lands and Vienna, and the Church Congress was the single plausible body for Serbs to look to for political guidance and cultural cohesion.

The autonomy of the Orthodox church in Hungary and Croatia was established in its modern form with Hungarian Law IX of 1868. Law IX placed control of the church in the hands of the higher clergy (the *jerarhija*). Subsequent laws of 1871, 1875, and 1908, among others, regulated the Orthodox diocesan administration, Serbian Orthodox schools, elections to the Serbian National-Church Congress, and the administration of the funds of the metropolitanate of Srijemski Karlovci, which encompassed all Croatia and southern Hungary. These laws established the Church Congress as the administrator of the church (under the presidency of the patriarch, who was appointed by the Hungarian government). The original law of 1868 nevertheless gave the Hungarian government the right of approval of all decisions reached by the Church Congress. The full Congress debated matters of general policy and voted on legislation prepared in the committees. The law stated that the Church Congress would have seventy-five elected members: twenty-five from the frontier, twenty-five from civil districts, and twenty-five priests.[35] The Congress still consisted of seventy-five elected members in 1906, although its internal composition was different, due to the demise of the frontier. Of the seventy-five, eight were elected internally to the Congress Committee, which governed the funds of the church and relations with the state; eight were elected to the Metropolitan Church Council, which governed the activities of the parishes; and six were elected to the Metropolitan

School Committee, which administered the Serbian Orthodox schools of the metropolitanate of Srijemski Karlovci.

In many important ways, the Serbs of Croatia/Slavonia were indistinguishable from their Croatian neighbors: they were for the most part illiterate peasants with few opportunities for social or economic advancement. More than 90 percent of Croatian/Slavonian settlements were peasant villages in 1880; in the Military Frontier, the figure approached 100 percent.[36] Figures for literacy do not discriminate between Catholic and Orthodox in Croatia/Slavonia, but in 1869, in Civil Croatia and Slavonia about 15 percent of the population was literate;[37] in 1880, about 25 percent of the population of Croatia above the age of five was literate; by 1890 that figure had risen to 32 percent. In 1910, the figure was about 52 percent. Between 1885 and 1910, about two-thirds of school-age children attended elementary schools in Croatia.[38] In the Military Frontier the situation was about the same: 15 percent literacy in the late 1860s.[39] The rapid rise in literacy masks the fact that it came late in the century and does not help us to negotiate the educational differences in the experience of Serbs and Croats. One way to reach such an understanding is to compare the data regarding numbers of schools. Between 1857 and 1874 (the last year that confessional schools existed in Croatia), the number of schools in Civil Croatia/Slavonia grew from 397 to 673. About 20 percent of all schools were Orthodox (137 in 1874), which was a better school-student ratio than for Catholics, as the Orthodox proportion of the population was about 17 percent.[40] That, however, did not include the Military Frontier, which we can only assume saw worse conditions. In 1857–1858, whereas 40 percent of school-age Catholic children attended Catholic schools, only 30 percent of school-age Orthodox children attended Orthodox schools.[41] And whereas about 22 percent of schools in that year were Orthodox, only about 14 percent of teachers and administrators were; there was about 1 teacher per school in Orthodox schools, and about 1.75 for each Catholic school.[42] Although the number of schools was rising in the second half of the nineteenth century, the ability of communities to support that growing number dwindled. This was especially true of communities that had to support both Catholic and Orthodox schools while only possessing the means to provide for one school. The figures all point to a more poorly educated Orthodox community; the situation was undoubtedly even less salutary, since the Military Frontier, which was about half Orthodox, does not appear in these numbers.[43] The educational situation was potentially much better for the Orthodox of the Military Frontier as one traveled eastward: the Lika, Otočac, Ogulin, and First Banija Regiments had the fewest schools (all fewer than thirty-two), while the Gradiška, Brod, and Petrovaradin Regiments had the most (all over eighty-four).[44] The Gradiška and Brod Regiments were two of the least Orthodox of the eleven Croatian/Slavonian regiments.

The metropolitanate of Srijemski Karlovci was responsible for Serbian Orthodox schooling; in fact, the metropolitanate considered schooling to be its fundamental right as cultural leader of Serbs in the monarchy. The metropolitanate organized schools according to bishoprics: Karlovac, Pakrac, and Srijemski Karlovci each controlled a number of school districts. In 1857, Pakrac, the central bishopric, administered seven districts with twenty-two elementary schools; Srijemski Karlovci to the east had only two districts, but twenty-eight schools; Karlovac, in the west, including the poorest districts of Croatia, was the worst off, with two school districts and only two schools.[45] Each of the eleven school districts was overseen by an Orthodox cleric. Until 1874, when the Croatian government secularized schooling in Croatia/Slavonia, the government could inspect Orthodox schools, but had no administrative control over them. As late as the late 1850s, the schools used "Slavo-Serbian" as their language of teaching, and they utilized prayerbooks and psalters for texts.[46] In the words of one Serbian historian, teachers were "for the most part unprofessional and insufficiently schooled, and occasionally even utter ignoramuses."[47] About all that could be certain under these conditions was that a minimum of students were nurtured in their faith. The church had certain basic requirements: that the Cyrillic script be taught to Serbian children, that schooling conform to the demands of the faith. The logic was simple: the faith had protected the Serbs of Croatia and Hungary, the most basic attribute of Serbianness was its Orthodoxy, and the church was the only acceptable conduit for education in one's responsibilities, which were to the nation and not to the state. As such, the subordination of Serbian schools to the metropolitanate was considered necessary by Serbian political and cultural leaders in Croatia through the early twentieth century.

Unfortunately, that perspective led them headlong into a struggle with the Croatian government, which proposed to secularize schooling in 1874 under Ban Ivan Mažuranić.[48] In proposing the Law on People's Schooling and Normal Schools of September 1874,[49] the *ban* wished to bring Croatia's education policy into line with the rest of Austria-Hungary, which had already secularized its schools. The law's two main features were four years of obligatory grammar schooling and the freeing of schools from clerical supervision, both Catholic and Orthodox, placing them instead under school committees composed of teachers and parents. The law was directed for the most part at Catholic schooling, for the Catholic church was dominant in Croatia. However, it also affected Orthodox schooling. The law thereby removed all Serbian schools from the control of the Serbian Orthodox church, which had controlled the schools through the Serbian National-Church Congress and whose autonomy in such matters as school and church affairs the monarchy had long recognized. Many Serbs reacted sharply in opposition to the new law; of course, the Catholic clergy also opposed it, since it was specifically directed against them. Orthodox schools assured the continued dominance of the church in the daily life and education of Serbs. Although the law impinged on the autonomy that the Serbian church had long enjoyed, the *ban* and the Croatian Sabor insisted that legislation passed in the Sabor superseded all precedents in the matter.[50] In 1888, a new law gave the Serbian Orthodox church administration limited authority once again over school personnel and educational material in Orthodox districts of Croatia.[51]

While the majority of the Habsburg Serbs were peasants, some were wealthy owners of estates. Their holdings were most likely to be found in southern Hungary and Slavonia, where there was fertile agricultural ground. The wealthiest people were also likely to be the most active politically, given the restricted franchise in Croatia and Hungary. Thus by the turn of the twentieth century, political organizations and monetary institutions were often part of the same larger network; in Croatia, the Serbian Independent party had its own circle of financial and cultural institutions, as did the Serbian Radical party and the Serbian Liberal party in Hungary. In Hungary, the first Serbian banks and lending institutions were founded in the late 1860s, after the Ausgleich and before the downturn of 1873. Novi Sad (5), Pančevo (2), Sombor, Kikinda, Veliki Bečkerek, Versecz, and other towns saw Serbian banks founded with Serbian investment funds. This region, known more generally to Serbs as the Vojvodina, was also renowned as the center of Serbian culture during the Ottoman period. Elsewhere, and especially in Croatia/Slavonia and the Military Frontier, the banking system opened its doors to Serbs in a more limited fashion: in Srijem (bordering southern Hungary), three banks capitalized in part by Serbian funds opened in 1869–1873, and in

Zagreb the Croatian Commercial Bank, which opened in 1873, included Serbian capital.[52] Beyond those, however, Croatia was a much poorer place than southern Hungary. Small Serbian savings banks opened between 1869 and 1876 in Ruma, Sid, Mitrovica, Zemun, and Srijemski Karlovci, all in Srijem; others in Karlovac, Ogulin, Petrinja, and Pakrac served western Slavonia and Croatia.[53]

For the most part, and especially in the late nineteenth and early twentieth century, these institutions were viewed by their founders as ammunition in a battle to maintain the nation. It was not so much that Serbs could not get loans as easily as Croats of a similar socioeconomic status and thus had to turn to their own, it was that the institutions were founded by people who wished to direct their attentions to Serbs. Thus Jaša Tomić, a Serbian politician in southern Hungary whom we will get to know better, believed it in the interest of the Serbian nation to build a network of cooperatives for Serbian peasants because it would help build or maintain Serbian national consciousness.[54] A concentrated effort to build a network of loan agencies, cooperatives, banks, and educational initiatives directed at the Serbian farmer was mounted at the end of the nineteenth century in Croatia, and its inspiration was indeed the belief that Serbs needed support in order to nurture the nation's consciousness. The Serbian Bank, located in Zagreb, was founded in 1895 with the aid of a politician from Serbia, Kosta Taušanović, a member of the Radical party of that kingdom.[55] With capital contributed by Serbs throughout the Habsburg lands, it ranked among the wealthiest banks in Croatia by 1910. In 1897, soon after its founding, the first of many Serbian farmers' collectives *(Srpske zemljoradničke zadruge)* was formed in Croatia. These organizations were designed to provide small-scale aid in the form of seed, feed, educational materials, and classes to Serbian peasants. By 1902, there were 140 such collectives, 51 of them in Croatia.[56] Linking all the collectives was the Serbian Economic Society and its newspaper, *Privrednik* (The Tradesman), located in Zagreb. It was launched in 1888 and was dedicated to the economic education and general advancement of Serbs.[57] Each of these Zagreb institutions (the bank, the farmers' collectives, and *Privrednik*) was founded by members of the Serbian Independent party. It is also true that most of the elected politicians among Serbs in Croatia were linked to some network of financial institutions.

Just as economic institutions tended to be the possessions of the elite among Serbs, so were cultural ones. The Matica Srpska ("Mother Serbia," for lack of a concise translation for this all-encompassing term), an organization founded in 1826 in Pest but located in Novi Sad (the Serbian "Athens") after 1864, was devoted to the nurturing of Serbian nationhood, defending Serbian culture from the assimilationist tendencies of Serbs' neighbors. The Matica was one of many such organizations founded in the early nineteenth century in the Habsburg monarchy as German romanticism filtered through to the east. The Matica became the centerpiece of ongoing projects dedicated to defining Serbianness: Vuk Karadžić, the great Serbian language reformer, was in regular conflict with members of the Matica who disagreed with his plans for a Serbian orthography. The Matica, at least, remained above the fray in day-to-day politics. Other organizations could not say the same. As the century progressed and the defense of the nation became a political as well as a cultural enterprise, cultural institutions became politicized. Such was the publishing house, the Srpska dionička štamparija in Zagreb, founded in 1892. It was a possession of the Serbian Independent party, and its publishing schedule reflected that: the newspapers *Srbobran*, the organ of the Independent party, *Privrednik*, and *Vrač pogadjač*, a satirical newspaper edited by Sima Lukin Lazić, one of the leaders of the Serbian Independent party and self-appointed historian of the Serbian nation; the yearly Serbian "national calendars"; and occasional printing jobs for books, journals, and articles from Serbia.[58] The Serbian Radical party of southern Hungary also had its publishing house: the Srpska štamparija dra Svetozara Miletića, in Novi Sad, which was most notable for its publication of pamphlets by Radical party leaders and of the party organ, *Zastava*. Together, the banking institutions, publishing companies, and party organizations served to segregate Serbs from their neighbors and inculcate an insular sense of community. They also promoted often vicious political confrontations within the Serbian community, confrontations that were partly ideological and partly practical.

Serbian National Identity

What exactly was a Serb? We have been discussing Serbs without adequately explaining the origins of the modern notion of Serbianness. It is to the ultimate despair of the outsider that one must acknowledge that Serbianness, as well as Croatianness, Germanness, and Frenchness (and the list goes on) is a self-defining category. Outsiders can only describe the phenomenon and note the essential capriciousness of national definitions. The simple answer is that a Serb is and was an Orthodox Christian speaker of the language we know as Serbo-Croatian. The complicating condition is that in southeastern Europe, the idea of the nation was brought to the masses by intellectuals who had the opportunity to pick and choose which elements of a collective personality they wished to emphasize. Only then was this personality communicated to the populace, which was becoming literate as it imbibed the nation-building educational efforts of newly formed state elites.[59] Thus this person whom we know as a Serb today might very well have become something else: a Croat, a Bulgarian, a Yugoslav, depending on the relative merits of the cultural and political arguments for the different options and the capabilities of those who influenced them. Obviously, the arguments are important, and their success or failure hinged on the cultural background to the process of nation building. In other words, one might try to convince Orthodox Christian speakers of Serbo-Croatian that they were Yugoslavs (and many did try), but if the definition seems to be, or is made to seem, irrelevant to the subject, it will fail.

Among the peoples of southeastern Europe without states in the nineteenth century (those of the Habsburg monarchy and the Ottoman Empire), Orthodox Serbs were perhaps the best prepared to make the modern transition from religious community to nationhood. They had strong cultural ties to an earlier era of statehood (the medieval Serbian kingdom) and an institution that had protected (probably even nurtured) a separate identity, the Serbian Orthodox church. After the Serbian revolutions of 1804–1815, a small state along the Danube River gave Serbs another advantage: a foundation for the propagation of a new state idea. Thus, in the nineteenth century, their church, their political history, and a new state establishment told Serbs that they were unique, they were Serbs, and thus their susceptibility to alternative national identities was relatively low. Benedict Anderson has suggested that the nation is an "imagined community," the synthetic creation of an intellectual elite.[60] If this is so, then among the small group of South Slavic peoples which could conceivably have imagined themselves a nation (including Croats, Slovenes, Macedonians, Bulgarians), Serbs had the most raw material to work with.

Yet there were competing ideas. When discussing Croatian and Serbian history, one cannot escape the various concepts that arose in the nineteenth century to define the relationship of the Croatian and Serbian nations. Some national thinkers proposed that Croats and Serbs (and Slovenes and even

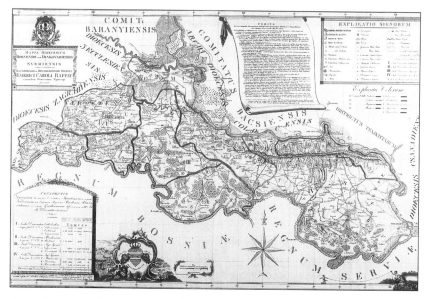

An early nineteenth-century map of Srijem. *Hrvatski državni arhiv, Zagreb*

Bulgarians) were so closely related that they may as well have been of the same nation. These formulations have received and maintained a generic designation as "Yugoslav" conceptions. Yugoslavism was strongest in Croatia; the stimulus to it was the relative political and cultural weakness of Croatia in relation to its neighbors, Austria, Hungary, and the Ottoman Empire. Serbs, who imagined themselves in a strong position with regard to their neighbors after the establishment of an autonomous Serbia in 1830, were less likely to champion a Yugoslav nationalism; rather, they envisioned the expansion of the borders of the Serbian state to include all of the Serbs (as defined by Serbs themselves: they often considered many or all Croats to be Serbs) of southeastern Europe.

The first in the catalogue of classic Yugoslav national ideologies was Illyrianism, a movement that flourished among a group of Croatian intellectuals in the 1830s and 1840s.[61] Led by Ljudevit Gaj, the Illyrians chose their appellation because they believed that first, it was the historical name of all the South Slavs, and second, it was an alternative that Slovenes, Serbs, Bulgarians, and of course Croats could use without threatening any individual national name. The Illyrians counted on a degree of cultural self-sacrifice by the various South Slav nations in order to help their movement gain momentum. The lasting legacy of the Illyrians was to adopt and establish the

Štokavian dialect of the Serbo-Croatian language as the Croatian literary language.[62] Croats were divided among those who spoke Kajkavian, Čakavian, and Štokavian; more spoke Štokavian than spoke the others, but Kajkavian had a rich literary tradition. Serbs spoke Štokavian exclusively, however, so Gaj saw it as a possible link between Croats and Serbs. Thus the move was dictated by practicality and then-current ideas which held that a nation was defined by its language. Štokavian could become the Illyrian, and not merely the Croatian or Serbian literary language. They hoped that such moves would entice the other South Slavs to acknowledge their shared nationality. Illyrianism, however, died as a result of Serbian and Slovene unwillingness to embrace the movement.

Vuk Stefanović Karadžić, a Serbian language reformer of the first half of the nineteenth century, also adhered to the proposition that language defined a nation. But Karadžić concluded that all Štokavian speakers were Serbs.[63] Thus, where Gaj and the Illyrians had envisioned Štokavian as a link between separate but related, complementary, nations, Karadžić viewed it as proof that all Štokavian speakers were of the same, Serbian, nation (his most famous article on the subject was entitled "Serbs All and Everywhere").[64] Gaj and Karadžić started from separate premises and drew their logical conclusions. The disparate conclusions were a metaphor for Croatian and Serbian attitudes toward their respective nationhoods in general: whereas Croats often saw portents of a future harmonious relationship between separate nations, most concerned Serbs interpreted those same portents as proof that the people in question were all Serbs.

Karadžić heralded a change in the substance of Serbian national thought. Before early nineteenth-century European national thinkers began to emphasize language as the sole indicator of a nation, Serbs had equated their nationality with their Orthodox faith; Karadžić reoriented Serbian nationalism to include all speakers of the dialect spoken by Serbs, including those Croats who also spoke it.[65] A further element in Serbian national thought became relevant with the foundation of a Serbian state in 1815. With this event, Serbs gained a focus for their national aspirations, and until at least 1918, the maintenance and expansion of the Serbian state became the foremost goal of Serbian nationalism. When this state was envisioned as including only Serbs (Orthodox speakers of Štokavian), this vision became known as simple Serbian nationalism; when it was envisioned as including other nations, whose nationhood, implicitly, would not be respected, the idea was denoted Great

Serbian nationalism. The latter implied that the state would include non-Serbs, but that those non-Serbs would be treated as if they were Serbs; in other words, they would be assimilated or treated as outsiders. Great Serbia and Yugoslavia would have encompassed many of the same territories, but reflected completely opposed concepts.

The most explicit statement of Great Serbian aims produced by a Serbian statesman was the Načertanije, written by Ilija Garašanin in 1844, when he was the Serbian minister of the interior.[66] In fact, Yugoslav historians have long argued whether the document was an expression of Yugoslavism, Serbianism, or Great Serbianism.[67] It is clear that Garašanin's document expressed Great Serbian sentiments, because he envisioned a Serbian state that included non-Serbs whose separateness would not be respected. Garašanin looked first to the liberation of Serbs under Ottoman control in Bosnia and Hercegovina; he assumed that all the South Slavs of the region were Serbs. Next on his schedule for liberation were the South Slavs of Kosovo and Macedonia. He did not wish to antagonize Austria, so he considered the union of the Serbs of Croatia and Hungary to be but a distant goal. He never betrayed any sensitivity to the fact that these lands included non-Serbs. Although Garašanin's statement was not made public until 1906, his ideas were certainly current among Serbs throughout the period.

The idea of South Slavic unity on a more reciprocal basis did not die with Gaj. In the 1860s and early 1870s, Bishop Josip Juraj Strossmayer of Djakovo, in Slavonia, sponsored a renewed version known as Yugoslavism. Strossmayer hoped that Orthodox Serbs and Catholic Croats could be brought together in spite of their obvious differences; he and Franjo Rački, his fellow prelate, envisioned a Yugoslav state centered in Croatia. Although they assumed the formation of a federal Yugoslav state in the future, they could obviously not propose that openly while the Habsburg monarchy yet existed. In the 1860s, they attempted to coordinate their activities with the Serbian government, then again guided by Garašanin, but their cooperation failed because Serbia was unwilling to carry it to its conclusion.[68] There was no chance for such cooperation to bear fruit without drastic changes in the European order. What remained was a legacy of tolerance and gentility, the character traits most often associated with Strossmayer.

Two territories that brought (and frankly still bring) nothing but grief to nationalists of all types among the South Slavs were Dalmatia and Bosnia. Dalmatia definitively entered the Habsburg monarchy as a result of the

Congress of Vienna, when it was taken from Napoleon's France and assigned to the realm of the Habsburgs. Until 1867, it suffered Habsburg political experiments along with the rest of the monarchy. The Ausgleich placed it in the Austrian half of the monarchy, a fact that rankled for Croats from then on. In fact, the attachment of Dalmatia to Croatia became the single most fundamental demand of Croatian nationalist politicians through the First World War. Yet the demand for union of Dalmatia and Croatia was not clearly just, for Dalmatia's ultimate place was disputed. Croats, Serbs, and Italians all claimed it.

One historian's estimate is that 89 percent of the population of Dalmatia spoke only Serbo-Croatian in 1874; about 8 percent spoke both Serbo-Croatian and Italian; 3 percent spoke only Italian.[69] Of its 457,000 inhabitants in that year, 17 percent were Orthodox, 82 percent Catholic. The Orthodox lived mostly in the south, on the Bay of Kotor and in Dubrovnik. They were also to be found in Zadar and Šibenik. Political conditions in Dalmatia were quite different for Croats and Serbs, who had to contend with a powerful Italian desire for the region. Although the Italian demographic presence was rather small, the cultural attachment of Italians to the Adriatic coastline was strong indeed. After all, Zadar (Zara), Šibenik (Sibenico), Dubrovnik (Ragusa), and Kotor (Cattaro) all had their Italian heritage. Given the Italian element and a conspicuous disinterest on the part of Austria, Croats and Serbs were much more capable of cohabitation than they were in Croatia proper. But Dalmatia would not become part of Croatia until the formation of the new Kingdom of Serbs, Croats, and Slovenes in 1918, and the battle over its national character could and would be just as hot as in other regions.

In 1878, when the Habsburg monarchy was allowed by the Concert of Europe to occupy and administer the Ottoman *vilayet* (province) of Bosnia (minus parts of the district of Yenipazar), the emperor felt himself compensated for having lost Lombardy-Venetia to Italy earlier in the century. In Austrian politics, the occupation of Bosnia was such a triumph for imperial prestige that it contributed to the downfall of the Liberal government that Franz Joseph despised. Bosnia was given special status in the no-man's land of dualism, as an imperial possession administered by the ministry of finance. Unfortunately, and in spite of Austrian efforts to make Bosnia a laboratory for efficient administration and modernization policies (the Austrian contribution to the White Man's Burden), Bosnia proved to be an ungovernable province as the era of ethnic nationalism dawned. Its population in 1870 was

48 percent Muslim (38 percent in 1879), 37 percent Orthodox (43 percent in 1879), and 14 percent Catholic (18 percent in 1879), and hopelessly mixed.[70] The Serbs predominated in the countryside, with the Muslim portion dominating the urban areas, of which there were few (Sarajevo, Mostar, Tuzla, Banja Luka, Travnik, and Bihać were the administrative centers of the Ottoman districts, known as *sanjak*s). Muslim emigration, indicated in the population figures cited above, contributed to the muddle, as Bosnia became more Orthodox and Catholic as the century progressed. Its ethnic mixture, the fact that it entered the Habsburg lands provisionally and with a unique constitutional status, and the ongoing competitive relationship of Croats and Serbs helped create a grand experiment in the art of national persuasion as Croats and Serbs attempted to make conationals of the large Muslim community. The competition for the soul Bosnia continues to this day, except that since 1941 a cultural battleground has turned physically violent.

Conclusion

All the debates about what constituted the Serbian or Croatian nation, who spoke which language, which territories comprised Serbia, Croatia, or Yugoslavia, did not occur in a vacuum. Political life among the South Slavs of the Habsburg monarchy was, however, rather predictable throughout much of the nineteenth century. People in the Habsburg lands acted as groups, defined according to a variety of categories: first as social classes—aristocracies, peasantries, city dwellers; then perhaps as national or religious communities; always, however, as groups, and never as citizens or individuals. By the end of the century in Austria and Hungary politicians and intellectuals began to move away from such political orientations, embracing instead the idea that the individual is the primary political and social actor and that values, not historical, religious, or cultural communities, define citizenship and ultimately nationhood. It goes without saying that within the Serbian and Croatian communities of the Habsburg monarchy there would be no intellectual and political explosion such as that which produced the French Revolution and the values associated with French national identity today. Among the Serbs and Croats of the monarchy, the central novelty of the French Revolution, the notion of the individual as the foundation of citizenship, would be applied in a much more simplistic fashion: in the struggle for constitutional governance in Croatia, for a form of government that would eliminate the ability of Habsburg governors to manipulate ethnic communities.

This book should not be read only as a narrative of the relations of two Serbian political parties and their relations with their Croatian neighbors. Instead, it offers an analysis of the only period in the history of the modern relations of Serbs and Croats in which one side or the other (actually, both) attempted to push collectivist ("ethnic") conceptions of politics to the margins in favor of an individualist, constitutionalist ("civic") ethos. In other words, political leaders who valued the characteristics of the individual over those of the nation (or ethnic group) attempted to foster those values in their constituents. In practice, they attempted to wean their constituents from a political style that emphasized one's cultural distinctiveness and collective nature in favor of a style that emphasized the merits of political behavior based on natural law, the notion that individuals possess certain rights as individuals, not as collectives whose value takes precedence. The distinction that I make between the civic and ethnic types of nationalism is certainly not novel: Hans Kohn described the two types as political (civic) and cultural (ethnic) nationalism, and other commentators since, culminating most recently in the stimulating work of Liah Greenfeld, have adopted it (and occasionally altered it in the process). In essence, they describe a civic or political type of nationalism that aspires to nationhood based on shared political values and an ethnic or cultural nationalism that posits the cultural nation as the basis of statehood. In the latter, political values are secondary, to be worked out once the nation, in its cultural purity, has a state to mold.

Perhaps the French Revolution came to Austria in 1848; it certainly did not come when it came to France. Even in 1848, however, the revolutions in the Habsburg lands rarely strived to establish the principles of an end to privilege and of representative government. Instead, for instance, the Hungarian revolution was a nationalist revolution that merely redefined the privileged. The end-of-the-century Habsburg monarchy produced a number of movements that hoped to rapidly catch their peoples up to the rest of Europe in political terms. Aligned against those nationalists who relied on states' rights as their foundations, Tomaš Masaryk in Bohemia, the Austrian Social Democrats Karl Renner and Otto Bauer, Oscar Jaszi in Hungary, and others argued instead that the modern age demanded universal suffrage and representative government, which would contribute to the solution to the national question by providing solutions to social questions that seemed to mirror national grievances.

In Croatia, political leaders with a less convincing foundation in political philosophy and less interest in the socioeconomic understructure to national conflicts adopted Masaryk's approach, which called for the politically active to abandon the stale states' rights approach to political action. Less in the interests of general progress, more as a method of ameliorating national antagonisms, the Serbian Independents, the Croatian Progressives, the Croatian Peasant party, and others moved toward the politics of participation, abandoning the politics of elite bargaining and negation of others. Their behavior reflected a belief in a civic rather than ethnic foundation in politics and statehood, but it should be noted early on that the Croatian and Serbian politicians who favored cooperation and constitutionalism did not share the same political values in the sense that, for instance, French and American nationalism is rooted in shared values. Their nationalism ("Yugoslavism") was not a fully formed civic idea. Instead, some Serbs granted the validity of the Croatian political nation long enough and deeply enough to enable them to work with the Croatian opposition, with its entrenched fondness for Starčević's politics of state right. The fact that their shared values were tenuously nurtured would turn out to be a fatal flaw in their cooperation later. Nonetheless, their insistence on the primacy of the individual over the nation or ethnic group marked them as innovators, innovators whose initial foray might have provided a new foundation for Croatian and Serbian politics, and ultimately a successful Yugoslavism.

The various options facing Serbs as well as Croats continued to be debated through the late twentieth century. The fact, however, was that Serbs always enjoyed a much stronger self-identification. This in turn made them much more coherent political actors. In other words, without the confusion that reigned, for instance, among Croatian intellectuals and politicians about their national character, Serbs were capable of defending their own national character much more ably. The reason is straightforward: Serbs possessed an uncanny collective sense of the attributes that made them Serbs: their faith, their script, their history and their interpretation of that history, the pervasiveness with which historical and cultural imagery permeated their folk and later official culture. In Croatia and Hungary, where their community was well marked culturally (if not physically), they strived to maintain their separateness. All other offers (to think of themselves as Croats or Yugoslavs, for instance) they rejected because the new imagery could not compete with that which was already deeply rooted in their collective sense and memory. Thus they rejected Illyrianism and later Yugoslavism. As politics became popular, they carried their consciousness of their separateness forward with them. Which takes us to the realm of politics, where the subject of this book becomes actual: the interplay of nationalisms and politics, of national diversity in a changing political climate.

2

SERBS AS POLITICAL ACTORS, 1867–1903

The Political Life of Serbs in the Habsburg Monarchy

MODERN POLITICAL LIFE began for Serbs in the Habsburg monarchy after 1867, when the Ausgleich established two separate entities within the monarchy. The first political parties emerged in Croatia and Hungary after 1868, the year of the Nagodba. Serbs had certain advantages in politics over their Hungarian and Croatian neighbors. Their community was spiritually (if not physically) well defined. They could look back on a shared history, in which Orthodox Serbs were, by definition, outsiders, without ties and obligations in the Habsburg lands, and their population was relatively undifferentiated in socioeconomic terms. The first modern Serbian party in the Habsburg monarchy was the Serbian Liberal party, led by Svetozar Miletić, one of the modern Serbian national heroes. Miletić was a nationalist, and eventually a persecuted one. His party attempted to work in a Hungary in which the law respected differences of nationality but the political system and intellectual life rejected all national ideas but the Hungarian one. Under such conditions,

Serbian politics in Hungary faced insurmountable odds: Serbs could only rarely be elected, and when they were, they were marginalized in a Hungarian parliament in which the only political nation, the Hungarian, had a voice.

Serbian politics in Croatia were acted out in conditions established from above—which was the norm in a monarchy in which political change had been characterized by imperial experimentation since the late eighteenth century. The final experiments were the Ausgleich and the Nagodba. After the Nagodba, Croatia enjoyed the trappings of autonomy, but in fact was governed from Budapest. The ban (viceroy) was appointed by the emperor with the advice of the minister-president of Hungary. The ban was not responsible to the Croatian Sabor in any political sense, although theoretically he could be removed if found by the Sabor to be in violation of criminal codes.[1] The Croatian government was empowered to administer Croatia's internal affairs, education and religion, and justice, with the help of three department heads appointed by the ban. Croatia and Hungary shared responsibility for economic decisions, banking, transportation, and defense. Thus the Hungarian presidency, ministry of finance, ministry of defense, ministry of trade, and ministry of agriculture were declared to be joint ministries of the Hungaro-Croatian government. The cabinet of the Hungarian minister-president also included a minister for Croatia. After 1888, when the Croatian Sabor attained its final configuration, it had 88 representatives. The Sabor then elected 40 of its members to take part in the Hungarian Parliament, which had 453 members altogether. In addition, there were 44 "peers" in the Sabor; 3 went on to the Hungarian Parliament with the Croatian delegation. When the Hungarian Parliament met with its Croatian delegation, the joint government of Croatia and Hungary was created.[2] An electoral law that allowed only 2 percent of the citizens of Croatia to vote assured that the Sabor and the Croatian delegation to the Hungarian Parliament would be acceptable to the Hungarian government. Since the ban himself had to be approved by the Hungarian minister-president, Hungary could be sure that Croatia's autonomy was quite limited. Many Croats represented and unrepresented in the Croatian Sabor opposed the compromise, and this opposition grew stronger as it became evident that Hungary did not view the Nagodba as a guarantee of Croatian existence as a state, but rather as the first step in the transformation of Croatia into an integral part of Hungary. Nonetheless, the Nagodba itself did not necessarily lead to the political subjugation of Croatia, which, after all, had not been an independent or even autonomous state before 1868. The attitude of the Hungarian government after 1868, however, did endanger the autonomy guaranteed by the Nagodba.

Serbs did have one legislative body all to themselves: the Serbian National-Church Congress, which governed the activities and funds of the Serbian Orthodox metropolitanate of Srijemski Karlovci. Unlike the Hungarian Parliament and the Croatian Sabor, the Church Congress represented all areas in which Serbs lived in Hungary and Croatia. By the 1890s, when Serbian political parties in the monarchy had developed and become intensely competitive, the Church Congress came to be the object of that political competition. Because it was elected by universal adult male suffrage, the Serbian parties, which were unable to elect a substantial number of representatives to the Hungarian Parliament and the Croatian Sabor (which had restricted franchises), could stoke their competitive fires in the Church Congress. Thus the Congress always played a large role in Serbian politics in the Habsburg monarchy. The autonomy of the Serbian Orthodox church, which enabled the Congress to exist and function, was also a constant concern of the Serbian parties in the monarchy, for national, ideological, cultural, and political reasons.

The low point in Croatia's modern history was the period from 1883 to 1903, the twenty years of the banate of Károlyi Khuen-Héderváry. Khuen-Héderváry came to office on the heels of disturbances that broke out in summer 1883 in Croatia as a response to the gradual unification of the Croatian and Hungarian financial administrations.[3] After the Hungarian government invoked martial law, Khuen-Héderváry was made ban in December 1883. His mandate was to stifle all opposition to the Nagodba, opposition that had grown as the creeping severity of Hungarian assimilationism became apparent. Instead of supporting the Croatian majority, Khuen-Héderváry reckoned that he could win over enough Serbs so that the Croatian opposition would concentrate its hatred of his regime on them. Combining these Serbs with the Croats of the older, now compromised National party, Khuen-Héderváry created in the Sabor a governmental party which, by virtue of its wealth and social position, could be easily and repeatedly elected via Croatia's limited franchise. Khuen-Héderváry was the first ban who was not linked to any political organization in Croatia—he built his own after coming to the position backed only by the confidence of the Hungarian government and with the assignment to create a strong faction that would support policy formulated in Budapest. His success stifled Croatian political and economic development until 1903.

Khuen-Héderváry's choice to promote Croatia's Serbs followed tradition in the Habsburg monarchy, in which the monarch balanced regions and historical interests by manipulating grievances with one hand and dispensing privileges with the other. Khuen-Héderváry assured his success with the electoral law of 1887 that gave him a compliant majority in the Sabor.[4] The law limited the right to vote to those who paid a very high tax rate, or about 2 percent of the population. It also gave the right to vote to civil servants working in the bureaucracy in Croatia. Finally, the law gerrymandered the electoral districts so as to further limit the possibility of the election of candidates not amenable to Khuen-Héderváry's government. This electoral configuration contributed to the election of many Serbs, who then, by and large, supported Khuen-Héderváry in the 1880s. It did not hurt that after 1881, the Serbian state and its ruling Obrenović dynasty were tightly allied to Austria-Hungary. But the relationship of Serbia and Austria-Hungary gave both Khuen-Héderváry and his Serbian supporters one more justification for their orientation: the Serbs could contribute to Serbian national policy emanating from Belgrade by cooperating with Khuen-Héderváry, and Khuen-Héderváry could link Serbs more tightly to the Austro-Hungarian monarchy.

By selectively favoring people who would support him, Khuen-Héderváry built his National party, which was united not by a program but by the national and self-interest of its members. Within the National party was the Serbian Club, consisting of Serbian "magyarones," so named for their service to the Khuen-Héderváry regime. To gain the support of these representatives, Khuen-Héderváry assured them of his support in Budapest. In placing the Hungarian government rather than the Croatian Sabor in the service of Serbian interests, Khuen-Héderváry drew these individuals into the Hungarian, rather than Croatian, administrative context. Serbs felt that they no longer had reason to act in the interests of Croatia. Serbs became visible representatives of the Khuen-Héderváry system.[5] However, Khuen-Héderváry's favoritism gained Serbs only two tangible victories: in 1887 and 1888, the Sabor passed two laws, one legalizing the use of the Serbian language and Cyrillic alphabet, the second assuring the existence of Serbian Orthodox schools in districts where Serbs predominated.[6] Such favoritism may have seemed advantageous in the short run, but in the long run it merely supported a regime whose antagonistic behavior toward the Croatian majority made its own demise inevitable.

The first Serbian opposition party in Croatia was founded in August 1881 at a congress in Ruma (in Srijem, the Military Frontier) sponsored by Svetozar Miletić's Liberal party, which was based in Novi Sad.[7] The imminent incorporation of the Military Frontier into Croatia and the growth of the Serbian population of Croatia prompted the formation of the party, called the Independent Serbian party and led by Milan Djordjević and Stevan Dimitrijević, followers of Miletić. The platform of the Independent Serbian party (which later became the Serbian National Independent party) included the basic demands of all Serbian oppositionalists in Croatia: church and school autonomy, budgetary support of Serbian institutions in Croatia, the equality of the Cyrillic alphabet with the Latin alphabet, the right to display the Serbian flag, and revision of the Nagodba. The party also demanded the eventual unification of Dalmatia with Croatia and Slavonia and called for the application of the principle of self-determination in deciding the future of Bosnia and Hercegovina. Indicative of the unimaginative politics of this first incarnation of the Independent party is the fact that its later leader, Pavle Jovanović, was once elected to the Sabor (in 1892) with the help of Khuen-Héderváry and the National party. He was one of only two Independent Serbs elected to the Sabor from 1883 to 1901, suggesting that the Independent party was not a significant factor in Croatian politics during that period.[8] In part, Khuen-Héderváry's use of coercion in elections locked out the Serbian opposition. But it was electoral laws favoring wealthier citizens that really kept opposition Serbs and Croats out of the Sabor. Furthermore, in public statements and literary activity, the members of the party demonstrated that they could be as narrowly chauvinistic as any member of the Serbian Club. Thus they offered no alternative for Serbian voters. The Independent party virtually disappeared in the 1890s, since its role was usurped by the Serbian National Radical party, which was formed in 1887 in Novi Sad and quickly became the "radical alternative" to the Liberals (and therefore to the Independents).

The Radical party formed as the result of conflicts following the retirement of Miletić.[9] The Radicals were originally the left wing of the Liberal party, which split over the question of the inclusion of social and economic issues in the party program. But even though the Radicals first emerged as a socially conscious wing of the Liberals, eventually the critical element of their politics was their fundamental belief in the validity of the privileges described in chapter 1. Under the leadership of Jaša Tomić, the party's program focused on the question of leadership in the Serbian National-Church

Congress, the body that administered Serbian Orthodox church and school autonomy in the entire Habsburg monarchy and the only stage on which the Serbian parties productively interacted, given their impotence in the Croatian Sabor and Hungarian Parliament. In attacking clerical, magyarone, and, later, Liberal domination of the Church Congress, the Radicals revealed the character of their politics until 1914: theirs was a battle for control of the Church Congress and its resources, which included funds, but also cultural resources such as church policy and parochial schools. Because the Orthodox church was seen by most Serbs, including the Radicals, as the protector of the Serbian nation in the monarchy, the Radicals easily portrayed their work as beneficial for the nation. The Radical party, unlike the Independent party, was not active in Croatia and had no reason to support the Nagodba. Instead, it based all of its political activity on the foundation provided by the privileges, which the party believed implied that Serbian church autonomy would someday be extended to the political realm and be the basis for territorial autonomy.

The Radical party took on the character of its leader, Jaša Tomić: combative, with limited horizons, very much devoted to the defense of his nation and its culture. Tomić was born in Vršac (Hungarian: Versecz), northeast of Belgrade, in a region whose fate shifted as the political winds did.[10] When Tomić was born in 1856, it was part of the Serbian Vojvodina, that administrative invention of the Bach absolutist regime in the post-1848 Habsburg monarchy. It had earlier been part of the Temesvár Generalcy of the Hungarian Military Frontier. Its population was approximately 25 percent Serbian, the rest being Romanian, Hungarian, and German. His family, Orthodox Christian of course, was well-off, having thrived in trade in Vršac. He was involved in the Bosnian uprising of 1875, after which he briefly and inattentively attended university in Vienna and Prague. Thereafter, he was most involved in politics in the Serbian community of southern Hungary. Combining interests in socialism and Serbian national politics as did many of his generation (Svetozar Marković and Nikola Pašić, for instance), he eventually found himself much less a socialist than a Serbian nationalist. His resume included a sentence served for murder: in 1890, following a drawn-out series of provocations regarding the honor of his wife, Tomić stabbed to death a Liberal political rival, Miša Dimitrijević, in Novi Sad. He spent five years in prison for the crime, emerging in 1896 with no loss of political enthusiasm.

When the Radicals and Liberals split in Hungary, the divide echoed through Croatia among members of the Independent party. The monied leaders of the party arrayed themselves with the Liberals. They also withdrew their financial support from the Independent party newspaper in Zagreb, *Srbobran* (The Serbian Defender), in 1888 because its editor, Jovanović, supported the new Radical party. The Independent party became even less visible, since its newspaper was now edited by a renegade with little financial support.[11] Although the Radicals now replaced the Liberals as the patrons of the Independent party, personal conflicts between Jovanović and the leadership of the Radicals led the latter to form its own Croatian organization during and after the 1892 elections for the Croatian Sabor. With that the Independent party's influence in Croatia virtually disappeared. Thus the Serbian Independent party affected no change in Croatia before 1903, partly because the party was buffeted by developments within its patron parties in Hungary, partly because it had little to offer. Personal rivalries and lack of finances stalled the possibility of acting vigorously and consistently, and the parties in Hungary, which guided Serbian politics in Croatia, were immersed in their battle for Church Congress spoils. So it would remain until 1903, when new conditions and new people rejuvenated the Independent party.

The primary foundation for the claims of the Radical party was the set of privileges granted by Austrian Emperor Leopold I in 1690. According to the Radicals' Autonomy Program of 1897, Serbs could justly seek "the right of autonomy not only in the church/school and property/financial [fields] but also in the political arena."[12] The Serbian National-Church Congress therefore would be the governing body for Serbs of the monarchy in all areas. Since the privileges predated the Ausgleich and the Nagodba (the pillars of dualism), the Radicals believed that the Nagodba had no validity for the Serbs of the metropolitanate of Srijemski Karlovci, which crossed the border between Croatia and Hungary. The Radicals' interpretation of Serbian privileges was controversial—they held, for instance, that the Serbs entered the monarchy on the basis of a previous agreement. Most Croats asserted that Serbs had been uninvited guests and had gained church autonomy *after* their arrival. Regardless, given their assumptions, the Radicals could not sincerely support the maintenance of the Nagodba. The question was never particularly divisive, however, since the Radicals had a keen eye out for their own material interests, which often called for compromise and even cooperation with the Hungarian government (and therefore implicit recognition of the Nagodba). In 1903, after several years of tenuous unity with the Independent party, the Radicals formed their own organization for Croatia and Slavonia under the leadership of Djordje Krasojević.[13] The Independent party, in the Radicals' view, could not be the sole representative of the entire Serbian population in Croatia. The two parties fought mainly over Srijem, a part of the old Military Frontier inhabited by large numbers of Serbs. The Independent party later became more popular in the poorer western regions of Croatia (Lika, Kordun, and Banija).

The Radicals had already set out to eradicate the influence of other Serbian parties in the National-Church Congress, which had elections in May 1902. In those elections, the Radicals formed a loose alliance with the Independents. In addition, they probably gained the cooperation of Khuen-Héderváry in Croatia, although this could not have helped too much.[14] Khuen-Héderváry reasoned that support for the Radical party could only increase the conflict between Croats and Serbs in Croatia proper, since the Croatian opposition despised the Radicals at least as much as they hated the Serbian magyarones. Also, the Hungarian government had been known to dislike the Serbian Liberal party (now led by Mihailo Polit-Desančić) more than the Radical party, because the Liberals, as a more moderate Serbian party, were more likely to put up an effective opposition. The Radicals could be trusted to alienate most possible allies, and they let off more Serbian nationalist steam than the Liberals. In any case, the Radicals won a convincing majority in the Congress, which convened following the elections. The focus of the Radicals' work in the Congress was threefold: to fill as many committee seats as possible with their men, to dispute the authority of Patriarch Djordje Branković, who, like previous patriarchs, had been appointed by the Hungarian government in consultation with the Congress, and to shift the funds and publishing activities of the Congress to Radical-controlled houses. The funds of the Serbian church were controlled by the high clergy, who in turn depended on the Hungarian government for their authority. The Radicals envisioned taking control of the funds away from the clergy, thus threatening the Hungarian government, which did not wish to see such funds in the hands of an anticlerical, nationalist party.

The victory of the Radical party in the Church Congress elections of May 1902 initiated its period as the "governing party" in the metropolitanate of Srijemski Karlovci, a position that the members of the party had tried for more than a decade to attain. Although it had always been a politicized body, from 1902 to 1914 the aggressiveness of the two main parties in the Congress (the Radicals and, after 1906, the newly rejuvenated Independents) often paralyzed its work. The accomplishments of the Congress from 1902 depended less on the healthy cooperation of the parties than on external factors. Furthermore, for the Independents, the Church Congress was only a stage on which to destroy the influence of the Radicals in all fields, not merely that of the administration of the church. For the Radicals, service in the Church Congress served as an end in itself.

By the 1880s, Serbs, a minority in Croatia, had profound influence in Croatian politics because this was the desire of the Hungarian government and its exponent, Khuen-Héderváry. Of course, this influence was not the work of the Serbian opposition but of the Serbian Club, Khuen-Héderváry's magyarones. Those Croats in opposition to Khuen-Héderváry lashed out against Serbs. The conflict between Croats and Serbs was caused by more than government favoritism of Serbs, however; the respective responses to Khuen-Héderváry's methods revealed a fundamental difference in Croatian and Serbian approaches to their own nationalism and nation-building processes. Croatia's Serbs insisted above all on maintaining their own culture as they perceived it, as represented by their Orthodox faith and Cyrillic alphabet. Serbs' behavior in Croatia was rooted in their fear of losing their collective identity. They were conscious of their history and proud that they had maintained their identity through centuries of Ottoman and Habsburg administration. The character of their national movement owed much to the fact that Serbs were dispersed throughout lands other than Montenegro and the Kingdom of Serbia, the two Serbian national states. Croatia's Serbs, in their own view, could do nothing but accept Khuen-Héderváry's patronage, given the attitude of the most popular Croatian political parties and their leaders.

The position of Croatian nationalists after 1878 was total resistance to granting any recognition to Serbian institutions and cultural characteristics without previous acceptance by Serbs of the concept that in Croatia the only "political nation" was the Croatian, the historical explanation for this assertion being that as a state of long standing in Europe, Croatia's medieval "nation" *(natio)* had been its Croatian aristocracy. Thus, in the modern context, the only nation in Croatia was the Croatian one (there had been no Serbian aristocracy in Croatia). In essence, by utilizing such a test of citizenship, the Croatian nationalist opposition merely requested that Serbs acknowledge that they lived in a Croatian state and were willing to treat it with respect: to behave as citizens of Croatia. The Croatian opposition's strongest party was the Party of Right, the "right" being Croatian state right. In the view of this party, Serbs could either accept that concept or remain complete outsiders in Croatian politics. The Serbian political and cultural elite refused to acknowledge such an obligation, of course. The logic of Croatian and Serbian intransigence was simple: Serbs feared the loss of their identity in the Croatian political nation, whereas Croats would not welcome Serbs unless Serbs accepted that they were part of the Croatian political nation. The result was a stagnant land in which the regime bought its ruling class and the opposition was fragmented. The question of guilt for this situation, so often assessed in Yugoslav historiography, is irrelevant in the face of such hard-headed obstinacy on both sides.

The Croatian opposition from the late sixties to the middle nineties of the nineteenth century consisted of two parties: the Party of Right and the Independent National party. The politics of the Party of Right cannot be understood without reference to the leader of the party, Ante Starčević. Starčević was born in Lika, the most benighted portion of the Military Frontier, in 1823, of a Catholic father and an Orthodox mother. His political activity was partly motivated by his resentment of Karadžić's assertion that all speakers of Štokavian were Serbs; he eventually became the charismatic leader of a movement that claimed historical rights for Croatia within the Habsburg monarchy. He, and his followers after him, asserted that Croatia, as a historical state, had the right to throw off Habsburg governance. Starčević saw the Habsburgs as tyrants. The activity of the Party of Right began in earnest after the Rakovica rebellion of 1871, in which one of its leaders, Eugen Kvaternik, was killed. From that point, Starčević led the party and dominated the stage of Croatian nationalist politics. As a product of their reading of Croatian history, the *pravaši* (members of the Party of Right), with Starčević as leading ideologist, did not accept that Hungary had any legal claim to govern Croatia and therefore had no right to negotiate the Nagodba.[15] In practice, this meant that the Party of Right took little part in the work of the Croatian Sabor, which was how they eventually earned their reputation for being uncompromising and impractical. The Party of Right also refused to acknowledge the existence of Serbs—not simply in Croatia, but anywhere: all Serbs were actually Orthodox Croats. This of course was the flip side of assertions often leveled by Serbs (first and foremost by Vuk Karadžić) that all Croats were really converted Orthodox Christians, and thus originally Serbs. The practical result was that until 1905 no *pravaši* would work with "self-proclaimed Serbs," and no Serbs would cooperate with a party that denied their existence. The Party of Right was nonetheless the most popular Croatian party from the 1880s until 1905 and after, and its fervent Croatian nationalist teachings produced most of the politicians who formulated the New Course.

The second Croatian opposition party, the Independent National party, emerged out of the ruins of the National party, which had divided before the temptation of cooperating with the Magyars in the 1870s. Those who joined the party's Independent wing held that the Nagodba, although repulsive, was the only basis for realistic political behavior in Croatia. The Independent Nationals included Josip Strossmayer (until 1873, when he retired from politics) and Franjo Rački, the two Croats who are most often identified with Yugoslavism in the latter half of the nineteenth century. Thus the Independent Nationals seemed to be the only hope for accommodation between Serbs and Croats during the Khuen-Héderváry era. Although these two men were known as spirited intellectual warriors, they and later leaders of the party were unwilling to expand the base of their party to include more than the intellectuals and priests who formed the core of the party in the beginning. The *pravaši* filled this gap, their program and activities being directed to less illustrious Croats.

Although these parties were in constant contact (the Serbian parties included), there was very little action toward alliance of any sort until the 1890s, when the Party of Right began to suffer because of the old age of Starčević and squabbling among its minor leaders for precedence. In 1895 this battle reached its crescendo, with the party splitting into two wings, one headed by Josip Frank that was called the Pure Party of Right, and the other, which had no dominant leader and which remained the Party of Right (its members were known as the *domovinaši* after their newspaper, *Hrvatska domovina*, [Croatian Homeland]).[16] The *domovinaši* were by and large younger, still hotly opposed to the Nagodba, but more inclined to seek agreement with Croatia's Serbs.[17] The *frankovci,* as the members of Frank's faction were known, turned Starčević on his head, and at first tacitly, then openly favored ties with the Habsburg dynasty and Vienna. Frank's party also brought the *pravaš* policy of denying the existence of Serbs to a more vocal level. One could generalize and say that whereas the Independent Nationals had remained static, the Party of Right had spawned two radical new groupings,

Josip Frank, leader of
the Pure Party of Right.
From Josip Horvat, Politička
povijest Hrvatske *Zagreb:*
August Cesarec, 1990.

both of which questioned the essentially negative character of the *pravaš*
opposition. The *domovinaši* looked to alliances with Serbs and a more positive, active policy in the Sabor; the *frankovci* hoped to achieve their success
through Vienna.

To conclude: politics in the Habsburg monarchy traditionally focused on
corporate competition: groups (religious, territorial, feudal) sought imperial
favor, which would result in the granting of privileges or rights on the basis
of imperial authority. The behavior of Serbs and Croats in the nineteenth
century conformed completely to that model. Croatian (and Hungarian) state
right politics postulated the primordial existence of territorial units and aristocracies associated with them; those units and groups then acted as unitary
entities in negotiations with the emperor. Thus the people of Croatia were
subordinate to the corporate Croatian *nation*. Croatia's existence was regulated by the relationship of the Croatian political nation with its monarch, who
in turn guaranteed that existence. The Croatian Party of Right took this concept one step further, asserting the right of Croatia to independence from its
ruler, the emperor, but that was merely an extension of the principle that the
Croatian political nation preceded all other political actors. It then decided
whether or not it would be governed by the Habsburg monarch. The Pacta

Conventa of 1102 was one such agreement, and most Croats used it as a starting point in making claims in the name of their nation. And although the Nagodba satisfied very few Croatian nationalists, it was the type of agreement that all Habsburg subjects understood, because it was negotiated by elites in the name of corporate rights. Serbs operated from the same premise: that they made up a unique, separate community in the Habsburg monarchy which then had the obligation to barter for the conditions of its existence. Thus the very settlements of Orthodox immigrants had been regulated by imperial decrees. The privileges were the product of negotiation between a monarch and a collective, in this case, Orthodox Christian. When the Radical party insisted on the validity of the privileges, it was speaking a language that the *pravaši* could understand quite clearly, because they operated from the same assumptions. Those assumptions were to be challenged by the turn of the century by an old political notion, new to Croatia: natural law, with its practical corollary, popular, representative government.

Enter the *Omladina*

Emperor Franz Josef visited Zagreb in October 1895,[18] and two demonstrations occurred in his honor: one to express loyalty to him but opposition to Hungary and the Nagodba, and one directed at Croatia's Serbs. Two different groups participated: youthful Croatian nationalists prepared the anti-Hungarian movement, and the *frankovci* worked up the anti-Serbian riot. In Croatian historiography, the day is most often noted for the burning of the Hungarian flag by the group of youths, headed by Stjepan Radić, today a Croatian favorite son. The demonstration against the Magyars introduced a new generation of young politicians who would dominate Croatian and then Yugoslav politics for decades. The secondary, anti-Serbian, demonstration is rightfully seen as merely another in a line of such occurrences.[19] The flag burners were banished from the Croatian university in Zagreb; they were able to continue their education in Prague where many studied with Tomaš G. Masaryk. Members of the group who were not expelled continued their studies and their political activity in Zagreb. The group in Prague included Radić; the one in Zagreb counted Svetozar Pribićević and Ivan Lorković among its members. In the early stages, these youths *(omladina)*[20] merely attacked the *pravaši* for their factionalism, but as they progressed they developed a full critique of the *pravaš* opposition, concentrating on the emptiness of a policy that proposed no realistic political strategy or goals. They also reevaluated the *pravaš* negation of the existence of a Serbian people.

The Zagreb collective made its appearance in February 1896 with a celebration of the seventieth anniversary of the birth of the Serbian leader Svetozar Miletić. The Serbian *omladina* organization invited the Croatian to take part, and together they produced in 1897 a volume entitled *The National Idea*.[21] Shortly after the celebration, the two *omladina* organizations fused to form the United Croatian and Serbian Youth. Its leaders included two Serbs, Pribićević and Jovan Banjanin, and two Croats, Lorković and Lav Mazzura, all of whom would distinguish themselves as leaders of the Croato-Serbian Coalition after 1905. The ideology that governed the budding politicians combined political realism and a heightened concern for social problems. The former emerged in reaction to the politics of the Party of Right; both concerns can be attributed to the influence of Masaryk. With the exception of Radić, these men would allow social concerns to fall by the wayside as their movement gained influence. Masaryk's influence was felt most of all regarding state right policy. He was a virulent critic of such politics in Bohemia, having built his political reputation as a leader of the realist refutation of the Young Czech party, which relied on the Bohemian historical state right tradition. Masaryk also emphasized the danger of German expansionism to the Slavic world and instructed his Southern Slav pupils to bury their quarrels in order better to oppose the Germans.[22] His influence is detectable in the *omladina*'s work, which clearly opposed state right politics and explicitly called on Croats and Serbs to end their antagonism.

Svetozar Pribićević would become the most active and influential Serbian politician in Croatia from late 1902. He was born in Kostajnica (Banija, in the Military Frontier) and named after Svetozar Miletić.[23] His youngest brother Adam (there were four altogether—Valerijan, five years older than Svetozar; Milan, two years younger; and Adam, five years younger) described Svetozar as unmanageable but highly intelligent as a child. Their father and mother "raised us to have deep devotion toward the Serbian national idea and fully uncritical love towards Montenegro, Serbia, and Russia." He attended school in Petrinja and Zagreb, whence, after fighting with Croatian students in his class, he was kicked out and moved to Serbia for a short time. He returned poorer soon thereafter, finishing school in Karlovac and then university in Zagreb. As the son of a pensioned citizen of the Military Frontier, he rated a stipend through high school. By all accounts a charismatic, dynamic personality, the young adult Pribićević cut a somewhat sinister figure—his dark hair, mustache, and short beard were stylish, but gave him a suspicious appearance. His career before the First World War has not been well documented, but his postwar activities have received much attention. Pribićević was one of the more intriguing Yugoslav politicians of the interwar period. From 1919 until 1926, he served as a minister in successive Radical cabinets as minister of education and minister of the interior. He himself was the head of the Independent Democratic party. During his years in government, he worked to centralize the government of Yugoslavia. Given his prewar experience, he was considered an expert on Croatia, and his appointed task was to dismantle Croatia's autonomous government immediately after the war. During this period, Pribićević's loyalty to the Karadjordjević dynasty became legendary. Among Croats, he also became one of the most hated politicians in interwar Yugoslavia. However, after the assassination of Stjepan Radić (until recently his most virulent critic, but at that point his political ally) in 1928, Pribićević entered into hard opposition to the dynasty and the central government and supported the creation of a federal Yugoslavia with an autonomous Croatia. Thus, he turned completely around in his politics. Such turns characterized his political career throughout his life: August Cesarec, the Croatian writer who passionately loathed Pribićević, once asked "Why, why, why—the question could be asked ad infinitum" regarding Pribićević's convictions and actions.[24]

In *The National Idea*, Pribićević's ideas appeared for the first time in print, promoting *narodno jedinstvo* (national oneness), the notion that Serbs and Croats were really one nation. This remained his preferred slogan and would enjoy a stormy existence as the intellectual foundation of the Croato-Serbian Coalition.[25] Here, in an article entitled "The Guiding Thought of Serbs and Croats," Pribićević attempted to explain *narodno jedinstvo* and to sketch out the political program that he believed logically followed the acceptance of the idea. He asserted that the victory of the national idea, the force behind the unifications of Italy and Germany, could be denied only at the risk of battle between those who fight "in the name of legitimacy on the one hand, and in the name of the progress of civilization on the other."[26] Legitimacy was the old order—states built by dynasties without regard for nations (and "civilization"). Pribićević stretched the usual notion of the Serbo-Croatian relationship when he explained that Serbs and Croats were really one nation: "There is probably not one thinking man among Serbs and Croats," he wrote, "who does not recognize that the Serbo-Croatian conflict is damaging to one and the other."

> If Serbs and Croats were two different nations . . . then conflict would already have found justification in that fact, and to seek a method of alliance would be all that remained. . . . An alliance would be able if not to solve a conflict, then at least to postpone it for awhile. But such relations do not exist between Serbs and Croats, and the Serbo-Croatian conflict cannot be considered a national question, because Serbs and Croats are not two different nations but parts of one and the same nation.[27]

Since Croats and Serbs did not appear to share his belief in their oneness, he proposed that some sort of primordial feelings of unity therefore had to be rediscovered, nurtured, and asserted: "something is sought, confirmation of life; that is, national consciousness. That consciousness consists of subjective feelings of oneness, in the impulse and desire for unity. We do not have that."[28] Pribićević suggested that the fact of oneness and a little education would evoke that consciousness, and that forces that wished to break up the Croato-Serbian nation would have to destroy it spiritually. By insisting that Croats and Serbs were members of the same nation and yet were still Croats and Serbs, Pribićević made a distinction that was too fine for most of his conationals (whether Croatian, Serbian, or somewhere in between). Like many other such formulations, Pribićević's should probably be viewed as a rhetorical basis for his concrete political action.

Several writers in *The National Idea* attacked the concept of Croatian state right and especially its role in Croatian politics from the 1870s to 1890s. Pribićević, of course, was one such writer.[29] The Serb Danilo Dimović, later a prominent politician in Bosnia, dedicated an article to the question, arguing against state right in a fashion more characteristic of Croatian dissenters from the *pravaš* style of politics.[30] Dimović counterposed "historical state right" to "natural right," the former derived from privileges granted throughout history to the Croatian state and its feudal classes, the latter from one's humanity. The former limits what a nation can accomplish, the latter broadens all horizons; the former is meaningful only to those who have the privileges, the latter is felt by all members of a nation.[31] Furthermore, "it is more dignified of a man and a nation to achieve with their own effort and work, to create conditions for a better future on the basis of consciousness and independent work, not depending much on the past."[32]

The authors of *The National Idea*, finally, invoked the foreigner as the cause of Croato-Serbian discord. Pribićević wrote that the supposed differences between Croats and Serbs were invented by foreigners who wished to dominate them, clearly referring to Germans and Magyars.[33] In his introduction, Dusan Mangjer argued that the Croato-Serbian conflict only hurt their mutual progress, in all spheres, to the benefit of foreign governors.[34] Dimović, as we have seen, also attributed the state right idea to foreign dominators who would limit Croatian and Serbian aspirations. Instead of accepting the domination of foreigners, Pribićević argued that Croats and Serbs needed to see that "one nation has the same needs, the same needs bear one idea, one idea leads to one ideal. Our national needs, as also the ideal of our national future, demand that one idea span Belgrade, Zagreb, Split, Sarajevo, Cetinje, and Prizren."[35]

Although the two *omladina* organizations united, some of the articles in *The National Idea* foreshadowed future conflicts among members of the group. Specifically, the question of the future of Bosnia and Hercegovina, which had induced conflict between Croats and Serbs in the 1870s and 1880s, appeared again. Pribićević expressed fear of Hungarian actions intending to bring Bosnia and Hercegovina into its orbit, that is, into Croatia, thus controlling the region "on whose fate depends also the fate of our [Croato-Serbian] nation."[36] He subtly accused Croats who had wished for the incorporation of Bosnia into Croatia of supporting attempts of the monarchy to gain a foothold in the Slavic south, the Balkan peninsula. "It is necessary not to lose from view that this question is most fateful for us, because when it is decided, the question of where the focus of our [Croato-Serbian] national position will fall will be decided, and with it the question of our national future."[37] Pribićević thus emphasized that the focus of South Slavic aspirations must be Serbia, because the Habsburg monarchy would have impure motives for gathering South Slavs within its borders. "We must also come to the conviction that it is in fact absurd that some desire to fight for things Serbian in a camp which is decorated with the flag of the Hungarian state idea."[38]

The critical aspect of Serbian contributions to *The National Idea* is that here Serbs claimed to wish to work for Croatia not as if in a foreign land, but as citizens of Croatia. For all the intrinsic differences of opinion on questions like the future of Bosnia, Pribićević accepted the validity of a Croatian state. We have seen that the magyarone Serbs had decided to concentrate on their own interests to the detriment of Croatia's economic and legal development, and that the *pravaši* insisted on Serbian acceptance of Croatian political nationhood. Here were Serbs who, although not willing explicitly to accede to *pravaš* conditions, accepted them in substance and proclaimed their desire to work for the betterment of their land, Croatia. When one understands the fact that Croats and Serbs are one nation, Pribićević wrote, "with joy we will sing from the heart '*Lijepa naša domovino* [the Croatian national anthem].' Under the concept of homeland, therefore, we understand the whole nation. We do not recognize a wider or narrower homeland."[39] Of course, this (Croato-Serbian) homeland also included Serbia, Montenegro, and any other place in which the South Slavic people lived. Nonetheless, these few young Croatian Serbs claimed that they had abandoned the magyarone tradition of serving Budapest to further one's own interest. In that alone, they had come some way toward bridging one of the deeper chasms lying between them and the Croatian opposition.

The *omladina* introduced a truly revolutionary notion into Croatian politics. That notion, a century old in most of Europe, was that the individual, not the corporate entity (based on faith and/or territorial nobility) is the fundamental political actor. Their strong opposition to the politics of state right and their support of natural law as a guiding principle in politics marked them as political moderns. The ramifications of this position were far-reaching and would be most notable in the politics of the Serbian community of the monarchy. Conflicting visions of Serbianness characterized the competing political strategies of two parties as they fought for the heart of an electorate which was, in their view, threatened. The Serbian Radical party, led by Jaša Tomić, represented a tried and true vision of Serbianness: that the Serbian community was Orthodox, isolated, threatened with assimilation, and needful of vigilance. Under the leadership of Svetozar Pribićević, the Serbian Independent party would, after 1903, represent a newer vision of Serbianness, by which Serbs were actually part of a larger nation, the Serbo-Croatian one, which was bound by the notion of *narodno jedinstvo*. The Independents also believed that Serbs were threatened—but their solution was, at least rhetorically, to propose that Serbs work with rather than against Croats to assure their mutual defense against outside, predatory nations (Germans and Hungarians). Their political strategies were also quite different and reflected their radically divergent visions of Serbianness. The Radicals assiduously supported the politics of the privileges: Serbian existence could only be assured through reliance on historically proved precedents, mainly the privileges that had been granted by Austrian emperors over the centuries to the community of faith that Serbian Orthodoxy represented. The Independents rejected such reliance, instead proposing that Serbs rely on modern political processes—participation in constitutional government, electoral politics, with natural law rather than privilege at its core. When Svetozar Pribićević suggested that there was a fight on between legitimacy and progress, privilege and natural law, he characterized the struggle between the Radicals and the Independents.

1903: A Year of Troubles and Opportunities

For the Serbs and Croats, the year 1903 was a significant turning point. Taken individually, the year's events were not necessarily positive—the period was one of troubles that begot opportunities. The entire South Slavic world was involved: a young Bosnian Serb intellectual, Croatian peasants, Serbian assassins, and a few insightful Dalmatian politicians. When 1903 ended, Croatian-Serbian relations and both Croatian and Serbian politics were fundamentally altered, giving a new generation of Yugoslav-oriented South Slavs an opportunity to take center stage.

Borba do istrage

The troubled period began in August 1902, when the *Srpski književni glasnik* (Serbian Literary Herald), the leading literary journal in the Kingdom of Serbia, published an article by a certain "N. S." entitled "Serbs and Croats."[40] Later, it was established that it was written by Nikola Stojanović, a Serbian student from Sarajevo, the capital of Bosnia. Stojanović, who later became one of the leading Serbian politicians in Bosnia, would also be a member of the Yugoslav Committee in London during the First World War. In 1902, however, he was merely a student in Sarajevo; the uproar he provoked undoubtedly satisfied his desire for notoriety, for in his article, Stojanović proposed to explain in detail how Serbs would inevitably assimilate Croats, whose weaker culture and national consciousness precluded their development into a nation. Using a phrase that has echoed through Yugoslav politics ever since, he declared "war" on the Croats "to extermination, ours or yours" *(borba do istrage, naše ili vaše)*. Stojanović proposed to be dispassionate, even scientific in his analysis, beginning his article using the language of compromise: "without the customary sentimentality," "without pretension," "wishing for serious discussion." Yet his tone was far from scientific, and the needling he engaged in was passionate indeed: referring to the fact that Croats made Josip Jelačić a hero, he notes that "that nation which finds its ideal in a servant to foreigners cannot hope for more than to become its ideal —a servant." Or: "Their leaders note that before union with Hungary, Croatia was an independent state. The fact is all the sadder because it is true; and after all this time, political identity has not become cultural identity." He annoyed Croats because so many of his points were true, so well-designed to get under the skin of Croatian nationalists. Croatian national identity was still inchoate; Stojanović made his point with every jab. Ultimately, he believed that the very weakness of the Croatian identity would result in Croats being seduced by the Serbian national idea. His "war to extermination" was a cultural war. Croats who cared about Croatian individuality were right to fear his predictions. Stojanović used language familiar to followers of the late Croat leader Ante Starčević, the language that denied the validity of competing nationalisms. In a commonplace reversal of Freud's "narcissism of minor differences," Stojanović was guilty (like the *frankovci* and other *pravaši*) of the cultural hegemonism that wished those same differences away with slick semantics ("Serbs are Orthodox Croats"; "Serbs All and Everywhere"). Similar sentiments were bandied about in Serbian and Croatian politics on a regular basis, so, except for the declaration of war, there was little new in the article. In fact, Svetozar Pribićević was accused of this type of Serbian nationalism later in his career—when, as a so-called unitarist, he denigrated Croatian identity and statehood. It is worth noting now that this type of nationalism was just as foreign and revolting to Serbs like Jaša Tomić, who wished for nothing more than a solid stone wall between his Serbs and other nations, as it was to Croatian nationalists.

When *Srbobran* chose to reprint the article without comment in September 1902, large-scale demonstrations against Serbian businesses and institutions in Zagreb ensued (the "September Events" in Croatian lore). Historians have attributed much of the destruction to economic rivalry: Croatian businessmen took advantage of the chaos to weaken or eliminate some of the competition. The demonstrations were large and well organized. According to *Obzor* (the most-read Zagreb daily newspaper), some of whose writers did their best to incite the riots, up to twenty thousand people took part.[41] And more than the usual suspects played a role: *frankovci* proudly and openly urged on the demonstrators, but many others joined in. After the Croatian press pinpointed those Serbs who financed *Srbobran*, Frank and others encouraged Croats to attack Serbian businesses. Even Stjepan Radić implied that Croats should end contacts, economic or otherwise, with Serbs in Croatia. The atmosphere in Zagreb encouraged troublemakers, so they made trouble. The riots lasted several days (the night of September 2–3 saw the worst, although they lasted from the first to the fourth of the month). On September 3, martial law was declared, the army having been called in two nights earlier. The Serbian Bank, many Serbian businesses and homes, and the local council of the Serbian Orthodox Church were destroyed.

The Independent Nationals and *pravaši* accused Khuen-Héderváry of arranging to have the article published to further divide Croats and Serbs, but that made little sense, since the article first appeared in a journal published in Belgrade and was then reprinted in *Srbobran*.[42] Both the Croatian and Serbian *omladinas* and the entire Croatian opposition condemned the article. All the Croatian political parties justified the ensuing demonstrations. Because the *pravaši* propounded a philosophy akin to Stojanović's, they reacted the most fiercely—they of all people had to do so, since Stojanović hit very close to home. Using the same form of argumentation, they arrived at utterly opposed conclusions. For Josip Frank, the article represented only the most recent episode in the battle between "the Croatian idea and the Serbian idea," the Serbian idea seeking "victory on terrain where there was no place for it."[43] Frank was the son-in-law of Ante Starčević, but had little of his charisma or prestige among Croats. He was born in Osijek, a German-speaking Jew, and became a lawyer and then a politician in the 1870s, founding two German-language newspapers. Frank was a political opportunist whose only clear goal was to keep Croatia loyal to the dynasty and the Habsburg state. He, like Starčević, denied the existence of Serbs, but he did this less from conviction than to prosper in Croatian politics. By the turn of the century, he had inherited part of Starčević's constituency, but he was a much less admirable figure. His Pure Party of Right would dedicate itself to disputing Hungarian governance of Croatia and to supporting Vienna. For Frank, *Srbobran* published the article in an attempt to divide Catholic Croats from "Greek-eastern" Croats (Orthodox Serbs) in Croatia. What most appalled him was that the article was "imported from Belgrade."[44] To this provocation, undertaken by "foreign elements," Croats reacted appropriately, according to Frank. "What would happen in Belgrade, in Budapest," he asked, "if a similar article appeared there in an enemy newspaper?" Furthermore, added Ante Starčević's son-in-law, "I do not even hesitate to admit that the Pure Party of Right also took part in the front lines of these demonstrations." The demonstrators "did the Croatian nation a great favor, since they rehabilitated the nation for the outside world."[45]

Mile Starčević, the *frankovac* nephew of the founder of the Party of Right, elaborated on Frank's claim that Serbs in Croatia comprised a foreign element whose activities were funded by the Serbian government. "Who carries the Serbian idea into Croatia? Who aids it? Who subsidizes it? The Kingdom of Serbia and the Montenegrin principality subsidize it. . . . Who founded *Srbobran?* The Belgrade hireling Pavle Jovanović." The Serbian Bank in Zagreb, according to Starčević, acted as the conduit for Belgrade's mercenary funds, "with the obvious intent to restrict and disable Croats' economic development."[46] Thus the article reprinted in *Srbobran* was yet another alleged salvo in Belgrade's war on Croatia's statehood and the Croatian nation. The Serbian intelligentsia in Croatia, according to this view, was guilty of importing this disease.

August Harambašić, a poet with a biting wit and one of the most effective *pravaš* speakers (he was not a *frankovac*), offered a ray of light in an otherwise gloomy time. In the course of the Sabor debate on the demonstrations, he made an offer: "I say to them [Serbs]: here is your carte blanche . . . , your blank page, just write down all of your desires, and I as a brother Croat will sign all of them. Write down ninety-nine [desires], but listen then to the one desire of your brother Croat . . . simply declare that you are Croatian citizens, that your homeland is Croatia, and that you are in that regard political Croats."[47]

This was the relaxed definition of Croatian political nationhood in play: do not fear assimilation (your "ninety-nine desires" will assure your identity), but do work for Croatia, in Croatia's interests, as a loyal citizen of that state and no other. For Harambašić, as for many *pravaši* and nearly all the Independent Nationals, Serbs had to stop following the example of the Serbian Club, for whom exclusivism and opportunism had pushed aside any Croatian patriotism; they must behave as civil Croats. The door was open, just a crack, for the new generation, the Serbs who wished to participate in a constitutional Croatia.

Among Croats who wished to explain away Serbian cooperation with Khuen-Héderváry, the favored method was to blame foreigners for provoking conflict between Croats and Serbs. Marjan Derenčin, a revered Independent

National, held that the demonstrations "were justified, insofar as there had to be a deserving reaction against this fantastic effort of Serbian irredenta . . . otherwise we most sharply and decisively condemn them." His colleague Fran Vrbanić believed that "this discord . . . appeared under the influence of a foreign element," that element, according to Vrbanić, not being Serbs but Magyars who, in the 1870s, drove a wedge between Croats and Serbs in order to create a unionist party favoring Croatian ties with Hungary. Thus they had bribed Serbs who would become members of the magyarone Serbian Club within the National party. Derenčin took Vrbanić one step further: "You here [in the Serbian Club of the Sabor] are not Serbs, you are rather adherents of Count Khuen-Hédervary, and with such adherents we will not solve this conflict."[48] Conflict between Croats and Serbs was a "child of the modern era," not rooted in their historical relationship. According to Vrbanić, even the demonstrations were a product of foreign interference: "The demonstrations . . . included elements who could not have cared less about Serbs and Croats . . . foreigners. . . . people who spoke German and Magyar."[49]

The Radicals reacted to the demonstrations of September 1902 in predictable fashion. Although the sympathies expressed in the article by Stojanović could not have warmed Radicals' hearts (whereas Stojanović longed to see Croats become Serbs, the Radicals would have built a wall between the two peoples in order to maintain the purity of Serbdom), they shared a common disdain for Croatian culture and ultimately feared the Croatian people. The Radicals chose to view the demonstrations, in the words of their historian, Lazar Rakić, as "a crazed orgiastic pogrom against Serbs and all Serbian institutions in Zagreb" in which "Khuen-Hédervary's policy of the dissemination of discord triumphed."[50] The Radical party chaired a meeting in Novi Sad in late September 1902 at which Tomić, Djordje Krasojević, and even Pribićević spoke. The Radical resolution, which Pribićević did not support, included the threat that if the government in Zagreb could not protect Serbs from attacks like those of early September, Serbs would be forced to seek the protection of some government other than the Croatian; presumably, this indicated the government of the Kingdom of Serbia.[51]

The response of the *omladina* to the Stojanović article was related to other developments in the youth movement. Early in 1900, the newspaper of the United Croatian and Serbian Youth, *Glas* (The Voice), stopped publication in Vienna. With that, the Croatian and Serbian *omladina* organizations

Karolyi Khuen-Héderváry, ban of Croatia, 1883–1903. *From Josip Horvat*, Politička povijest Hrvatske *Zagreb: August Cesarec, 1990.*

separated, and the Croatian group formed the Progressive Youth, which remained apart from political parties but began its own organized activity. The Serbian organization's members found the going difficult: in late 1901, Pribićević and Banjanin approached the Serbian Independent party, which declined to admit them.[52] Pribićević's attacks on the Independents' retrograde politics were not easily forgotten.

The publication of "Serbs and Croats" therefore found the authors of *The National Idea* dispersed, attempting to work their way into their respective national political organizations. In the article, Stojanović, ironically, praised the Croatian *omladina* for its work. Along with his provocative rhetoric, he identified a process that he believed was leading to the disappearance of those who considered themselves Croats. One example was that Croats had made the "Serbian" language (Štokavian) their own literary language during the Illyrian movement of the 1830s. Others identified this process as the gradual adoption of "Yugoslav" principles and the "growing together" of Croats and Serbs, or, in another variant (favored by Svetozar Pribićević), the reassertion of the forgotten or ignored fact of Croato-Serbian unity. Stojanović himself represented a deceptive brand of Serbian "Yugoslavism" that confused integral Serbian nationalism with Yugoslavism. Thus the usually unstated assumption that all Croats were in fact Serbs allowed the Serbian government to claim that its national policy rested on Yugoslav principles. Similarly, Croats who received their political education from the Party of Right at times accommodated Starčević's contention that all Serbs were in fact orthodox Croats by claiming that this made Starčević and his theories Yugoslav—in that he believed that all Croats and Serbs were of one nation. It was often a matter of semantics.

Stojanović saw the integration of the Serbian nation being furthered in Croatia by the Progressive Youth: "There is among Croats a fairly large conscious intelligentsia that is quickening the process, comprehending that only the Serbian national idea means economic, political, and cultural independence and salvation from German encroachment. . . . Serbs can only wish them success and offer them aid in that work."[53] Stojanović's discussion provocatively mirrored many of the assertions of the *omladina*, both Serbian and Croatian. Focusing on natural law rather than state right, the youth had indeed evolved a conception of citizenship that rejected the collective membership in some nation in favor of respect for the individual. Nevertheless, time would show that neither side envisioned the withering away of one nation in favor of the other. National distinctions would have to be retained. The Progressive Youth, to whom Stojanović's remarks were dedicated, did not appreciate this misrepresentation of their ideas and activities. Certainly no Croats shared Stojanović's assessment of the work of the *omladina*. The result of the article and the demonstrations was to set back collaboration of the Croatian and Serbian *omladinas*. The Progressive Youth condemned the article, but, perhaps to defend themselves against Stojanović's unwanted recommendation, they did not publicly object to the demonstrations.[54] After September 1902, the Progressive Youth initiated a movement to publicize their views on the political situation in Croatia; in November 1902, Lorković and Večeslav Vilder began publishing *Narodna obrana* (The National Defense) in Osijek to counteract the magyarone newspaper there, *Die Drau* (The Drava). In January 1903, the Progressive Youth fused with the Independent Nationals and *domovinaši* to form the Croatian Party of Right.

One young member of the Croatian *omladina*, Stjepan Radić, separated from his colleagues at this point. He had been part of the Zagreb-Prague connection, although by 1903 he no longer spoke for the Progressive Youth, having already moved away from them in formulating his own political philosophy based on the latent political strength of the Croatian peasantry. Radić founded the Croatian People's Peasant party in March 1905 with his brother Antun. Various obstacles would arise to cooperation between the Radićes and the rest of the Croatian and Serbian *omladina*. Because of the power of Catholicism in the Croatian peasantry, the Peasant party could not afford the anticlericalism of the Progressive Youth. Later, the Radićes would disagree with the direction of the New Course, favoring either a triune Habsburg monarchy or a Danubian federation of some sort. At the time of the September demonstrations, however, Stjepan Radić's conception of the role of Serbs in Croatia did not differ greatly from that of the Progressive Youth. Radić shared the position of the Progressive Youth regarding the demonstrations. His critique of Stojanović's article and assessment of Croato-Serbian relations in Croatia, entitled *Croats and Serbs*,[55] can be accepted as a valuable statement of their position regarding the demonstrations. For Radić, the most horrifying aspect of the history of Croato-Serbian relations was that "everything around us . . . testifies that the battle is leading to extermination, yours *and* ours."[56] "It is obvious that conflict, or rather battle, can only appear among such Croats and Serbs who are 'Croat-onlys' or 'Serb-onlys'."[57] Radić noted that while Serbs ignored the fact that their culture was disappearing in Hungary, they concentrated their anger on Croats, who actually threatened them less.

At the end of 1902, the younger generation of Serbs around Pribićević and Banjanin were faced with an unforgiving political situation in Croatia. Their Serbian forebears in the Serbian Club and the Serbian Independent party propounded a philosophy whose exclusivity was shared by Stojanović —even if less cerebrally, and to different ends (separation rather than assimilation). *Srbobran*'s publication of "Serbs and Croats" in August 1902 provided ample evidence that the Independent party had not substantially altered its point of view regarding Serbo-Croatian cooperation and nationhood, even though it had undergone recent renovations designed to mitigate its harsh Serbian nationalistic tone. During the demonstrations, Khuen-Héderváry halted publication of the paper, and when it began publication again in December 1902, it had a new name, *Novi Srbobran* (The New Serbian Defender) and a new editorial structure headed by Pribićević and Banjanin.[58] From that point, Pribićević was secretary of the party, whose president remained Bogdan Medaković. The transfer of power was nearly as subtle as it sounds: almost invisibly, the Independent party had radically shifted gears administratively and ideologically. The Independent leadership had been forced to make drastic changes and accept the youth leaders into its organization.

Pribićević we know already; his colleague, Jovan Banjanin was the editor of *Srbobran* until 1913. He and Pribićević worked as a team between 1903 and 1913—Pribićević being the politician, Banjanin the propagandist of the Independent party. At a time when the party newspaper was the most read and most influential mode of communication in Croatia, having a good man with the scissors, as Pribićević once described Banjanin, was critical.[59] One might expect Banjanin, as the editor of the party rag, to be somewhat cynical, but he later demonstrated his own consistency when he opposed the party's tendency to collaborate in the years immediately preceding the First World War. As a result, in 1913 Pribićević banished him from the offices of *Srbobran* and Banjanin left the Independent party. For Banjanin, *narodno jedinstvo* implied the need for complete union with Serbia: during the First World War and after, his support for Serbia was unsurpassed among Croatian Serbs. In the interwar period, he supported King Aleksandar's dictatorship when others who shared his reverence for the dynasty (including Pribićević) moved into opposition.

The September Events settled nothing. They represented expressions of rage against the Serbian population of Zagreb and Croatia. That rage was motivated in part by economic fears, but in part by the frustrations of being a Croatian nationalist in a time when Croatian national identity was still very insecure. Yet the September riots did perhaps motivate many politicians in Croatia to abandon the language of national competition and hatred that had become the lingua franca of opportunistic but exhausted political strategies: those of the Party of Right, the Serbian Club, the Serbian opposition, and even the Independent Nationals. Many Croats and Serbs realized that the petty psychological benefits of wrecking a competitor's business or of printing an inflammatory article were not going to alter the fundamental political situation, resting as it did on the Nagodba and relying on mutual Croato-Serbian loathing. The September riots were a sign of Khuen-Héderváry's success, but the Khuen-Héderváry era was just about over.

The Croatian National Movement

In both 1883 and 1899, Croatia was the stage for rebellions: in 1883, peasant unrest had been enough to prompt the imposition of a commissariat (Khuen-Héderváry then became ban); in 1899, the demonstrations were less widespread and encompassed no larger towns or cities. In 1903, a more pervasive rebellion wracked Croatia. Beginning in March, a series of incidents gradually built into what is collectively known as the Croatian National

Movement.[60] Some historians point to social causes, some see it as national. Most agree it was unfocused. Most also agree that it was doomed by its geographic limitations, lack of support from the majority of Croatian political parties, and its failure to attract Serbs. There is general agreement on the probable causes of the movement: the world economic crisis of 1900–1901 had contributed to the impoverishment of Croatia; relations with the Hungarian government continued to be poor (or perceived as such) and, during 1903, negotiations were held to renew the financial terms of the Hungaro-Croatian Nagodba; and finally, some Croatian politicians (but certainly a minority) chose the spring of 1903 to mount a *skupština*[61] movement designed to provoke opposition to Hungary.

Given the unrelated root causes of the movement, it is not surprising that it was never really exploited and never achieved a focus. When in February the Hungarian government rejected the proposals of the Croatian government in negotiations for the financial Nagodba, the Progressive Youth held a series of well-attended public meetings. First in Zagreb and Osijek, then in other cities and towns of Croatia, the Progressives organized meetings designed to focus Croatia's anger over its mistreatment by Hungary. After the Zagreb meeting on March 11, the government banned further public skupštinas. Nonetheless, from early March through early April, the meetings went on: first in Zagreb in the north, then in Osijek in the east. Then, on April 11, in Zaprešić, a small village that is today a suburb of Zagreb, police killed one peasant when locals tried to remove the Hungarian-language sign over the railroad station. By May, Varaždin, Križevci, and Karlovac had all seen demonstrations, many of them leading to violence. As one historian noted, "It seemed as though Croatia was on the verge of a general uprising. But it did not happen."[62]

Croatian historians have since berated the Croatian opposition parties for their inability to harness this energy. The leaders of the Progressive Youth (including Lorković and Mazzura, plus Franko Potočnjak and Milan Marjanović) were jailed by May, thus disabling their open support for the movement. The older opposition (Independent Nationals and *domovinaši*) gave only cold support, due likely to their fear of a mass uprising that could threaten even them. Yet the failure of the movement was not simply the result of fearful "bourgeois" politicians. In fact, the movement was ruined by two other fundamental flaws: first, it was geographically limited; and second, Serbs ignored it. In much of Slavonia, even the Progressives were unable to get a skupština movement going; and throughout Srijem, Lika, Kordun, and Banija, Serbian leaders refused to incite their own people to action as the Croats had. Thus Slavonia and much of the southern rim of Croatia remained aloof from the action. Zagreb, the Zagorje (north of Zagreb), Gorski Kotar (Rijeka's hinterland), and the Bjelovar districts were involved in the disturbances.

By June, the movement began to wane, given the fact that political leaders who were not jailed refused to lead it. The government of Khuen-Héderváry did not shy away from force in dealing with the rebellions. Blood was shed, and thousands were jailed. However, just as the movement peaked, Khuen-Héderváry was plucked out of Croatia and made minister-president of Hungary. Although many in Croatia believed that they had overthrown the Khuen-Héderváry regime, in fact his removal was motivated by the emperor's desire for a loyal figure to govern Hungary. Nonetheless, the despised Khuen-Héderváry was out. Why should the Croatian rebels not rejoice? This was their ultimate goal anyway. Unfortunately, the new ban, Teodor Pejačević, was a new face, but the essential elements of the Khuen-Héderváry regime remained in place. With the waning of the movement, he did release most prisoners and relax other measures such as the censorship of the press.

The Croatian National Movement might not have achieved clear and positive results, but it did provide a stage for the Croatian and Serbian *omladina* to publicize their ideas and demonstrate their willingness and ability to work together. Although the Serbs of Croatia remained out of the fray initially, the Serbian Independent party under its new youthful leadership sponsored several large public meetings in late 1903 and 1904 and took part in others initiated by members of the Croatian *omladina*, including Radić, Milan Heimrl, and Lorković.[63] The movement of 1903 was the first political trial for the *omladina*, and in it they gave evidence of strong organizational activity in the field and the willingness to join each other on the political stage. These meetings were not enough to affect the outcome of the movement, but they did seem to prove the vitality of the *omladina*.

In late May 1903, the Serbian *omladina* organizations for Vienna, Prague, and Zagreb planned a reconciliatory meeting with the Croatian *omladina* at Zagreb University. Given the attitude of the new leaders of the Independent party, it is no surprise that when this meeting occurred on May 25, they neither welcomed nor condemned it, saying only that the youth should not move too fast, since Croato-Serbian relations had still not been put on a solid footing. The Independents probably feared that the *omladina* would outdistance the party. In any case, Pribićević and Banjanin could undoubtedly have halted the plans for the meeting if they had wished. As leaders of the Independent party, however, they felt constrained to demand that reconciliation proceed slowly and by negotiation.[64]

Pribićević found himself in a contradictory position. He, like the rest of the Serbian opposition, was leery of supporting a movement that was perceived as strictly Croatian. Yet he was an opponent of state right politics; he was a proponent of the notion of *narodno jedinstvo;* most of all, he supported participation by Serbs in the affairs of Croatia. Should he not have thrown himself directly into the movement, pressing his followers to support the Croats as conationals? As a savvy politician, he knew he could not. He initially worked only to prepare his Serbs for cooperation with Croats, his skittishness the result of his desire not to give up too much too fast to the other Croatian opposition parties. At a meeting in December 1903 in Dvor, he first asked his constituents to entrust leadership to him, for "the national soul is a real tabula rasa . . . on which the most fundamental political ideas have not been noted. . . . constitutional life is the best road for the Serbian people under the guidance of its leaders to find an exit from its unbearable position and its national, civil, social, and economic subordination."[65]

Pribićević wished first to nurture the national identity of his Serbs, simultaneously fostering within them a respect for the possibilities inherent in participation in a Croatia governed constitutionally. Then, he believed, they would be ready to play a role in events like the National Movement, during which these words were uttered. Simultaneously, Pribićević warned that Serbs would not participate in any cooperative venture with Croatian parties until the Croatian opposition endorsed true constitutionalism in Croatia. The Croats who were involved in the National Movement regularly chastised Croatia's Serbian leaders for their failure to bring their constituents into the movement. Thus, in August when the Independent Nationals proposed that the Croatian and Serbian opposition parties form a coalition immediately, Pribićević responded in *Novi Srbobran:* "They forget that first of all there must come healthy, sincere national consolidation . . . and that only then can the great, successful battle for state and constitutional rights be begun. . . . [For now] Serbs will organize as an independent constitutional factor and battle as much as possible by themselves for the state and constitutional

rights of their [Croatian] fatherland."[66] This was a threat and a promise—
Serbs would work for the Croatian land, but only when a "sincere" effort was
made by Croats to bridge differences could the real constitutional fight begin.

The Independent party did not hesitate to make absolutely clear that explicit recognition of Serbs and their culture in Croatia had to be made before
any political alliance against the magyarones could be formed: "the Serbian
nation, regardless of the good will involved, cannot fight for imprecise goals,
not even if these goals are presented through a prism of brotherly harmony."[67]
Medaković held out hope that the Croatian *omladina* would be the solution
to the problem: "Among [Croats], a group of younger people have appeared,
who realize that alliance with Serbs is stronger than all state rights."[68] In fact,
the Independents need not have looked farther than many *pravaši*, including
August Harambašić, whose "ninety-nine desires" speech seemed to open the
door to the sort of negotiation Pribićević and Medaković demanded. They
could count on the fact that one of the main lessons of the failed Croatian
National Movement was that Croatia's Serbs should not be ignored.

Serbia, 1903: A Brutal End to the Obrenović Dynasty

Interestingly, while many in Croatia characterized Croatian politics under
Khuen-Héderváry and state right opposition to him as debilitating and im-
potent, Serbia suffered the same sort of symptoms. Stifled by the leadership
of a weak and self-indulgent Obrenović dynasty, many Serbian political, intellectual, and military leaders felt that Serbia's potential greatness had been
sacrificed in the interests of a stable relationship with an outside power:
Austria-Hungary. The Obrenović dynasty had produced two consecutive
unstable personalities as kings: Milan, who governed from 1868 to 1889, and
Aleksandar, who became king in 1889 and ruled until 1903 (both were limited by regencies early in their reigns). After 1878, when King Milan was able
to enlarge Serbia's territory at the expense of the Ottoman Empire with the
aid of Austria-Hungary, he allowed Serbia to be dominated by the Habsburg
monarchy. In foreign affairs, Serbia's freedom of movement was limited by
secret agreements with Austria-Hungary, and trade treaties of 1881 and 1892
linked Serbia tightly to the monarchy.

Having a patron was never necessarily an embarrassment for small states,
but parading your weakness before the world was. And by the turn of the
century, Serbian politics, the Serbian dynasty, and Serbian weakness in general had become legendary (if exaggerated) in Europe. The trials and tribu-

lations of Milan, his wife, Natalia, and Aleksandar, would have been tabloid fare in the late twentieth century. When Aleksandar determined to marry the woman he fell in love with, all the humiliations that Serbs had suffered over the years seemed to come into sharper focus, for Draga Mašin, the love of Aleksandar's life, was deemed by Serbs to be too ordinary for the king of a powerful state. She was twelve years older than he; she was a widow; she was known to have a "shady past"; she may have been unable to bear children; and she was Aleksandar's mistress. The marriage was viewed by virtually all influential figures in Serbia as simply degrading.

In July 1900, the marriage took place. To no one's surprise and to almost no Serb's horror, on June 10, 1903, the royal couple was slain by conspirators from among junior officers in the Serbian army. Among the leaders of the coup was to be found Dragutin Dimitrijević (also known as "Apis," the bull). There is no question that the main reason for this coup d'état was the conviction of the officers in question that Serbia under the Obrenovićes (not merely Aleksandar) would not be strong enough to fulfill their version of Serbia's destiny: the unification of Serbs in a single state. Virtually all Serbs accepted the logic of the conspirators and the event itself—which underscores the importance of the issue for Serbs in 1903.[69] The assassinations, and the resulting dynastic change, was one of those events that made 1903 so meaningful in Serbian and Croatian history.

Although the rival, native Serbian Karadjordjević dynasty had no known part in the coup, Petar Karadjordjević became king on June 25, 1903, after being elected by a unanimous vote of the Serbian Skupština (assembly). As is often the case with dynastic changes, this one implied shifts in internal and external policies that were rooted in the inclinations and loyalties of the new king. First, a relatively new generation (although certainly not a young one) made up of members of the Radical and Independent Radical parties in Serbia—open enemies of the Obrenovićes—came to the fore. And King Petar and the Radical parties all tended to look to Russia for support, a fact that implicitly drew Serbia's weakening ties to Austria into doubt. It would not take long for those who wished to test Serbia's ties with Austria to flex their muscles. The most recent trade agreement between the two states would expire in early 1905, and the conclusion of a new one was a high priority for Austria. Leaders of the Radical and Independent Radical parties in Serbia hoped to free Serbia of Austrian economic domination. The first step taken by Serbia was to conclude a customs union with Bulgaria. They accomplished this in June 1905 (the treaty was to take effect in March 1906). In concluding an agreement with Bulgaria, Serbia broke its treaty of 1881 with Austria: it did not obtain Austrian acquiescence. At the same time, Serbia began to search for a provider of arms. The choice came down to Škoda or Schneider-Creusot, or more to the point, an Austrian or a French manufacturer. To press Serbia, after sporadically closing its border with Serbia during 1905, Austria finally closed it for good in January 1906, when the Austro-Serbian customs war (also known derisively as the "Pig War") began. The Austrian tie was essentially severed.

Many Croats viewed the changes in Serbia with approval. Specifically, the change of dynasties boded well for the younger generation, which desperately needed Croatia's Serbs to turn against the magyarone regime. One source of strength for the Serbian Club had been that Serbia under the Obrenovićes supported its activity morally and financially with the blessing of the monarchy's governors. Tension between Austria and the Karadjordjevićes could only contribute to the aggressiveness of Serbs who opposed the Serbian Club. For Croats who were appalled by the negative reaction of the world press to the September demonstrations and by the weak response of the opposition in Croatia to the national movement of 1903, the change in dynasties in Serbia was salutary. According to Frano Supilo, a Croatian political leader, Petar Karadjordjević was "a liberal man, a good Serb, a good friend of the Croats."[70] In the words of Miroslav Krleža, the great Croatian writer, with the fall of the two dynasties—that of Khuen-Héderváry and that of the Obrenovićes—"for the first time, striking, positive dynamic possibilities appeared on the national horizon."[71] It remained to tap that rich vein of opportunity.

The Birth of a New Course

By virtue of the Ausgleich, historical Croatia (Dalmatia, Croatia, Slavonia) was divided between Austria and Hungary. That division contributed to the paralysis of Croatian nationalism in action in the late nineteenth century. For Croatia to become one again in the eyes of its nationalists, the dualist system established in 1867 would have to be destroyed. With Dalmatians forced to work within the Austrian system, and Croatia and Slavonia part of Hungary, Croats' (and Serbs') attentions were divided—some looked to Vienna, others looked to Budapest. As long as the dualist cease fire between Austria and Hungary lasted, there was little opportunity for Croats from both sides of the divide to maneuver. By 1903, an equally pressing problem was the depressing cynicism and venality that had descended over Zagreb as a result of Khuen-Héderváry's capable management of Croatia's politicians. In other words, dualism had permeated the flesh of Croatia's body politic —and Dalmatians, for whom collaboration had never become the norm, sensed that Zagreb had lost its vitality.

The National Movement, in tortuous fashion, began a process that bridged the differences that divided Dalmatian and Croatian nationalist politicians. Dalmatians had grown dissatisfied with Viennese administration.[72] The region was in 1903 the poorest and least developed in Austria. The monarchy's plans for railroad development seemed designed to leave it with no valuable transportation connections. Other slights rankled: Dalmatia was governed by a military commissar rather than a civilian appointee, and an Austrian trade agreement with Italy had destroyed much of the Dalmatian wine industry. From the ineffective National Movement Dalmatians learned that they could hope for no benevolence on the part of the Habsburg dynasty toward the Croatian lands and people: when several Dalmatian politicians resolved to go to Vienna to present a petition to the emperor on behalf of the movement in Croatia, they were turned away on the basis of a court formality.[73] By all accounts, this was the final straw: Vienna was unconcerned with Dalmatia or Croatia. So the Dalmatians formulated an actual strategy to pull Croatian politics out of the doldrums of recrimination. For these men, the passivity of the established parties in civil Croatia to the National Movement of 1903 confirmed the need for a new and dynamic orientation. They also believed that no such initiative would come from Croatia itself. According to one, the movement of 1903 had "evoked among us [Dalmatians] a true spiritual revolution in political conceptions, [whereas] Croatia had neither learned anything nor profited from its own movement." For the Dalmatian leaders, convincing Zagreb to accept their new ideas would not be easy: "It was said," this man noted, "that we had to conquer Zagreb, to impose ourselves on their soul and outlook, so strange for us."[74]

Under the influence of the National Movement, many Croats from both sides of the great dualist divide wished to forge a union in political strategies that might precede a union of the two halves of the historical Croatian kingdom. This strategy, known as the New Course, proposed simply to unite the Croats of Dalmatia and Croatia along with any other ethnic group that wished to form a cohesive bloc in order to create a united (and ultimately independent) Croatia. Originally directed at Hungarians who opposed dualism, the New Course also offered an opening for Croatia's Serbs to reintegrate themselves with the Croatian opposition parties. The New Course was concocted in 1903, put into action in 1905, and had flamed out by 1907, and it was never considered a strategy for Croato-Serbian reconciliation; but it became the entry point for those Serbs who favored a constitutionalist strategy in Croatia. And the Serbs who took advantage of that opening remained actors in Croatia's politics long after the New Course had withered.

The strategy worked out by the Dalmatians (including Frano Supilo, Ante Trumbić, Pero Čingrija, and Josip Smodlaka) called for all who felt threatened by German expansionism to ally: the slogan called for defense against the German *Drang nach Osten*.[75] The strategy was heralded by Trumbić's speech in the Dalmatian Sabor on November 7, 1903, the central theme of which was the threat that German civilization posed for all non-Germans of the Habsburg monarchy.[76] Trumbić also appealed to the Magyars, who, he believed, had to realize that "it is better to be a loved friend than a hated ruler." Finally, he asked Croats to "pacify domestic disagreements, which do not have real value, which do not emerge from true national needs. All of that which belongs to the past and has no actual value" should be left to historians. This final call, it should be noted, was directed at contentious Croats. Serbs were among his prospective allies, but Trumbić had not accepted the assertion of their oneness. This strategy, as yet merely an idea, clearly looked to the Hungarians as plausible allies against Vienna. The Dalmatians could not hide their desire to fuse the nascent movement of the Hungarian opposition parties (see below) with Croatia's own (new) movement for unity. Such an orientation would not sell well in Croatia proper, however, where the Croatian and Serbian opposition alike uniformly viewed the Hungarian government as their archenemy.

While Croatia lumbered hesitatingly toward a fundamentally new opposition orientation based on the rejection of dualism, new forces in Hungary propelled that country to the forefront of the antidualist movement. Although the Ausgleich of 1867 had determined Hungary's political relationship with Austria, every ten years a new financial agreement had to be concluded between the two components of the monarchy. The negotiations for the financial Ausgleich of 1897 provided the occasion for strong Hungarian sentiment for financial independence. In that year, the Hungarian minister-president, Kálmán Szell, successfully avoided a crisis for the monarchy by temporarily satisfying the Hungarian factions which favored financial independence. In the elections for the Hungarian parliament held in late 1901, the Independent party of Ferenc Kossuth and the nonaligned group of Gabor Ugron made noticeable gains at the expense of the Liberal party of István Tisza, which had governed Hungary since 1867. The Liberals still retained a large majority in parliament. By early 1903, support for the Independents (the leading party in a coalition of several that sought Hungary's independence from Austria) had grown with the help of public meetings they sponsored throughout Hungary. The parties favoring radical revision of the financial Ausgleich (and some military changes as well) apparently had overwhelming support of the Hungarian voters by 1903. The next elections would not be held until January 1905.

The demands of the Magyar coalition were threefold: it demanded that Hungary be made an independent customs unit, that Hungary have its own national bank, and that the imperial army units in Hungary have a Hungarian officers' corps, use the Magyar language, fly the Hungarian flag, and take an oath to the Hungarian constitution. Such demands obviously would have given Hungary much more independence than it had, and they betokened further demands of ever more separation from Austria. Thus the monarchy's ruling circles correctly perceived the coalition to be a threat to dualism, which amounted to a threat to the existence of the monarchy. That fact alone proved to have great appeal to many Croats, who had already concluded that dualism had to go before Dalmatia and Croatia could be unified.

The emergence of a strong Magyar opposition to the dualist Liberal party in Hungary prompted the Dalmatians to consider alliance with the hated Magyars. If there were a Hungarian government that favored the alteration of the dualist basis of the monarchy, the Dalmatians reasoned, then perhaps an alliance with them would further the unification of Dalmatia and Croatia, which were in separate halves of the monarchy. Such unification would require a modification to the monarchy's order. The New Course thus took concrete form as an alliance of the antidualist Magyars and the Croatian opposition. "Slogan: Struggle for respect of the law! Alliance with our brother Magyars! Down with the provocateurs of disharmony between the Croatian and Magyar peoples!"[77] The New Course was an odd combination of wishful thinking and realpolitik: imagining themselves hard-driving practical politicians, Croatian oppositionists would ally in order to obtain ill-defined concessions from those who seemed least likely to respect their alliance, Magyars.

It took a charismatic person to sell this new strategy. Supilo filled the bill.

Frano Supilo was a Dalmatian, born near Dubrovnik in 1870. He was of a poor family, and his future success attested to his personal dynamism and intelligence. As a young supporter of Ante Starčević, he began working for *Crvena hrvatska* (Red Croatia, the newspaper of the *pravaši* of Dubrovnik) in the 1890s. He founded *Novi list* in Rijeka in 1900. Supilo and Ante Trumbić formulated the concept of the New Course between 1903 and 1905; Supilo then led the Croato-Serbian Coalition from 1905 through 1909. After leaving the Coalition in January 1910, he faded from public view, but later emerged as a leader of the new Croatian and Serbian *omladina* until 1914. During World War I, Supilo helped form and lead the Yugoslav Committee (again with Trumbić), but left it and died in late 1917.

Supilo was somewhat isolated even in his years of active involvement in Croatian politics. He was not easy to get along with; even his best friends conceded that. But he brought unbelievable energy to his work. Supilo was probably the only member of the Coalition who honestly believed that Croatia could wrest independence from Hungary; his was a politics "founded on a romantic, misty, Garibaldi/Mazzini-like, 1848-ish hypothesis."[78] He was also probably the only member of the Coalition who did not have any material interest in seeing the organization succeed. Had Supilo survived into the interwar years, he would undoubtedly have been one of the most energetic opponents of the Serbian-dominated government of the Kingdom of Serbs, Croats, and Slovenes. He accepted the idea of *narodno jedinstvo* in principle, but the differences between the two brother-nations led him to the obvious conclusion that Croats and Serbs, even if one nation, had nurtured such diverse cultural and political characters that practical cooperation was difficult. Serbs had long been the focus of Supilo's anger over Croatia's divided and subordinate position in the monarchy and Croats' underling status in their own country. To Supilo, who was the most charismatic Croatian politician of the period, can be attributed the roles of coformulator and driving spirit of the New Course; later he was the unchallenged leader of the Croato-Serbian Coalition through 1909. The way in which Serbs fit into this new strategy depended on how Supilo conceived of their role.

Supilo undoubtedly shared the belief that Croats and Serbs were one nation, but his conception of the implications of that belief was clearer than most. "We all know that Croats and Serbs are blood brothers," he wrote in 1902, "and that there is nothing more unfortunate than brothers fighting each other in the service of strangers." But no one "will ever erase from our national history of recent times the fact that whenever anyone needed to slap Croats on the hand . . . there were always Serbs in reserve, *our* Serbs, who, invited and uninvited, always gladly rushed to perform this unthankful and unbrotherly task."[79] Supilo understood and clearly conveyed that although Croats and Serbs may have been blood brothers and comprised one nation, they had yet to behave as if they respected their brotherly bond. Unlike Pribićević, Supilo did not propose that Croats and Serbs be educated in their oneness, nor did he concede to Serbs their right to legal guarantees.

For Supilo, as for many *pravaši*, a turnabout in Croato-Serbian relations could only come when "from the Serbian side announcements are heard that the autonomy of Croatia is in the interest of the Serbian as well as the Croatian branch, then it can be assumed that these phrases have begotten an idea. And that idea is neither hollow nor barren. It contains the call to action."[80] Supilo, like his *pravaši* forebears, demanded that Serbs recognize their united interest with Croats in the progress of their country, Croatia. Unlike his predecessors, Supilo did not require from Serbs a legalistic recognition of Croatian state right, and furthermore, in the regenerated Independent party, Supilo knew that there were Serbs, namely the Serbian *omladina* of Pribićević and Banjanin, who were willing to work for Croatia as well as for themselves.

Events in Serbia and Hungary gave the formulators of the New Course hope: the Dalmatian Supilo welcomed the Serbian dynastic change, for he now not only had a stage on which to carry out his New Course (the events surrounding the independence movement in Hungary), he had the Serbian government, with which he communicated, to discipline the unruly Serbian opposition in Croatia. The New Course, designed to extort the unification of Dalmatia and civil Croatia from the monarchy's unwilling leaders, also was now marked by an apparently genuine consensus between many Croats and Serbs. Unfortunately, as in the Serbo-Hungarian case, so in the Croato-Serbian, definitions and expectations of cooperation were divergent, and Serbia, Hungary, and Croatia were destined to disappoint each other. For Croats, especially those whom Supilo had to convince to adhere to the New Course, the value of cooperation with Croatia's Serbs was that the Serbs implicitly agreed to work as political Croats. Croatia's progress, unity, and eventual independence was their end, *narodno jedinstvo* a means.

Conclusion

The transition in Serbian politics in the Habsburg monarchy represented by the behavior of the Serbian Independent party under the leadership of Svetozar Pribićević in 1903 and 1904 can be understood in a variety of ways. Choose a perspective: from that of the *pravaši*, here was a party finally willing to recognize Croatian statehood, to demonstrate a willingness to fight for it. From the perspective of Habsburg politics, Pribićević rejected the politics of barter, the politics of reward and punishment whereby Serbs could protect themselves from assimilation as a group by swearing loyalty to the emperor (rather than a state or a constitution) who would personally assure their safety. From the perspective of the Radical party of Jaša Tomić, the Independents were giving up their essence, their Serbianness, in the name of a state idea (the Croatian) that threatened to swallow them. Once having recognized a Croatian state idea, according to the Radicals, they could never again reclaim their Serbianness without being accused of treason by Croats. From the perspective of Pribićević and the Independents themselves, they were opting for modernity, for citizenship in a modern state. Recognizing Croatian statehood was the first step in becoming citizens of the state in which they lived—until that point, they would be traitors. *Pravaši* beware: in recognizing Croatian statehood, the Independents did not intend to relinquish their Serbianness. Radicals be assured: the Independents would not sacrifice their culture on the altar of assimilationism, but they would try to assure its long life in a modern state, with rights of citizenship guaranteed by a modern constitution.

3

THE BIRTH AND SHORT LIFE OF THE NEW COURSE, 1903–1907

Initiation

THE NEW COURSE emerged as a full-fledged political strategy designed to take advantage of political conditions in turn-of-the-century Austria-Hungary. The background: in 1897, Austria-Hungary and Russia agreed not to let Balkan conditions draw them into war (an agreement that put the Balkans "on ice"); in 1903, they agreed at Mürzsteg to support reforms in Ottoman administration of Macedonia, thereby hoping to remove that region as a source of conflict. Each of these European powers had compelling reasons to limit its competition in southeastern Europe: Russia had recently been hurt by its involvement (or meddling) in Bulgarian affairs and wished to turn its attentions to eastward expansion, which eventually led to the catastrophe of its war with Japan in 1904–1905. Austria was already entering an era of constitutional reform that dominated the attention of its statesmen. The agreements to limit competition in the Balkans thus froze the existing situation there, a situation in which Serbia was firmly, if not happily, attached to Austria-Hungary.

The monarchy's politicians were preoccupied with internal affairs. After 1867, Hungarian leaders were temporarily satisfied with the level of Hungary's autonomy within the Habsburg monarchy. But other nationalities in the monarchy viewed the Ausgleich as either a betrayal of their interests (the Croats felt this way) or a promise of a similar agreement in the future (the Czechs probably hoped for such a turn). In fact, however, as detailed in the previous chapter, even the Hungarians were dissatisfied with the Ausgleich by the 1890s. After the fall of Kálmán Tisza in 1890, Hungarian leaders began to strive for ever more independence from Austria. They usually expressed this in the economic sphere, and in 1897 and 1907, the financial Ausgleich had to be renegotiated, opening the door to political conflict. The fall of the elder Tisza marked the beginning of an era in which financial conflict would lead to the growth of a more nationalistic, more combative element in Hungarian politics. This new consensus challenged the dualist basis of the monarchy. With this restructuring of the Hungarian political spectrum, which occurred between 1902 and 1905, the role of Croatia in the dualist system naturally came into question. Austrian and Hungarian leaders alike profoundly hoped that Croatia would not make dualism an issue, but of course their hopes were in vain.

While leaders of the monarchy's two halves clearly wished to maintain the status quo with Serbia and in Croatia, politicians in Serbia and Croatia alike (if for different reasons) viewed that status quo as an obstacle to be confronted and conquered. Serbian politics were not monolithic: there was no consensus behind the stifling relationship between Serbia and Austria, and as time passed and Serbian political parties contended for power, that relationship would be questioned more and more openly, especially by the emergent Radical party of Nikola Pašić. Thus Serbian leaders hoped to break the bonds that tied them to Austria. In Croatia, the conflict between the dualist forces and Hungarian nationalism could only provide Croats with room to maneuver for more autonomy of their own. Furthermore, by 1900, political leaders recognized the strength of nationalism as a political mobilizer. The very notion of a conflict between Hungarian nationalists and Austro-Hungarian "dualists" implied that new forces had to be considered: dualism was a product of unresponsive elites, whereas Hungarian nationalism was the product of the masses—whether manipulated or not. In an era of mass politics (most European states had universal male suffrage by 1907), old restrictive relationships negotiated by elites could only come into question.

Arriving at a Fortuitous Consensus

It was in these circumstances that the New Course emerged. It must be said that the New Course was never a well-articulated policy. In spite of the importance that it and its organizational progeny, the Croato-Serbian Coalition, are given by historians, and in spite of their relative prominence in Croatian (and Yugoslav) political memory, the strategy's importance was more symbolic than actual. The New Course as such only lasted from late 1905 to mid-1907. In fact, as a strategy, it rested on highly unspecific private agreements between an isolated group of Dalmatian politicians and Hungarian oppositionists (and Dalmatia, remember, was in the other half of the monarchy and thus had no legal relationship with Hungary). More important, and more memorable, was the structure that attended the strategy: that is where the Croato-Serbian Coalition came in for the tenuous agreement between the Dalmatian Croats and the Hungarian opposition prompted the formation of a radically new sort of opposition coalition in Croatia. Initially meant only to represent all those forces in Croatian politics which supported an antidualist policy, the Croato-Serbian Coalition mobilized Croatian and Serbian political parties which represented "oneness," the idea that Croats and Serbs were Yugoslavs. The New Course was dead by 1907, but the Croato-Serbian Coalition carried the torch of *narodno jedinstvo* until 1918.

The New Course's directive was simple: Croatian parties would cooperate with non-Croatian parties in order to achieve some of the most basic Croatian desiderata, which included the unification of Croatia and Dalmatia and the gradual achievement of economic, then political autonomy. If the directive was clear, the means were not: the strategy could not succeed without a vehicle of some sort, and as yet, there were no signed alliances, no political parties formed to implement the strategy. In fact, it was nothing but hopes and ideas, and even those were limited to a small circle of Dalmatians, responding, as described above, to the failed promise of the National Movement of 1903. The Hungarian challenge to dualism opened the door to concrete action. Following the victory of the Hungarian independence coalition over Tisza's Liberal party in the elections of January 1905, Supilo and Trumbić began to court that coalition. Supilo believed that Croatia should play a role in Austro-Hungarian rivalry similar to that which Piedmont had played in the Crimean war: take a side, play its necessarily limited role, and thereby place the Croatian question on the monarchy's agenda by rattling the cage of dualism's cultivators in Vienna and Budapest.[1] In a March 1905 article, Trumbić proposed to the Magyar coalition an alliance with Croats whereby "we [Dalmatia] get some sort of true autonomy and unification with Croatia, you get us, with Croatia and Dalmatia as a new and supporting unit of the Magyar crown."[2] The Magyars could not afford to overlook the offer—it would give them a long and valuable Dalmatian coastline that was then in Austrian hands. Supilo approved the article as "statesmanlike" and noted its friendly reception in Budapest.[3] But Croats were reluctant to agree to such a plan. The problem was simple: Croatian oppositionists from the *frankovci* to the *omladina* considered Hungary their mortal enemy. This sentiment precluded easy acceptance of Supilo's initiative by the parties of Croatia. Supilo's challenge was to convince them that the new Hungarian opposition group represented antidualism more than it represented the old oppressor, Hungary itself.[4] There would be long months of negotiation before the parties of Croatia proper would come around to Supilo's thinking. "[Antidualism] was the one [and only] point of agreement of the Magyar opposition with Croats," Trumbić later wrote.[5] The proposed New Course indeed rested on shaky ground.

The Dalmatians had thought in 1903 that the economic abandonment of Dalmatia by Austria and the National Movement in Croatia would be enough of a catalyst for the acceptance of their strategy in Zagreb. At least, they assumed, Croatian, Serbian, and perhaps Italian parties in Dalmatia and Croatia could unite on the basis of hostility toward Vienna. However, in Croatia only the Progressive Youth attempted to take advantage of the movement—and they were yet to be convinced that the New Course, implying cooperation with Hungarians, Serbs, and Italians, could accomplish more than a unified Croatian opposition could. One sign of life came in spring 1904, when Ivan Lorković and some younger members of the Croatian Party of Right founded the newspaper *Pokret* (Movement). Their major initiative was to force the pace of cooperation with Croatia's Serbs.[6] They did so not with the intention of pushing along the New Course, but as their own initiative stemming from their interest in Croato-Serbian cooperation. For Lorković and the Progressives, historical state right might have appeared radical in its time, but it was in fact economically and socially conservative.[7] *Pokret* gave extensive positive coverage to various events promoting South Slavic unity, such as the South Slav Art Exhibition in Belgrade in May 1904 and the celebration of the one hundredth anniversary of the Serbian uprising of 1804, both of which were attended by Slovenes, Croats, Serbs, and Bulgarians.

Ivan Lorković, leader of the Croatian Progressive Party. *From Josip Horvat*, Politička povijest Hrvatske *Zagreb: August Cesarec, 1990.*

Adopting the constitutionalist orientation of the new Serbian Independents of Pribićević and Banjanin, they ridiculed Croats who ignored the strong Serbian presence in their land. In a series of articles entitled "The Serbian Question in the Croatian Context," they explained their position.[8] Asking Croats to dare deny that the "Serbian question" was the cardinal problem in Croatia at that time, the writer warned Croats not to deny Serbian presence in Croatia, for that was the same tactic used by Magyars toward Croats. Such parallels "would have made Jelačić roll over in his grave."

The focus of Lorković's attentions was the Serbian Independent party. He and his colleagues believed that the Serbian Radicals had too much invested in national particularism and were too unwilling to work with Croats on the basis of recognition of Croatian statehood. The Independents were asked to concede that Croatian and Serbian interests in Croatia proper were identical; agree to work to revise the Nagodba; join the battle for a free press, freedom of assembly, an independent judiciary, and the secret ballot in Croatia; strive for local administrative autonomy; work for economic reform (that is, the revision of the financial Nagodba); work for the rights of all non-Magyars in the Croatian Sabor and Hungarian Parliament; and stand for the principle of the "East to the Eastern Peoples" in Habsburg foreign policy. In return, the Independents could expect Croatian support for full equality of Serbian citizens, churches, and schools; full equality of the Serbian name by law in the Kingdom of Croatia and Slavonia; school and church codes guaranteeing a separate Serbian administrative hierarchy; inviolability of Serbian church and school property; freedom to fly the Serbian national flag; and the use of Cyrillic. Finally, *Pokret* suggested that the question of Bosnia and Hercegovina be set aside for the time being, since the Croatian and Serbian viewpoints were irreconcilable, with each firmly believing Bosnia was its destiny.

The program of the Serbian Independents already supported the revision of the Nagodba, and in other areas the demands were hardly controversial—in fact, the concept "the East to the Eastern Peoples" was traditionally associated with the Serbian Radical party in Hungary, and had also been proclaimed as a principle of foreign policy in the Kingdom of Serbia by the Radical party there. On the other side of the equation, all that was offered to the Independents was already guaranteed by law. The offer, however, implicitly represented a distinct change in tone for a Croatian party. It took Harambašić's "ninety-nine desires" a bit further. While granting recognition to Serbian demands of long standing, it dropped the legalistic request that Serbs accept Croatian political nationhood, in its place simply asking that Serbs recognize that their interests coincided with Croats', which was, in essence, the same thing. That actually represented a significant shift in rhetoric, and rhetoric, after all, was what Croatia's politicians excelled in. It was an important transition.

Lorković commenced selling the proposal not to Serbs, but to Croats, since no other Croatian party was thinking so convincingly along these lines after the Croatian National Movement. To those who claimed that Serbs all tended to magyaronism, the future Progressives simply denied that such was the case: many young Serbs, these Croats knew, realized that their interests coincided with Croats' in all areas and rejected magyaronism. In December 1904, they founded their Croatian Progressive party, which lent more substance to their appeal. Lorković became president of the party, which stood on an explicitly anticlerical, middle-class foundation, with what support it could muster coming from urban areas: Zagreb, Osijek, Sisak, Karlovac. Its program called for the autonomy of Croatia, financial independence from Hungary, and productive work in the Hungarian Parliament (as opposed to pro-forma obstruction). The new Progressive party maintained contact with

Stjepan Radić, who formed his Croatian People's Peasant party at about the same time. However, cooperation between these two offspring of the Progressive Youth was necessarily limited, since the Peasant party concentrated on the peasantry, and thus declined to join the Progressives in their anticlericalism. Indeed, the Progressives found the going rough in general, since they based much of their appeal on their ability to attract urbanites, who were already strongly represented by existing Croatian parties.

While the Progressives and their initiatives might have been refreshing and their pro-Serbian orientation salutary, the fact remained that they were peripheral political actors. The New Course demanded the adherence of the Croatian *pravaš* mainstream. While harmonious relations among Croats and Serbs were an important by-product of the emergence of the *omladina*, they were considered marginal by the initiators of the New Course, who were more interested in sweetening the relationship between Croatia and Hungary. While Supilo and the Progressives chipped away at resistance to the New Course among the Croats of Croatia, other initiatives began to bear fruit. Serbia itself had, in rather coincidental fashion, become a logical and indeed important actor in the leadup to the New Course. It was not that new post-coup Serbian leaders had fallen under the spell of *narodno jedinstvo;* it was not that they cared in the least whether Croatian oppositionists threw in their lot with the Hungarians; it was simply that the new leadership in Serbia had staked its future on rejecting Serbia's recent tradition of subservience to Austria. As a result, Serbia needed to find new allies in a dangerous world. The customs war, which was about to begin, was the first gauntlet that Serbia would have to run in sloughing off Austrian tutelage. Concurrently, Serbian leaders recognized that an independence-minded Hungary offered a logical ally against Austria.

The Hungarian crisis offered Serbia concrete but limited opportunities. Were the Austro-Hungarian customs union to disappear, Serbia could utilize Austria against Hungary, using a small power strategy of dividing one's larger neighbors. But, as the Serbs knew, the leaders of the independence movement in Hungary wanted Hungary to form a Danubian confederation including the various states of the Danube basin. Serbs no more wanted to be tied to Hungary than to Austria, but believed they could easily maneuver between the two. Further limiting a possible Serbo-Hungarian relationship in the future was the socioeconomic composition of the Hungarian coalition. The coalition consisted of industrialists and landowners who all had reason to desire economic independence from Austria: the industrialists needed a free hand to compete in foreign markets; the agrarians wanted to protect their products. Serbia, an overwhelmingly agricultural country, could only have temporary political interest in linking its fortunes to Hungary's agrarians, although it did not fear Hungary's industrialists. Any Serbo-Hungarian relationship could only last until its basic goals (the breakup of the Habsburg customs union) had been achieved—beyond that, Serbia and Hungary were competitors at best. At worst, Hungary could eventually try to tie Serbia to itself as Austria had. In this would-be marriage of convenience, Hungary and Serbia wished to use each other to pressure Austria.

As early as spring 1904, at the urging of the Serbian Consul Vasiljević in Budapest, a meeting was held of Serbian businessmen and Hungarian politicians, including members of the Hungarian Parliament.[9] Although the Serbian government wished all such meetings to be strictly unofficial, the consul and Serbian politicians in Hungary allowed them to be perceived otherwise by the Magyars. Nikola Pašić, Serbia's premier at the time, sent a personal emissary, Giga Geršić, to Budapest to scout the territory. Geršić met with the Croatian delegation to the Hungarian Parliament and Serbian politicians and attended a large meeting of Serbian and Hungarian businessmen which included ministers in István Tisza's government. The timing is important: Geršić met with a Croatian delegation still consisting of magyarones and representatives of a Tisza government that had not yet been voted out. Serbian behavior was not idealistic. Serbia did not differentiate the various factions in Croatia and Hungary at first—it would have negotiated with any authoritative group that expressed willingness to listen. But among the new generation of Serbs in Croatia, the actions of the Serbian consul and businessmen were controversial: the consul requested that the Serbian newspapers in Hungary and Croatia, *Zastava* (Banner, newspaper of the Radicals), *Branik* (Rampart, newspaper of the Serbian Liberal party), and *Novi Srbobran*, refrain from criticizing the meeting. *Novi Srbobran* refused to do so, which illuminates the fact that many of the Serbs of Croatia, including those youth around Pribićević and Banjanin, had different agendas than the Serbian government at that time. Obviously, the Serbian government felt the need to search for options to Viennese tutelage even before the Hungarian independence coalition or the New Course jumped into the picture.

Nonetheless, as soon as the Hungarian opposition came to power in January 1905, the policies of Serbia and the hopes of the backers of the New Course coincided. And Supilo, whose visionary streak included the hope (if not the expectation) of forging a true, unified Yugoslav approach to Croatia's problems, grasped the opportunity. He went to Belgrade to use old acquaintances to try to influence the Serbian parties of Croatia and Hungary.[10] Josip Frank later accused Supilo of treason on the basis of this visit. Supilo claimed that he had only visited Pašić, and that for five minutes—long enough for Pašić to make clear that he was busy. That may have been true, but Supilo certainly carried on talks at other times with other Serbian politicians. Three weeks later, he wrote Trumbić that an emissary from Belgrade had visited him, and that Serbia was considering the situation and wanted to "see how far the Magyars will go."[11] The emissary could have been Jaša Prodanović, a member of the Independent Radical party in Serbia, who had been the conduit for Supilo's correspondence with Ljuba Stojanović, the Serbian premier after March 1905. Stojanović himself had come to Rijeka in early 1905 to discuss with Supilo possible work with the Magyars. Josip Smodlaka and Franko Potočnjak, two Croatian supporters of the New Course, also maintained contacts in Serbia. Dušan Popović of the Independent party is also known to have mediated between the Radicals, the Independents, and the Serbian government in the interests of a coalition of the two Serbian parties.[12]

Serbian leaders had not wanted to become too implicated in talks with the members of the Hungarian coalition until the coalition won the elections of January 1905. When it actually came to power, unofficial overtures continued and official negotiations for an anti-Austrian alliance began. They mixed enthusiasm with caution. Jovan M. Jovanović, an official of the Serbian Ministry of Foreign Affairs, wrote in May 1905 that although the Hungarian coalition was seeking independence, a goal with which all small nations could sympathize, it brought nothing new to their relations with the smaller nations within Hungarian borders. Thus Serbia should be careful. When the Hungarian independence coalition won the elections, Jovanović wrote, it "developed a program that did not differ in essence from the program of the [Hungarian] Liberal party: magyarization of the non-Magyar nationalities." "They emphasize," he continued, "the principle of equality and fairness in their struggle against Austria, but forget to recognize the same principle for Serbs, Romanians, and Croats." "Those in Zagreb," he advised, "should not kid themselves. . . . Both Vienna and Pest offer the world; necessity knows no law."[13] Jovanović was calling attention to the fact that the unity of interests between the Hungarian coalition and the Croats was destined to be of short duration.

In June 1905, Supilo wrote Trumbić that he had convinced influential

Serbs to work with him: "they are with us."[14] The one great service that Serbs from Serbia could provide Supilo was to help pacify ongoing infighting between the Serbian Independents and Radicals in Croatia. The Radicals were the most intransigent. In 1905, the Serbian government asked the Radicals to take the uncomfortable step of allying with Croats. Months later, Supilo boasted that "had I not hopped down to Belgrade in time and run from Pašić to Živković and Ljuba Stojanović, our Serbian parties in Croatia proper would still be scuffling and calling each other all sorts of names. . . . But they were pressed to reconcile by Serbia."[15] Pribićević's Independent party needed no convincing to adhere to the New Course. The Radicals were tougher to convince, since they were not ideologically predisposed to cooperate.

Forming the Croato-Serbian Coalition

By October 1905, all the pieces of the political puzzle were momentarily in place—the Radicals, the *pravaši*, and of course the Progressives and the Independents. The Rijeka conference, which heralded the new alliance and strategy, was convened on October 3. All Croatian and Serbian opposition parties represented in the Croatian and Dalmatian Sabors were invited by Ante Trumbić and Pero Čingrija to send representatives. Hardheadedness and technicalities assured that some parties would not participate. Because the Serbian Independent and Radical parties were not represented in the Croatian Sabor and the Hungarian Parliament, they were not invited. The Serbian National party of Dalmatia, which was represented in the Dalmatian Sabor, refused to attend because Frank's party was asked to come and the Serbian parties of Croatia proper were not. For his part, Frank refused to attend because he disagreed with the strategy being formulated. So, in the end, neither the *frankovci* nor any Serbs attended the Rijeka conference. The fact that the Serbian Independents were not invited at all is indicative of the fact that the New Course, as proclaimed at the Rijeka conference, was not a strategy of reconciliation of Croats and Serbs, but was designed to enable Croatia to progress as a country in ways that the Croatian opposition found meaningful. In other words, this was not a declaration of a new phase in a Yugoslav national movement, it was a Croatian political strategy.

On October 3, the deputies at Rijeka presented a resolution formulated by Trumbić.[16] The main premise of the resolution was that the Croatian parties represented at Rijeka sympathized with the efforts of the Hungarian coalition to enhance Hungary's autonomy in the Habsburg monarchy. Cooperation between Croatian and Hungarian deputies in the parliaments "having been attained, there is laid down as a condition the speediest reincorporation of Dalmatia and the Kingdoms of Croatia, Slavonia, and Dalmatia." The resolution called for the implementation of electoral reforms, judicial reforms, freedom of assembly, and freedom of the press. It did not demand the abandonment of the Nagodba, because the resolutionists sought the strict enforcement of the Nagodba along with the unification of Dalmatia and Croatia proper. Thus they demanded "the punctual and strict fulfillment of the rights of the Croatian nation as contained in the existing Croato-Hungarian Nagodba." The resolution stated that a committee of five had been designated to negotiate with the Hungarian independence opposition. At Rijeka, therefore, the Croatian opposition, harmonious except for the *frankovci*, threw in its lot with the Hungarian opposition. There was no mention of Serbs, *narodno jedinstvo*, the national problem. Croatian strategy would be directed toward the attainment of the unity of Dalmatia and Croatia.

Two weeks after the Rijeka Conference, the Serbs who had not attended met in Zadar, the capital of Dalmatia, and formulated their own resolution, which they passed on October 17.[17] The Zadar Resolution, formulated by the Independents, Radicals, and members of the Serbian National party in Dalmatia, was a response to the Rijeka Resolution, not an independently formulated statement of Serbian initiatives. The Serbian delegates at Zadar declared their support for the Hungarian coalition, but, unlike the Croats at Rijeka, they demanded that the Magyars also "place their relations with the non-Magyar nations of Hungary upon a just basis, with a view to guaranteeing the latter's national cultural existence and development." This critical point dealt with a purely Serbian problem: Serbs had a more direct interest in convincing the Magyars to treat the nationalities of Hungary more fairly, since there was a strong Serbian presence there—and the Serbian Radical party, which represented those Serbs, was present at Zadar.

The Serbian delegates did put forth a condition to the Croats. The single most portentous passage of the Zadar Resolution read: "Concerning the demands of our brother Croats for the reincorporation of Dalmatia to Croatia and Slavonia . . . the Serbian parties are prepared to [support this], if the Croatian side. . . . bindingly recognizes the equality of the Serbian nation with the Croatian."[18] Thus the signatories of the Zadar Resolution agreed to act as political Croats, in return for that which most Croats had offered (remember Harambašić's "ninety-nine desires" in 1902): recognition of Serbian cultural individuality in Croatia. Understood by "recognition of equality" was the equality of the Serbian church, schools, name, and alphabet on Croatian soil. The Serbian delegates elected a three-man committee to negotiate with the Croatian signatories of the Rijeka Resolution. On that committee were Ante Puljezi of the Serbian National party of Dalmatia, Pribićević of the Serbian Independents, and Milivoj Babić of the Serbian Radicals.[19]

Although by virtue of the Zadar Resolution the Serbs did in fact join the Croats in the New Course, there was some dissension regarding the goals of the alliance. Whereas the Radicals wished the Zadar Resolution to focus most on cooperation with the Hungarian opposition, the Independents were less forceful on that question and more interested in simply joining the Croats for the sake of participation. As we have seen, the Radicals were much more goal-oriented where the New Course was concerned: they stood to gain in very tangible ways (in the Church Congress) by supporting the Hungarian opposition. On the other hand, the Independents under Pribićević stood to gain little of note except a contributing role in the formulation of Croatian opposition strategies. Niko Nardelli, the Austrian commissar in Dalmatia, suspected with reason that the Serbian Independents had in Zadar joined the New Course simply for the sake of participation in Croatian politics and the maintenance of a hard-won friendship with the Croats.[20]

Nonsignatories attacked the Rijeka Resolution. The reason is simple and clear: the signers intended to form an alliance with Magyars of the independence coalition, who opponents of the Rijeka group believed were no different than their forebears in the Liberal party. Opponents of the resolution included Radić's Peasant party, the *frankovci* in the Pure Party of Right, and the National party. Josip Frank attacked the resolution on two counts: first that it declared friendship with Magyars, second that it implied friendship with Serbs. Frank could not understand how those who had dealt with Hungary for so long could not see that the members of the Magyar coalition were fooling them: now that the coalition was in power in Hungary, it would remember its intolerance toward Hungary's minorities.[21] Mile Starčević expanded eloquently on Frank's point that the Rijeka Resolution was not the work of skilled strategists but of weak politicians: "Common sense says that the Magyars will be more friendly and more inclined to that party which yields to them the most; common sense says that the Magyars will not give more than is included in the Nagodba."[22]

Their fear had been shared by those who signed the Rijeka Resolution. Harambašić, a member of the Croatian Party of Right and the Croat who had done the most to sell the New Course to the *pravaši* of Croatia proper, explained the motives of the signatories: "representatives of the Croatian people have to persevere so that their nation not only does not suffer any sort of damage in this [Austro-Hungarian] crisis, but that in that crisis, which is shaking the constitutional foundations of our monarchy, they extract as much advantage as possible."[23] The resolutionists wished to bargain with the Magyars on the basis of the Nagodba, which, they believed, legally guaranteed all that Croatia needed, but which the Hungarians had not respected.[24] The resolutionists were counting on the promise of cooperation with the Hungarian coalition parties, nothing more.

Frank's second reproach to the signatories of the Rijeka Resolution was that they had allied with Serbs.[25] Harambašić, who took his role as interpreter of the New Course in the Sabor uncharacteristically seriously, responded to Frank's accusations regarding the role of Serbs in the New Course. One of the great successes of Rijeka, Harambašić said, was "to achieve alliance between Croats and Serbs in Dalmatia, an alliance forever unshakable because each brother sincerely and honorably recognized that which he had to recognize."[26] Harambašić was not willing to go much further than that, however. For the *pravaši* who signed the resolution, the agreement was not a proclamation of unity or nationhood. It was a declaration of a Croatian political strategy—Serbs and Magyars were allies. "[The Zadar Resolution] was only a complement, a commentary on our resolution," said Harambašić; Serbs had finally come to the proper conclusion that an alliance with Croats was the only way for both peoples to achieve Serbian national goals in Croatia. The thrust of his argument was that Serbs in Croatia had joined the Croats in a political endeavor, nothing more.

Frank's objections were predictable. But, ironically, at least one of the *signatory* parties at Zadar was unhappy with the direction politics were taking. Tomic's Radicals had no faith that the Croatian opposition would seriously undertake to give legal guarantees of Serbian individuality in Croatia. They also did not like the fact that the Rijeka Resolution did not mention Serbs at all. However, the most cogent Serbian criticism came from a respected outsider to the proceedings, the leader of the Serbian Liberal party, Mihailo

Polit-Desančić, who questioned why any Serb or Croat would trust the Hungarian Independent party: "Have any Magyar statesmen or the Kossuthites yet given the smallest sign that they are in agreement with the demands of the Croatian opposition, that they want to support the Croatian opposition at all, and especially in the question of the unification of Dalmatia? . . . We who have led the struggle for years for Serbs and for Croats in the Hungarian Parliament, we know how the Kossuthites think, how they breathe."[27]

In spite of much valid Serbian criticism, on November 14, 1905, Bogdan Medaković, the president of the Serbian Independent party, received from Ante Puljezi, the president of the Serbian National party in Dalmatia, a note stating that the Croatian and Serbian representatives in the Dalmatian Sabor had agreed that "the Serbian nation is recognized as completely equal with the Croatian. The Serbo-Croatian conflict has accordingly disappeared, and the club of Serbian Sabor representatives has agreed to unification with Croatia."[28]

This agreement cleared the way for the formation of the Croato-Serbian Coalition, which was announced on December 14, 1905. Signatories of the Coalition's declaration were: the Croatian Party of Right, the Croatian Progressive party, the Serbian Independent party, the Serbian Radical party, the Social-democratic party, and Franko Potočnjak, an independent representative.[29] The stage was set for the New Course to be put into action—the elections for the Croatian Sabor of May 1906 awaited.

The Coalition in Action: The Temptations of Power

The first step of the Croato-Serbian Coalition after its formation was to emerge from the elections of May 3–5, 1906, as a significant factor in the Croatian Sabor. The initial goal was simple—to be rid of the National party, the detested magyarones, the pillars of dualism in Croatia. Although the Coalition did not gain even a plurality, it was the second strongest grouping in the Sabor. Of the eighty-eight seats in the Sabor, the governing National party gained thirty-eight, the Coalition gained thirty-one, and the *frankovci* nineteen. Of the Coalition seats, the *pravaši* won twenty, the Independents six, the Radicals two, and there were three nonparty candidates (Vladimir Nikolić-Podrinsky, Count Miroslav Kulmer, and Franko Potočnjak). The Progressives gained no seats.[30] The Coalition's showing at the polls, although apparently weak, was notable given the apathy in Croatia to that point. It was such a convincing repudiation of the National party that the magyarones disbanded their organization, leaving the Coalition to attempt to cooperate with the *frankovci* in the Sabor.

In Croatia, the government was not responsible to the Sabor; its members had to be acceptable to Vienna and Budapest, since the ban and his cabinet ministers were appointed by the emperor in consultation with the Hungarian minister-president. On May 29, the Coalition agreed to allow the current ban, Teodor Pejačević, to remain in that position.[31] The agreement reached between the Coalition and Pejačević was momentous, since it represented the first step in a trend toward cooperation between the Coalition and some members of the old regime. The members of the Croato-Serbian Coalition were utterly unused to being the "government party." Early on, Supilo noted that they would have to go outside their own ranks to create a government, for two reasons: they themselves were incapable of filling the functions, and Budapest and Vienna would only accept a limited degree of change in Croatia. The Coalition willingly admitted that it was forced to retain Pejačević, who had replaced Khuen-Héderváry in mid-1903.[32] However, in forcing an agreement on the ban, the Coalition could claim that it had established the basis of constitutional government in Croatia, since it had bound his hands and made him responsible to the Sabor majority.

The agreement itself stipulated that Pejačević step out of the National party and remain outside of party politics; assure that the Sabor would meet following the meeting of the Hungarian Parliament in June; support constitutional reforms, presumably regarding the union of Dalmatia and any further revisions of the Nagodba, as well as the freedoms of assembly, speech, and secret ballot, and the independence of the courts, which were part of the Coalition's platform; assure that such reforms, when passed in the Sabor, would not be rescinded by imperial rescript (the critical yet impossible obligation); and fill the seats in his government in consultation with the Coalition.[33] The final stipulation was a face-saver: the Coalition had to accept men who were acceptable to Vienna. Although the agreement with Pejačević promised some stability for the Coalition in the Sabor, the general consensus was that he was an unimpressive figure. According to Supilo, he was weak and self-indulgent. "It is necessary to surround him with honest and capable people, which are hard to find in the [Coalition's] parliamentary club."[34] "He has the intelligence of the average count," one hostile witness reported, "evil of heart and very hypocritical."[35] After negotiations with Pejačević and the Hungarian government, the Coalition supported Vladimir Nikolić as vice-ban

for internal affairs, Milan Rojc as departmental chief for religion and education, and Aleksandar Badaj as departmental chief for justice. "These [latter]
two are among the most capable [in the] Coalition," wrote Supilo.[36] Unfortunately, they had neither declared themselves members of the Coalition nor
been elected to the Sabor (yet). They each gained their seats in by-elections,
after being named to the government.

Nikolić was the least likely choice of the three. One of Khuen-Héderváry's
Serbian allies, he served as the magyarone *veliki župan* (county administrator) of the *županija* (county) of Modruš-Rijeka from 1895 to 1905; at the time
of the Croatian national movement of 1903 he distinguished himself for the
industriousness with which he jailed rebels in Ogulin.[37] He left the National
party and his position after a clash with Nikola Tomašić, the head of the National party, in 1905. His connections with Vienna, however, recommended
him for the post of vice-ban, and Supilo nominated Nikolić after being informed by Pejačević that he had to be present in the government for Vienna
to accept it.[38] He was never a sympathetic choice for Supilo, who accused him
later of having been a disruptive influence and gossipmonger in the Coalition. Nonetheless, he became one of the organization's leaders after 1910,
when Supilo left the Coalition.[39] Rojc also had strong connections with the
magyarone National party and had once been saved from prosecution for
corruption by one of Khuen-Héderváry's *veliki župani*.[40] For his part, Badaj
had served Khuen-Héderváry in Zemun. These men reflected gross com-
promises with the ideals that the Coalition claimed to represent. Their elections to the Sabor were handled in a disingenuous fashion by the Coalition,
which wished them to be elected but could not support them openly and remain consistent with its stated principles.

Not only was the government top heavy with borderline magyarones,
but the Serbian Independent party in 1906 was a radical organization only
on the surface. Except for Pribićević, Banjanin, and Dušan Popović, the
party's leaders had been members since the foundation of the organization.
Medaković and Vaso Muačević were hardly to be thought of as critical new
minds in the party—rather, they were veterans of the turbulent 1880s. Furthermore, even the Independents quietly absorbed new members who had
been in the National party previously. Dušan Peleš, for instance, was elected
to the Croatian Sabor in May 1906 as a member of the National party, but by
November, he was elected to the Serbian National-Church Congress as an
Independent.[41] Another future leader of the party, Bude Budisavljević, had

been a magyarone until 1903, when he joined Pribićević and Banjanin to work on *Novi Srbobran*.[42] The Independent party gained young members in the years to follow, but many of these one-time Khuenites remained in the leadership.

Supilo was often alone in understanding the wisdom of this complicated mix of idealism and opportunism. He was surrounded by the contradictory desires of his allies: many of his partners (the *pravaši*, for instance) did not want to appear to sell out to the magyarones; others (ex-magyarones, some other Serbs) wished the collaboration to take some more concrete form. After the pact with Pejačević was signed in Budapest, Supilo wrote that "the majority of our people are not equal to the situation. The Serbs, [Grgur] Tuškan, [Bogoslav] Mažuranić [both *pravaši*], and another two or three helped me."[43] Later, after leaving the Coalition, Supilo wrote that in the most complicated situations and tenuous moments for him as leader of the Coalition, "the Serbs in the Coalition most generously supported me, and many of my opportunistic tactics and maneuvers would not have passed without their recommendation and support. . . . my proposals found much more support among them than among the Croats, except for a few personal friends."[44] Supilo could simply be indicating that the Serbs put aside their differences when supporting him; he was certainly attributing to the Serbs a predilection for opportunism.

Among the members of the Coalition, interests were so varied that it was no wonder that there was conflict regarding the direction of the organization's policies. The maximum and minimum aims of the New Course contributed to this variance. The minimum aim was the unification of Croatia and Dalmatia in a Croatia still respectful of the Nagodba; from there, in no particular order, the goals continued from the desire for Croatian control of its own tax revenues, shared decision making with Hungary regarding investment in Croatia, fairer contributions of Croatia to unified Hungaro-Croatian expenses, complete financial independence of Croatia, to the maximum aim which was Croatia's political independence. We have already seen that for many *pravaši*, the Rijeka Resolution signaled a new phase in Croatian politics in which Serbs would help their brother Croats to achieve the unification of Croatia and Dalmatia within Hungary, but no more. The charismatic and independent Supilo, on the other hand, would have brought Croatia to financial and (eventually) political independence if it proved possible.

The only common trend among the politicians in the Coalition was their economic interest.[45] Banks and other lending institutions in Croatia tended to be run by people who were also associated in politics and business. Khuen-Héderváry, as an exponent of the Hungarian Liberal government, controlled or influenced several banks with which he provided many of the favors that drew the magyarones to him in the late nineteenth century. Institutions loyal to Khuen-Héderváry would likely have members of the National party in their directorates. The directorate of any bank in Croatia would include men from the same political party. Croats and Serbs maintained their national division in the financial sphere. We are already acquainted with the network of banks and lending agencies controlled by the Serbian parties: the Serbian Independent party controlled the Serbian Bank, which was situated in Zagreb and had many offices throughout Croatia, Dalmatia, Hungary, and Bosnia. The Serbian Bank also headed a network of agricultural lending banks as well as other small lending institutions and craft organizations designed to loan money to peasants, agricultural laborers, and craftsmen. The network of the Serbian Bank was fairly consolidated in Croatia proper, but the Radical party did have its own institutions, as did the Serbian Liberal party in southern Hungary. Unlike the Serbian Bank, which was centralized, the Croatian banking network was not unified, which reflected the situation of the Croatian political parties. The Serbian Independent party was able to call on its provincial network when organizing voters, explaining in part the great upsurge in support for the party from 1903 to 1914. Conflicting economic interests resulted in the opposite phenomenon among the Croatian parties, which by and large remained static over the same period.[46]

Although the New Course was clearly a nationalist strategy, both the minimum and maximum programs of its adherents envisioned a financially independent Croatia as an early step in the progress of the Croatian state and nation. The formulators of the New Course saw Croatia's progress as best served by the state first gaining control of its own revenues, and the various suggestions for the initial work of the Coalition reflected that fact.[47] Given that the institutions run by the National party and the government were connected with Vienna and Budapest, one suspects that the members of the Coalition who were associated with the institutions listed above expected those institutions to gain by Croatia's financial independence. The same phenomenon occurred in the context of the Serbian National-Church Congress. From the perspective of the Serbian Independents, the Croatian context was only half the canvas: the Coalition gave the Independents the opportunity to pursue its constitutionalist policy of activism in the Croatian Sabor and Hungarian Parliament. The other half of the canvas was its relationship with its Serbian constituency and the Serbian Radical party. Participation in the Coalition promised to give the Independents a leg up on their Radical rivals. It is to the Serbian context that we now turn.

The Parallel Universe of Austro-Hungarian Serbs

Within the protective confines of the Croato-Serbian Coalition, two Serbian political and world views struggled for predominance. One was distinctly conservative, the other demonstrably modern. Both were determined to see the Serbian nation protected from the perceived threats of Croat and Magyar assimilation. The Radical leader Jaša Tomić viewed his world as threatening, because he viewed it through the prism of his nation, his community. His community had always been nurtured by its ecclesiastic leaders; it had always been protected by its relationship with the Habsburg emperor, the Hungarian king. These guarantees were enough for him; they were the only such guarantees that had any sort of historical pedigree for him. He would rely on them in the future; his party, the Serbian Radical party, would represent and fulfill his essentially conservative vision. Svetozar Pribićević viewed his world through a different prism. He had been educated to believe that his nation was part of a larger and yet valuable community. He and his colleagues had heard Masaryk's admonitions that they abandon nationality as the basis of political work and adopt natural law as a guiding principle. Pribićević and his fellows in the Serbian Independent party therefore rejected Tomić's reliance on personal relationships of patronage that served only to isolate the patronized. They insisted that Serbs view their nationality in the context of their political unit, the Habsburg monarchy as a whole, and acting politically rather than resisting involvement with other nations. Of course, neither party could live up to its own vision of politics, but since the Radicals' vision was far less constraining, they behaved much more consistently over time. While the two parties were members of the Coalition, the clash of world and political views was played out in full force.

The Serbian contribution to the New Course, as a Croatian political strategy, was minimal. In fact, if there had been no Serbian parties in the Coalition, the New Course would not have suffered in the least (although Supilo might have had to scrap for support in the absence of his Serbian colleagues). The Serbs were too weak electorally to influence the course of the Coalition. The Croatian parties in the Coalition recognized that the participation of the Serbs was less important as a concrete contribution to the New Course than it was as a contribution to a new political and cultural climate in Croatia. Underlying those noble motives, however, the Serbian parties had their own distinct reasons for taking the positions they took regarding the New Course and the Croato-Serbian Coalition. Those reasons indicate clearly the two contrasting agendas in Serbian politics after 1903. Pribićević's Independent party wished to take part in the Croato-Serbian Coalition because it recognized that the Coalition represented its best chance to become a factor in Croatia's governance, and it believed that the inevitable popularity of the Coalition would enable it to kill the strength of its rival, the Radical party. The Radicals, on the other hand, joined the Coalition against their better instincts, fearing the participation in Croatian politics that the Independents desired. Their aim was strictly utilitarian: to maintain an alliance with Kossuth's coalition in Hungary.

Cooperation and Tensions Between Serbian Parties

After the announcement in December 1905 of the formation of the Coalition, the member parties concentrated their energies on winning the May 1906 elections for the Croatian Sabor. Most of the parties cooperated in meetings throughout Croatia. The Serbian Radicals, however, still petulantly questioned the wisdom of having joined the Coalition at all. Tomić publicly wondered why the Radical party had not been invited to the Rijeka Conference (of course, the Radicals would have declined to attend, due to the potential participation of the *frankovci*). And the Radicals were dissatisfied with the fact that neither resolution expressly denied the existence of the Croatian political nation (a demand that the Independents never made). The conditions placed by the Zadar Resolution on Serbian support of the union of Dalmatia and Croatia did not necessarily satisfy the Radicals. Given their distrust of the Croatian opposition, the Radicals would count only on a legal affirmation of Croato-Serbian equality, which they believed must follow a Coalition victory in the coming elections. The Radicals would actually expend most of their limited energy, as members of the Coalition, demanding in vain that the Coalition place legal equality of the Serbian name at the head of its agenda. The demand was completely in harmony with the party's history and ideology—a legal guarantee, a piece of paper with the emperor's signature was worth a parliament full of good will.

So the Radicals did not cease stating publicly their reservations regarding the New Course. It fell to the Independent party to take on the burden of bringing the Radicals into line—or driving them out of the Coalition. Pribićević, for one, welcomed the opportunity to alienate them, as the elimination of the Radicals was part of his dual-track strategy in Croatia. By March 1906 the Independents and Radicals had already begun feuding over the proper area for Serbs to concentrate their strength, in the legislative bodies of the Habsburg monarchy or in the Serbian National-Church Congress. *Novi Srbobran*, claiming for the Independents a "clearer vision" of the needs of the Serbs in Croatia, returned the attack of *Zastava*, the "reptilian" newspaper of the Radical party in Novi Sad.[48] Accusing the Radicals of wasting their energy in the Church Congress, the Independents voiced the opinion that it would be better if there were no such body. For the Independents, the Church Congress had served a purpose only insofar as Serbs had until 1905 no other stage on which to express themselves. The Radicals did not understand contemporary national needs, wrote *Novi Srbobran*.

The Independent party was led by more skilled politicians and was therefore successful in using the hostility between the Radicals and the Croatian membership of the Coalition to its advantage in what became a bitter battle with the Radical party for the Serbian electorate. "In fact, the Independent Serbs and the Radical Serbs hated each other to a ridiculous degree and attempted to trick each other at every turn," wrote Supilo later.[49] These rivalries, party and personal, were played out in the newspapers and in the numerous meetings that the parties held to gain support for their respective programs.[50] It is clear that when Pribićević took over the Independent party, the party's activity increased substantially. Thus in the fall of 1903, the party began a newspaper for peasants entitled *Srpsko kolo*, which was edited by Budisavljević and included Adam and Valerijan Pribićević, Svetozar's brothers (the first a journalist, the second an Orthodox priest), as correspondents.[51] For the Independents, the enemies were the magyarone Serbian Club and the Radical party. Both opponents brought out the most assertive in what would be a very aggressive party.

The competition between the Independents and the Radicals illuminated the regional basis of each party. The Independents were strongest in western Croatia (Lika, Kordun, Banija), from which their leaders came: the Pribiće-vićes were from Banija, Banjanin and Budisavljević were from Lika. They also attempted to move into Radical areas in Slavonia and especially Srijem, using the local influence of Dušan Popović, who was from Srijemska Mitro-vica, to help build their party in that region. Popović founded the newspaper of the Independents in Srijemska Mitrovica, *Sloboda*, in late 1906 for this purpose.[52] In the campaign leading up to the Sabor elections of May 1906, the Independents faced a Serbian electorate that had become conditioned to voting for the government candidate, since the Serbian Club had become the accepted representative of the Serbian people. Supilo noted that when the Independent candidates ventured into some Serbian districts, they read falsi-fied telegrams announcing that the government had collapsed and that a new government had been formed—led by the Independents. So the voters "sim-ply gave their vote to the new government." Thus, according to Supilo, the Independents were not elected as oppositionalists, they were elected as the government party, which among many Serbs had come to be perceived as their only protector.[53]

The real battle between the Radicals and the Independents was revealed in the context of other, side issues for the Coalition. The conflict tran-scended the campaigning for the Croatian Sabor. The Independent party was at odds with the Radicals over virtually every aspect of the New Course and the administration of the Serbian church. In June 1906 in Zemun, two Radicals (Jovan Radivojević-Vačić and Milivoj Babić) founded *Narodni glasnik*, the only major Radical paper in Croatia. They proclaimed the willingness of the Radical party in Croatia to suspend its negative judgment of the New Course for the moment. However, the lead article did not at-tempt to hide the Radical perspective: "we will seek recognition of natural and legally guaranteed rights and freedoms for our Serbian nation."[54] In other words, the Radicals in Croatia insisted on official guarantees that Ser-bian cultural characteristics would be protected by law.

One situation revealed both the distrust between the Serbian parties and the radical divergence in their ideological approaches. The occasion was a dispute over the Zemun mandate in the Croatian Sabor. Zemun is a city at the confluence of the Sava and the Danube, directly across the river from Belgrade. It was a mixed city, with large Serbian, German, and Croatian com-munities. In Serbian politics, Zemun was definitely a Radical town, far from the Independent strongholds of western Croatia. The Zemun Radicals broke Coalition discipline when a Croatian member of the National party, Fridolin Kosovac, announced that he wished to give up the mandate he had won in the May elections to another Croat, Aleksandar Badaj, who was not a member of the National party. Nor was he a resolutionist. Badaj, like Rojc, was to become a member of the Coalition government, so the Coalition supported his acceptance of the mandate. The Radical party, which had long been the only Serbian party in Zemun, fought tooth and nail for a new election to be called. In addition to their natural desire for a second chance at the Zemun mandate (which Babić had lost to Kosovac convincingly), the Radicals had a preelection agreement with the Independent party on their side.[55] The two parties had agreed in June 1905 in Slavonski Brod to run a Radical candidate in Zemun, thus implying that the Radicals would determine the fate of Zemun in Coalition negotiations. What the Radicals could not control, however, was the behavior of the Croato-Serbian Coalition, which had not yet been formed. Even in the first election, the Croatian parties had rather disingenuously supported the magyarone candidate, Kosovac, over Babić. At that time, the issue of Badaj's position in the government had not even arisen.[56]

The Coalition as a whole did not feel bound by the Slavonski Brod agreement between the Radicals and the Independents. Clearly, the Coalition supported the placement of Badaj in Kosovac's seat in the Sabor because it already intended to place Badaj in the government. The maneuver occurred without complaint, except for that of the Radical organization in Srijem. Interestingly, the Radical party must have understood the Coalition's position (Krasojević and Lisavac, the two Radicals elected to the Sabor, took part in the Coalition's meetings), thus one must wonder how much the Radicals cared about the fate of the Coalition, even at this early date. Participation in a coalition would impose self-denial on the normally self-indulgent Radical party. Technically in the right, the Radical party nonetheless opened itself to doubts.

Beside the practical issue of interpretation and implementation of interparty agreements, the scenario surrounding the Badaj-Kosovac-Babić debate revealed the hostile triangular relationship of the German, Serbian, and Croatian populations of Zemun, a city on the borders of Hungary, Croatia, and Serbia that was the political and economic center of eastern Srijem. Zemun had long been the scene of German-Serbian competition, in which Croats, as the smallest element, played the role of arbiter, providing one or the other side with a majority in the city administration. Until 1888, the city government was in Serbian hands, but in that year, the Germans won the local elections, after which the Croats mediated an agreement by which the Germans would govern with a Croatian mayor, Kosovac, and the Croatian variant (Ijekavian) as the language of administration. Badaj was instrumental in achieving this agreement.[57] This situation was never acceptable to the Radicals, who viewed their present electoral agreement with the Independents and their participation in the Croato-Serbian Coalition as a chance to reassert their domination of Zemun. After all, in coalition with Croats and other Serbs in the name of *narodno jedinstvo*, should the Radicals not have expected those parties to honor their electoral agreements? After the creation of the Coalition and before the elections of May, Babić peremptorily demanded that the administrative business of the city be conducted in Serbian (Ekavian) and Cyrillic and that the electoral district be considered the domain of the Radicals.

The Progressives viewed the situation in Zemun differently. They strongly felt that Badaj would make a better representative of the Coalition than Babić, a longtime Radical who had demonstrated a lack of brotherly feeling toward Croats. So *Pokret* changed the ground rules for the debate. Instead of arguing hopelessly that the Coalition behaved consistently in supporting a nonresolutionist, after writing off the Radical complaints about Badaj, they pointed the opponents of the Radicals in a new direction: because they opposed the Coalition candidate, the Radicals were agents of pan-Germanism! Babić and his Radical friends, asserted the Progressives, supported the German majority in the Zemun city council to the detriment of Croatian state interests. This was true to the same extent that Zemun's Croats had worked with their German neighbors, but for the sake of the polemic, past Croato-German collaboration was forgotten.[58] The issue now had changed: the Coalition resisted the German *Drang*, so the Radicals had to heel. Having initiated the debate in order to marginalize the Badaj question, the Progressives tossed the issue to the Independents. Certainly the more pressing problem in the eyes of the Croatian component of the Coalition was the Badaj affair, for it affected the Coalition representation in the Sabor and eventually the Coalition government of Croatia. So it was the Independent party that led the charge on the German question. But there were really two issues: one was the interparty arguments; the other was more substantial, and revealed once again the chasm between the world views of the two Serbian parties.

The German debate, which developed as an aftereffect of the Badaj affair, revealed that the Radicals viewed their role in local terms (looking at politics as defensive tactics designed to assure the domination of their nationality in a given area) rather than as participating in a Croatianwide coalition designed to assure the rights of individuals (looking at politics as a strategy to assure the development of the Croatian whole, for its citizens).

The Radicals claimed that their position on the German population of Srijem was dictated by the large number of Germans there with whom Serbs had to coexist. Additionally, Germans faced the same marginalization that Serbs faced when confronted with the exclusive idea of a Croatian political nation. Perhaps the Independents had accommodated themselves to such an idea, but the Radicals had not and neither had the Germans.[59] Serbs, according to the Radicals, had bargained away everything (that is, their nationality) in order to cooperate with Croats in a venture that stood to bear no fruit for the Serbian members of the Coalition. The Zemun Radicals made clear that they would take care of their own business in their region as they saw best, even if it meant working harmoniously with the notorious Germans of Zemun. The Independent party simply returned that the Radical party had a strange outlook if it could accept working with the enemies of Slavdom against the wishes of the coalition to which it belonged. The Radicals insisted on acting in accordance with time-honored principles: horse-trading, political bargains, personal politics. The Independents and Progressives attempted to turn the system of patronage politics in a constitutional direction. The Badaj affair had been of general importance for Croatia. The German question that followed was strictly a polemic, almost solely carried on by the Serbian parties, designed to place the Radicals in as poor a light as possible.[60] It was a skirmish in an ongoing interparty struggle for predominance in the Serbian community of the Habsburg monarchy. It was in this area that both parties were at their most aggressive.

The success of the Independent party in the contest with the Radicals is evident from the results of the elections for the Croatian Sabor and especially the Serbian National-Church Congress from 1906 to 1914. In 1903, when the Independent party began life under a new leadership, it was a dead organization with little support in Croatia. The Radical party in Croatia was not much better off (after all, the Independent party had been its organization), but it did have a historical base of support. By 1905, the Independents, under the aggressive leadership of Pribićević, had easily overtaken the Radicals in western Croatia. Slavonia was by 1905 a mixed area, the Independents gradually usurping the power of the Radicals. By the time of the Slavonski Brod agreement in June 1905, the two Serbian parties were warring for control of the Serbian community of Croatia. Their behavior in 1906 reflected certain tendencies: that the Independents were using their favorable position in the Coalition as a base from which to destroy the influence of the Radicals, and that the Radicals were not going to lose quietly; that the Radicals felt little loyalty to the Coalition if it did not give them that which they could not gain for themselves; and that for the Radicals, membership in the Coalition was a convenient expedient, whereas for the Independents it was an ideological and strategic prerequisite for them to ascend to the top in the Serbian community as well as to be an integral part of the Croatian political structure. Underlying all of this was the fact that the Independents saw the Croatian Sabor as their avenue to success, whereas the Radicals looked to the Serbian National-Church Congress for the same reason.

There was a certain irony in the Radicals' adherence to the New Course. Strictly speaking, they were in fact the first party to implement it, since they were the first to cooperate with the Hungarian Independence party. The explanation for this lies in the needs of the Radical party in the Church Congress. After its victory in the May 1902 Congress elections, the Radical party immediately went to work forcing through legislation in accordance with its Autonomy Program. Simply put, this legislation tended to remove control of the church's funds from the old majority consisting of members of the Liberal party and high clergy and to remove everyday control of the administration from the clergy to laymen.[61] Much of the legislation was designed to rationalize the finances and administration of the metropolitanate, but there was significant opposition to the behavior of the Radicals, mostly from the clergy, who believed that the Radicals were usurping their traditional role. In fact, one way that the Radicals intended to rationalize finances was to secularize the funds of the monasteries. The Autonomy Program consisted of points that would eventually form the Monastery Decree.[62] In the long battle to see the Monastery Decree come to life, however, the party needed powerful allies. Any decisions or decrees of the Sabor had to be signed into existence by the emperor and the Hungarian minister-president. To achieve this end, the party controlling the Congress would be best served by a patriarch who would support its legislation, since the Hungarian government appointed the patriarch. From 1902 to 1907, the patriarch was

Djordje Branković,[63] who cared little for the Radicals and their secularization plans. The Radicals could be even more certain if they had patrons in the Hungarian government. This explained their alliance with the Hungarian Independent party and its leader, Ferenc Kossuth. The logic behind Radical support for the New Course was not its focus on alliance with Croats, but on alliance with Kossuth; the Radicals simply entered the Coalition through a side door. Thus for a fleeting period from 1903 to 1907, the Radicals found themselves on the same side of the geopolitical fence with the Dalmatian founders of the New Course and much of the Croatian opposition. The logic of the Radicals' adherence to the Croato-Serbian Coalition was therefore entirely situational.

Although the Independent party had won seats in the 1902 Congress elections, it had not provided significant opposition to the Radical majority. Following those elections, Pribićević's arrival provoked a transformation in the Independent party. By the elections of December 1906, it had built great momentum in Croatia and looked to the Church Congress as the arena in which it would eliminate the influence of the Radicals in the Serbian community of the monarchy. In the Church Congress elections of December 1906, the Radical party won forty-one of seventy-five mandates, whereas the Independents gained thirty of the thirty-four opposition seats.[64] The Radicals thereby commanded a clear majority, although the Independents had made inroads. In Croatia, the Independents won twenty-six of thirty-eight seats that they contested in the Congress.[65] From the outset, the Independents disputed the role of the Radicals in the Congress. The Independents walked out of the Congress on February 1, 1907, after it became clear that the Radical party would neither tolerate dissent nor cooperate in any way with the opposition parties.[66] The Independents could do nothing but watch while the Radicals passed their Monastery Decree during the session, which meant that only governmental approval stood between them and their ultimate success. It became ever more important for the Radicals to cuddle with the Hungarian government. And for the Independents, the success of the Radicals in secularizing monastery and church funds would be a double blow: the Radicals would control more money, and they would gain in prestige.

But the battle between the two parties was not just a question of power. Although the Radicals clearly (and properly) viewed the Church Congress as the only body in the monarchy which they could dominate, they did have more honorable reasons for choosing to focus on it. Those reasons were ideological, and were summed up in a dispute between the Radicals and Independents that questioned one fundamental premise of the Croato-Serbian Coalition's majority: that Serbs and Croats were one nation.[67] Here was the crux of the matter for the Radicals as well as the Independents, whose participation in the New Course had been predicated on their interpretation of the relationship of Croats and Serbs.

The Quick Demise of the New Course: 1906–1907

Only the most opportunistic members of the Coalition could have been happy with the outcome of its relationship, ever so tenuous, with the Hungarian coalition government. In the elections of May 1906, the Croato-Serbian Coalition gained control of the Sabor (albeit without the benefit of a majority). In June of that year, the first Coalition government was formed. Until May 1907, the Coalition cooperated with the Hungarian coalition, through which the resolutionists hoped at least to achieve the legal unification of Croatia and Dalmatia. However, by the time of the May elections in Croatia, the Hungarian opposition coalition had already agreed to take part in a mixed Liberal/Independent government and thereby became a governing party in Hungary. The minister-president of this government was Sándor Wekerle, a Liberal. All the hopes of the Croato-Serbian Coalition thus hinged on the success of a party (the Hungarian Independents) that had already given up the battle in Hungary. Since this solution to the Hungarian crisis had been forced on the Hungarian opposition by the emperor, much of the threat that this opposition posed for the dualistic basis of the monarchy was now gone. Thus it has been said that the battle of the Croato-Serbian Coalition was over before it started, since its success seemed to depend on the continued militancy of the Hungarian opposition.[68]

The situation became somewhat clearer and much less salutary for the Coalition in the summer of 1907, when the Hungarian government proposed legislation known as the "railroad pragmatic," which in fact evolved to meet internal Hungarian needs but included an appendix making Magyar the official language of the railroads in Croatia. Although the paragraph offended the Croatian delegation to the Hungarian Parliament immensely, the legislation in its entirety was not intended to be anti-Croatian. The fact that the legislation emerged with the imprimatur of Minister of Trade

Kossuth, who was also one of the originators of the alliance between the Croato-Serbian Coalition and the Hungarian opposition, rubbed salt in the wounds of the Croatian delegation. The railroad legislation acted as a litmus test for the members of the Coalition. Many (including Supilo, the Serbian Independents, many *pravaši*, and the Progressives) considered it a call to outright parliamentary warfare; others (for instance, Harambašić, Stjepan Zagorac, and Ante Bauer of the Party of Right) felt that the New Course had failed and that further action was counterproductive, and they later left the Coalition; still others (the Radicals) left the Coalition because they wished to continue their cooperation with the Hungarian coalition in spite of the injury done the Croatian statehood by the railroad legislation.[69] The Croato-Serbian Coalition failed to advance its cause of 1907, and with that failure it no longer served the purpose for which it was designed: to wrest some degree of unity and perhaps independence from Hungary. The New Course was therefore done with, and the short-term goal for which many joined the Coalition no longer served to bind otherwise disparate groups. From 1907 forward, the Coalition operated as a grouping of what its members might have called "Croatia's progressive forces." Its original function no longer applicable, it saw those elements which viewed the Coalition in purely instrumental terms leave the organization. The older *pravaši*, the Serbian Radicals, and others for whom the Coalition was the means to an end were gone by the end of 1907. What remained was a core group that claimed, first and foremost, to represent the idea of *narodno jedinstvo*. This group included some *pravaši*, the Croatian Progressives, the Serbian Independents, Supilo, and other independents.

The only question was who would leave first and under which pretext. As it turned out, the Serbian Radical party would jump ship first, utilizing the ongoing discussion of the relationship of Croats and Serbs as its justification. The question was posed for the first time by Jovan Radivojević-Vačić in February 1907, which was a rather odd time to be opening a topic of discussion whose logic would inevitably force the Radicals to leave the Coalition (which they did not do until August). Perhaps the Radical party already sensed that it would leave. The basis for the discussion was the fact that the Radicals had always demanded legal guarantees for the Serbian name and cultural characteristics from the Croatian government, which in this case was the government of the Coalition, or even more specifically, the Croatian parties that controlled the Coalition. Presumably, the Radicals had noticed that two Sabor sessions (of May and November–December 1906) had passed without any movement on this pressing question. Worse yet, the *frankovci*, who had obstructed the work of the Sabor by refusing to allow the word Serb to be used as a noun or a qualifier, had ceased their obstruction, but only after the Independents had shown willingness to allow the Sabor to continue with its work at the expense of strict semantic maintenance of Serbian equality, which was hardly a legal guarantee. Various formulas were attempted: one, by which the Serbian and/or Croatian nations would be referred to as "the Croatian political nation, to which the Serbian nation belongs," was proposed by Nikolić in consultation with the *frankovac* Iso Kršnjavi. Another proposed by Vrbanić referred to the "entire nation, whether Croats or Serbs." The reason the obstruction had to end was that the simplest legislative tasks could not be taken care of.

Radivojević-Vačić began the debate (the "one [nation] or two" polemic) by clarifying the position of the Radical party regarding the nationhood of Serbs and Croats: "The Serbian National Radical party professes that in Croatia and Slavonia live *two* nations, two brother nations, two equal nations, not Serbs *or* Croats, rather the Serbian *and* Croatian nations."[70] Such a formulation was nothing new. The Radical party had never claimed any supposedly higher ideals regarding the nationhood of Serbs and Croats. However, to posit such fundamental differences between the two Serbian Coalition partners at a time when the two were already fighting like the bitterest of enemies in the Church Congress indicated that the Radicals were prepared to elevate their demand for guarantees to a new level, perhaps to make that demand a formal condition for their continued participation in the Coalition.

The Independent party had already addressed the complaints of the Radicals at length, but the Coalition simply had what it considered more pressing business. From his safe haven in Lika in September 1906, Pribićević had appealed for a looser definition of guarantees and a bit of slack—after all, the Coalition's name acknowledged the existence of a Serbian nation in Croatia. For more than that, the Serbian parties were dependent on the goodwill of their Croatian partners. Pribićević still joined the "one or two" polemic with gusto, asking the Radicals why they had ever joined the Coalition, knowing its position on the nationhood of Serbs and Croats.[71] Although Pribićević had a point, insofar as the Radicals could not have been under any illusions that their conception of the Croato-Serbian relationship matched that of their partners, in fact the Zadar Resolution did expressly call for legal guarantees of Serbian individuality.

The "one or two" polemic actually betrayed the fact that the basis of the Radicals' adherence to the Coalition was not philosophical but practical. For they had obviously known that their philosophical viewpoint did not accord with that of the Coalition majority. In this the Radicals resembled one faction of the Croatian Party of Right that also had adhered to the Coalition for strategic rather than ideological reasons. For the Radical party, the appearance of the New Course was a coincidental and fortuitous means to an end, since they were already allied with Kossuth's Independent party. The Radicals never changed a single portion of their program, never had to alter their viewpoint in order to join the Coalition. On the other hand, for the Independents, the New Course was not fortuitous, for that implies that luck was involved—and they helped formulate the New Course, which meant that for them it was not coincidental but a purposeful end.

The cumulative effect of the abuse that the Radicals suffered for any of a number of transgressions, which included their relations with the Germans of Srijem, their attitude toward the election of Badaj, the opposition they faced in the Church Congress, and the generally unsupportive actions of the Independents and Progressives, was to make them question their membership in the Coalition. By April, Supilo was aware that the Radicals were no longer with the Coalition majority (if they ever had been) and arranged a meeting with Krasojević and Tomić, presumably to attempt to bring them into line.[72] "The Serbian Radicals are naively running aground," he wrote Čingrija on April 3. "*This nation is one* [Supilo's emphasis]! It is no wonder that Khuen was able to smother it," he continued, obviously referring to the inability of Serbs and Croats to get along.[73]

On June 27, 1907, the Croato-Serbian Coalition issued a declaration announcing its move from alliance with to opposition to the Hungarian government because of the railroad pragmatic.[74] The situation had grown acute since the pragmatic was placed on the agenda in the Hungarian Parliament on May 13 by Kossuth. By then the conflict had reached the Croatian public. The Croatian delegation to the Hungarian Parliament began obstruction in that body on June 5, which placed in it in clear opposition and necessitated the resignation of the Pejačević government in late June. The new ban, Aleksandar Rakodczay, was sworn in on June 27, one day before the Coalition issued its declaration of opposition. By mid-August, the Radicals began to hint at their imminent departure. On August 18, the Radical party exited the Coalition.

In spite of their claims that they were forced out of the Coalition by the

Independents and the Progressives, the Radicals departed from the Coalition because it had not brought Serbs any visible benefits in the form of legal guarantees and in order to protect their position in the Church Congress.[75] On August 16, 1907, almost three weeks after the Coalition government fell, a party leader, Stanislav Novak, wrote an article for *Zastava* entitled "Dare We Continue Together?"[76] Novak bemoaned the inability of the Radicals and Independents to coexist. He particularly blamed three Independents (Banjanin, Popović, and Bogdan Stojanović) for attempting to destroy the Radicals. Furthermore, the Independent party had twisted its relationship with the Radicals by manipulating the Church Congress, the Croatian press, and the Coalition's committee meetings (in that order). What emerges clearly from this is that the Radical party had no intention of sacrificing its individuality for the sake of the Coalition. Because the Coalition demanded that not only national parties but also nations themselves suppress their individuality for the whole, the situation for the Radicals was untenable.

The Progressives and Independents were responsible for the Radicals' exit, *Narodni glasnik* reported a day after the party announced it was leaving: "the Croatian People's Progressive party and the Serbian Independent party. . . . both weak among their nations but very strong in the connivery of their young leaders, became more aggressive every day. . . . with the Serbian Independent party we have broken every connection . . . either them or us!"[77] So there was the reason for the Radicals' resignation from the Coalition. The Radical party did not accept national unity as a basis for the Coalition's existence; it did not envision disappearing as a party and, more importantly, abandoning the previous focus of its work, the Church Congress. Other explanations can be reduced to these facts.

When the Croatian delegation began its obstruction of the Hungarian Parliament, the New Course was clearly exhausted. The reaction of the Hungarians and Austrians was immediately to try to divide the Croatian and Serbian members of the Coalition. For instance, on July 2, a Hungarian representative offered to Pribićević and Popović Hungary's help in the formation of a Great Serbia if they would take their party out of the Coalition.[78] The two Independents declined and reported the offer to the Coalition's executive committee. In the first week of August, when Alois Lexa von Aehrenthal, the Austrian minister of foreign affairs, suggested that the Hungarian minister-president, Sándor Wekerle, threaten to appoint the government's candidate as patriarch of the Serbian Orthodox church in Srijemski

Karlovci and to disallow the resolutions of the Church Congress, he was pressuring the Serbian Radical party to be obedient.[79] On August 19, Supilo wrote Čingrija that the Radicals had resigned because of "the patriarch question."[80]

The departure of the Radicals meant very little to the success or failure of the Coalition. In fact, Supilo wrote on the following day, August 19, that "the resignation of the Radicals from the coalition . . . did almost no harm, except that we in Pest will lose Lisavac, who understands Magyar better than I."[81] Pribićević made the Radicals' resignation sound like more than it was—accusing them of betraying Croatia in its direst moments, of leaving for purely partisan reasons, and, most important, of leaving at the behest of the Hungarian Independent party and Kossuth.[82] Everyone, it appears, knew that Kossuth had promised to help the Radicals regarding the Church Congress. Succeeding weeks were filled with antagonistic polemics between the Independent and Radical presses as the Independents tried to paint the Radicals' "treason" in the darkest colors and the Radicals tried to justify themselves. Although the Radicals were barely represented in the Coalition and played a very small role in its deliberations, Supilo later wrote that their departure had "made a terrible impression in our public."[83] Perhaps that is true, but Supilo's earlier conclusion that the Coalition lost little with the exit of the Radicals seems most accurate.

After the Radicals left the Coalition, they suffered abuse from all the press of the Kingdom of Serbia except the Radical party of Pašić. Tomić responded with his own accusations of the Independents, to whom he attributed the same venal motives that the Independents attributed to his Radicals. Pribićević, he reported, had only opposed the Radicals because they would not hear of his brother Valerijan becoming the new Orthodox bishop in the soon-to-be founded bishopric of Zagreb, after which he would become patriarch.[84] There is no evidence that the Pribićevićes had negotiated either the formation of a new bishopric in Zagreb or for Valerijan Pribićević to become patriarch. Had such a deal been struck by the Independents and the Hungarian government, one supposes that Pribićević might have been proposed as patriarch soon after, which did not occur. Tomić later explained that the Radicals had left the Coalition because its actions did not accord with the desires of the Radical party—which was accurate.[85]

Conclusion

The year-and-a-half period in power was for the Croato-Serbian Coalition the beginning and the end of the strategy of the New Course. With the end of the New Course as a pragmatic political strategy, the Coalition, which was a strong consensual political formation regardless of its failure, had to defend its existence and create a new role for itself. Because the Coalition remained the only political organization that did not question the propriety of Croato-Serbian cooperation and the notion of national oneness, it was able to find a new role as the defender of *narodno jedinstvo*. Just as it had compromised some of its philosophical rectitude in applying the New Course, the Coalition would also face temptations in the next phase of its existence.

The Serbian Independent party had played a complementary role in the actions of the Coalition during its time as the governing party in Croatia. Pribićević, Banjanin, Medaković, and Dušan Popović had supported the policies of the leader of the Coalition, Supilo. The Independents concentrated on gaining the favor of Serbs in Croatia who had voted for magyarones in the elections for the Croatian Sabor and for Radicals in elections for the Church Congress. The Independents lived up to their promise to respect Croatian statehood and act as political Croats. They concurrently strived for predominance in the Serbian community of the monarchy, ably utilizing their more general popularity in Croatia as members of the Coalition to propel them to leadership among Serbs.

The Radical party, guided by its belief in the singularity of the Serbian nation and in the Church Congress as the only guarantor of that singularity, left the Coalition for two reasons: first, because it thought that it would have seen Serbs assimilated by Croats, and second, because of the seductiveness of working with rather than against the government to achieve their political goals. As opposed to the Independents, who proposed that the safest and best way for Serbs to maintain their nationhood was in cooperation with Croats and, importantly, constitutionally, through the medium of the Croatian Sabor rather than the Church Congress, the Radicals maintained that the Church Congress, as the repository of various semiarchaic privileges granted by Habsburg emperors, should be the focus of Serbian party and legislative work.

Both intellectually and practically, therefore, the Serbian Independents of Svetozar Pribićević lived up to the promise of their civic ideal. Building constitutionalism in Croatia by supporting Supilo's virulent defense of Croatia's rights, they then suffered along with their Croatian coalition partners when the New Course collapsed. The Radicals, on the other hand, illustrated their lack of faith in constitutionalism as well as their own practical inability to resist the carrot of Habsburg concessions. Vienna and Budapest offered both the Independents and the Radicals a piece of the pie of privilege; only the Radicals responded.

4

INTERLUDE

Persecution and Temptation, 1907–1909

Penance

FOR THE STATESMEN of the Habsburg monarchy, political stability was a political and territorial puzzle to be solved by manipulating the pieces. If the pieces did not fit, they could always be shaved down here, chipped away there, until some temporary semblance of order was reached. Such a system could also be described as one of rewards and punishments—when one served the needs of the empire, as personified by the emperor, the emperor would reward one with his pleasure. Such rewards were the basis of the formation of the Serbian Club under Khuen-Héderváry; such also, on a grander scale, were the privileges granted by Leopold I to the Orthodox Serbian migrants to his lands in the 1690s. Rewards are meaningless without punishments, however, and just as the monarchy granted the special requests of various bodies within its realm, it also punished on the same basis. Croatia's Serbs, in the name of the Croato-Serbian Coalition but especially the Serbian Independent party, were going to have to do penance for their intransigence in 1907.

As a result of its transition to opposition in the Hungarian Parliament, the Coalition, led by Supilo, Pribićević, and other members, blocked discussion of the renewal of the financial Ausgleich in the summer of 1907. If the Coalition could not benefit Croatia by opposing dualism in cooperation with the Hungarian coalition government, it would make it as hard as possible for the dualists to maintain their system in the monarchy. The Coalition's obstruction annoyed the governors of Austria and Hungary enough to make the destruction of the Coalition a serious goal of the Austrian and Hungarian governments.[1] The Coalition's move into open opposition in Budapest prompted the foreign minister of Austria-Hungary, Alois Lexa von Aehrenthal, and the minister-president of Hungary, Sándor Wekerle, to consider ways of pacifying Croatia through the formation of a new party or coalition that would work with Hungary and not threaten dualism. First they tried the time-honored Habsburg formula of enticing the Serbs to abandon their Croatian allies. As has been noted, a Hungarian politician approached Pribićević and Popović, hoping to divide the Independents from the Coalition to form a new Serbian magyarone party. The failure of that maneuver dictated a new tactic: Wekerle now planned the creation of a strong *pravaš* party that would be formed of the *pravaši* in the Coalition and the *frankovci*. The Independents and the Progressives would be isolated, their influence destroyed by a public campaign in Croatia.

Foreign affairs complicated the picture for Austria-Hungary's rulers. In October 1908, the Habsburg monarchy annexed the provinces of Bosnia and Hercegovina, which it had occupied on the authority of the Treaty of Berlin in 1878. Although the annexation was prompted by the offer of the Russian foreign minister, Alexander Izvolskii, of a deal by which Austria-Hungary would support Russian desires regarding the Bosphorus and Dardanelles, and although the eventual annexation of the provinces by Austria-Hungary had been assumed since 1878, the annexation provoked a war scare that lasted until March 1909 because Serbia and Russia would not accept the Austrian action. As a result of the annexation and the response of Serbia and Russia, internal events in Croatia became entwined with international issues: the efforts of the new Croatian government to discredit the Serbian Independents and the Croatian Progressives were belatedly turned also to the purpose of demonstrating a Serbian conspiracy emanating from Belgrade, which could justify a war with Serbia, should such a war break out. The years from 1907 to 1909 thus became characterized by attacks, both justified and unjustified, on the Serbs of Croatia and the Independents in particular.

Rauch and Serbian Politics in Croatia, 1907–1908

The new ban, Pavao Rauch, was named on January 7, 1908. Rauch made no attempt to fool Croatia that he was going to rule constitutionally (always a questionable term when applied in Croatian politics). He had long desired the banate, but he had never had a patron in Croatia on whom to rely for support. His family connections (his father, Levin Rauch, had been ban when the Nagodba was concluded in 1868) and loyalty to the dynasty recommended him for the post now, at a time when Aehrenthal required only a yes-man. Rauch was too thankful for the position to worry much about challenging orders from above, which he proved willing to execute, clumsily but enthusiastically (on occasion even too enthusiastically). Because he could rely on no political faction in Croatia, he was forced to name his cronies to government posts. His government thus became known humorously as the *servus društvo*, or "greetings society," because its members were drawn from among his drinking buddies.

Rauch was merely tolerated by the principals involved in his appointment: Aehrenthal, Wekerle, and Frank. He had alienated Khuen-Héderváry and his magyarones during the 1890s, when he had attempted to become ban, and the Coalition was aware that Rauch was to try to destroy it. The Coalition also opposed his appointment for the simple reason that the Sabor did not support him and he was thus an "unconstitutional" ban. In Croatia, the ban was not responsible in any tangible way to the Sabor—thus there was no such thing as a constitutional ban. Nonetheless, the opposition in Croatia never failed to note the unconstitutionality of those who were imposed against the will of the Sabor, which was almost always. The remainder of the Croatian opposition concurred. The people of Zagreb greeted Rauch with jeers, eggs, and stones upon his arrival, expressing their opposition to Hungarian and Austrian domination of Croatia. The Coalition played a role in the demonstration that awaited Rauch. Supilo, Zagorac, and Popović successfully pressured the mayor of Zagreb (the magyarone Milan Amruš), whose position required him to greet Rauch, to resign rather than join the delegation that met Rauch at the train station.[2] However, Croatian disgust with Hungarian methods was manifest, and not merely a Coalition ploy. But the demonstration served Rauch well. He placed the blame for it on the Serbian Independent party[3] and immediately commenced collecting evidence of "Great Serbian propaganda" in Croatia and Bosnia, publicizing the facts as

Sándor Wekerle, Hungarian
politician. *From Josip
Horvat*, Politička povijest
Hrvatske *Zagreb: August
Cesarec, 1990.*

he went. His intent was to prove that the Serbian Independent party was the
vehicle for such propaganda. The *pravaši* of the Coalition might then abandon the treasonous Serbs.

Despite his lack of support in Croatia, Rauch's first task was to hold elections for the Sabor, in which he hoped to see an obedient majority elected.
He believed that the *frankovci* and the Coalition would elect approximately
the same number of representatives.[4] His own candidates, members of his
newly formed and ironically named Constitutional party, would align with
the *frankovci* to form a majority in the Sabor. The men who ran as Constitu-
tionalists were members of his government and close personal friends.
Rauch also counted on any Serbian Radicals who were elected to contribute
to his majority. The elections, called for February 1908, were accompanied
by moderate government force to insure that Rauch's endorsed candidates
would win. The electoral battle was joined with enthusiasm by the Independents and Radicals. With the exit of the Radical party from the Coalition in
August 1907, the ever thinner veneer of courtesy that graced the relations of

the Independents and Radicals fell away, and the Independents immediately began openly to attack the Radicals in their home region of Srijem. The Radicals had placed themselves in an extremely weak position in Croatia by abandoning the Coalition, which enjoyed convincing support among voters. Furthermore, although they publicly denied it, the Radicals had allied with Wekerle in order to maintain their influence in the Church Congress. Eventually, it would become clear that in so doing, the Radical party had allied with Rauch. A Serbian political party in 1907 could not have made a poorer choice of ally than Pavao Rauch.

The Radical party nonetheless heightened its opposition to the Independents and the Coalition in late 1907, assuming that with Rauch's help it could regain ground lost to the Independents. In October, the party moved its newspaper, *Narodni glasnik*, from Zemun to Zagreb,[5] in order to better challenge the Independents and to attempt to extend its influence into western Croatia (Lika, Banija, Kordun), the Independent heartland, and regain its lost position in western Slavonia (the *županija* of Požega).[6] They boldly proclaimed their support for the Wekerle government in Hungary, which, in their opinion, would bring Hungary independence from Austria.[7] They disingenuously but accurately characterized their position as consistent with the Rijeka Resolution, which called for cooperation with the Hungarian opposition coalition; therefore they claimed to have remained loyal to the New Course. According to the reasoning of the Radicals, the goal of the Rijeka and Zadar Resolutions had been to create a new unionist party (one that favored the current relationship of Croatia and Hungary) that had "roots in the nation," unlike the old unionist National party, which was divorced from the nation. While they had a point (the Coalition had accepted the validity of the Nagodba), they chose to avoid addressing the ultimate goal of the Coalition's work, which had been to wrest ever more independence for Croatia from Hungary.

Before the elections in February, Krasojević, the head of the Radical party in Croatia, went to Budapest to negotiate with Wekerle and Rauch.[8] Krasojević desired their support for the Radical candidate for patriarch of the Serbian Orthodox church. In return Krasojević assured Rauch that the Radicals could win many, perhaps twenty, seats in the Sabor with Rauch's help (indicating the government pressure that was manifested during the elections).[9] Although Rauch was compelled by Kossuth to ally with the Radicals, he without question counted on the seats that the Radicals would take from the

Baron Pavao Rauch, ban of Croatia, 1908–1909. *Hrvatski državni arhiv, Zagreb*

Independents.[10] In February, the Radicals, perhaps unable to comprehend their anomalous position, allowed themselves to be included among the candidates endorsed in Rauch's newspaper, *Ustavnost* (Constitutionality), immediately before the elections.[11]

For their part, the Independents had to defend themselves against charges that they would leave the Coalition as a result of its break with the Hungarian coalition government; in other words, that they would mimic the Radicals.

At that point (1907), because of the Coalition's inability to work with the Hungarian government, Aehrenthal and Wekerle wished to destroy the Coalition by removing and nurturing the Independents as a loyalist grouping. But after the decision had been made to annex Bosnia and Hercegovina in the fall of 1908, they no longer wished to draw the Independents closer to them; rather they intended to eliminate them from active political life in Croatia and to maintain the remainder of the Coalition in support of Rauch. As late as February 1908, even the Pašić government would subtly urge the Independents to abandon the Coalition.[12] However, the Independents remained in the Coalition and cooperated in the obstruction of the Hungarian Parliament throughout 1907. Although the party would be tempted, out of exasperation with Rauch, to negotiate with Wekerle rather than fight it out with Rauch in months to come, it never took the advice of the Pašić government to leave the Coalition. There is evidence that Pašić stood alone in Serbia in his desire to see the Independents leave the Coalition. The remainder of the Serbian party press uniformly condemned the Radicals for leaving the Coalition.[13]

The Independents campaigned heavily in Srijem, the Radicals' center in Croatia, to attempt to extend their control of Slavonia. The war of public meetings, which had helped so much to increase the visibility of the Independents and the Coalition in 1906, was renewed by both the Independents and the Radicals. The Independents concentrated on Radical territories, since they were unchallenged in Lika and Banija and had prearranged the distribution of other districts with the parties in the Coalition. Their largest meeting took place in Srijemska Mitrovica on January 23, reportedly attended by six hundred people. Pribićević, Medaković, Banjanin, Popović, Budisavljević, and Muačević (the entire leadership of the party) spoke at the rally, which was staged in the center of Radical strength.[14] Another notable rally, this one in Udbina, the district in Lika represented in the Sabor by Banjanin, saw the Radical candidate attacked by supporters of the Independents after Pribićević sent a telegram to local electors calling for "battle to annihilation" in the region. One man died and five were injured in the melee.[15] In preparation for the elections in February, the Independents placed candidates opposite Radicals in nine electoral districts in Srijem; the Radicals placed candidates in several districts in Lika to challenge the Independents' predominance there.[16]

The elections were held on February 27 and 28, 1908. The government arranged for the districts in which Rauch's candidates were expected to win without a battle to hold their elections on the first day, in order to build some momentum for the ban; districts in which the Coalition was strongest would hold elections on the second day. Rauch and his candidates harangued Croatia with claims that the Coalition and especially the Independents were involved in anti-Croatian, pro-Karadjordjević conspiracies. In spite of this and intermittent pressure at the polling places, the Coalition won fifty-six of eighty-eight districts, whereas the *frankovci* won only twenty-four and the Radicals two. Rauch's Constitutional party won no seats at all.[17] Within months, the *frankovci* would split into two parties (becoming the Frankist Party of Pure Right and the Starčević Party of Right, headed by Mile Starčević), leaving Frank's party with only fifteen mandates. Obviously Rauch could not form a majority in the Sabor with such numbers. The Serbian Independent party alone won nineteen seats in the Sabor. Of the nine districts in which the Serbian Independents and Radicals had opposed each other, the Independents won six, the Radicals only two. The two elected Radicals, Mladen Lisavac and Jovan Radivojević-Vačić, were the last two Radicals to serve in the Croatian Sabor. The Radicals' defeat in eleven of the thirteen districts in which they ran illustrated their complete decline in Croatia. Soon after, they closed *Narodni glasnik*, their only newspaper in Croatia.

The Sabor elected by the February elections was postponed indefinitely on March 14, 1908, two days after it convened.[18] The elections, which certainly disappointed Rauch, Wekerle, and Aehrenthal, served their ultimate purpose nonetheless: the strength of the Coalition and the Independent party purportedly illustrated their contention that "Great Serbian" propaganda had taken hold in Croatia. At the same time, Rauch and his government reacted in a more practical vein, promising to remove the bureaucrats who were largely responsible for the strong showing of the Coalition.[19] However, Rauch could not disguise the fact that his regime enjoyed absolutely no support in Croatia. All that remained to them was to carry on in their task, which was to incriminate the Coalition in antimonarchical, treasonous activities in partnership with Serbia.

After his election debacle, Rauch began to openly denounce the Coalition and especially its Serbian Independent component. After the Coalition issued a proclamation to the Croatian people on March 20 announcing that it would continue "an irreconcilable battle against the unconstitutional government of Ban Rauch . . . and against the joint government in Budapest,"[20] Rauch initiated a press campaign in his newspapers *Ustavnost* and *Agramer Zeitung* accusing the Independents of treason and warning the Croatian parties in the Coalition that they could be implicated themselves should they not abandon the Serbian Independents.[21] The elected Independents responded with an open letter to Rauch dated April 10, 1908,[22] that granted Rauch some distinction as "an honorable man," but clearly suggested that he was a weak ban with no support from above. The letter accused Rauch of working "to demonstrate that [the Independents] are a dangerous and revolutionary element" in Croatia in order to justify to "competent factors" his own heavy-handed banate as a necessity to the integrity of the monarchy. In other words, the Independents thought that Rauch had fooled his superiors into believing in a Serbian conspiracy in order to maintain his position. Clearly the Independent party did not realize that the opposite was the case—that Rauch was necessary to "competent factors" because he would execute the task he had been given, to blacken the reputation of the Independents.

The open letter announced the intention of the Independents to "settle accounts with [Rauch] personally."[23] They demanded that the Sabor be called, their immunity be rescinded, and the charges made against them be proved in court. Rauch refused to provide proofs, which prompted the Independents to reissue their complaint, adding that they could only conclude that "Mr. Pavao baron Rauch . . . consciously and maliciously lied, slandered, and denounced" the Independent party. When Rauch responded by accusing Medaković and his party of maintaining treasonous links with Serbia, Medaković demanded proof. Little did he expect Rauch's response, which was to challenge him to an armed duel. Custom in such matters held that Medaković did not have to answer the challenge unless Rauch produced his evidence, so the duel never took place.[24] Rauch, however, claimed that his evidence consisted of state secrets, and therefore he could not produce it. This was the government's first public recognition that it was accumulating evidence of treason against the Serbs in Croatia.

Rauch's government also responded to the "treasonous" letter of the Independent party by attacking those Independents whom it could successfully remove from their positions. One in particular, Gavro Manojlović, a professor at Zagreb University, was suspended in early May 1908. This followed the pensioning of another professor, Djuro Šurmin, a member of the Croatian Progressive party. Both actions were undertaken for political reasons. Šurmin had stood by at the demonstration that greeted Rauch in early January, while Manojlović had signed the open letter of the Independent party. Rauch broke Croatian law when he mixed in the university's affairs, but such was the nature of his banate.[25]

Until this point it had been unclear whether Rauch was operating on his own initiative (in which case the Coalition could perhaps appeal to Wekerle) or on the orders of Aehrenthal and/or Wekerle (which, in fact, he was). The Independents now recognized that Rauch intended to discredit the Independent party and, through it, the Coalition.[26] The rest of the Coalition understood that he was attempting to force it to disown the Independents and join him in his patriotic endeavor.[27] Events to follow would reveal that attacks on the Coalition and the Independents were desired by higher powers in the monarchy.

The Leadership Crisis in the Coalition

Wekerle and Rauch manipulated the Croatian political spectrum in order to create a working relationship between the Croatian and Hungarian governments; their activities highlighted the contradictions inherent in the composition of the Croato-Serbian Coalition. The Coalition did not present a unified front in the face of persecution by the Rauch government. And, for a considerable period of time, no one understood the nature of Rauch's attacks. The most that could be surmised was that Rauch, who had long pined after the banate, had now achieved it and wished to justify his position by contriving a Serbian conspiracy against the integrity of the Habsburg monarchy.

Little did Supilo or Pribićević know that Aehrenthal and Wekerle were active participants in the outlandish game that Rauch was playing. Coupled with the confusion of the Coalition's members was the fact that even Aehrenthal was unsure of exactly how he wished to proceed. In early 1908, he still had not decided whether to retain Rauch as ban. In addition, the monarchy's upper echelons were as factionalized as Croatia's: besides Aehrenthal, the Coalition had to consider the roles of the Archduke Franz Ferdinand and his circle; dualist Hungarians such as Khuen-Héderváry; Magyar nationalists including Kossuth, who was in the Wekerle cabinet; Wekerle himself, who was a dualist but headed a nationalist cabinet in Hungary; and Croatian politicians and parties with loyalties to any number of combinations of the above actors. The result of the early confusion regarding Rauch's role and motivations was that each of the Coalition's factions attempted to navigate the situation by activating its own political connections. Several factions emerged during the preannexation era, but after late 1907 they became firmer.

One was Supilo, who, as it turned out, was indeed a faction in himself. A second group consisted of the three nonparty members of the Coalition, Nikolić, Kulmer, and Rojc. A third was the Serbian Independent party. Finally, several *pravaši* in the Croatian Party of Right (Zagorac, Harambašić, Bauer) comprised the fourth faction. Left dangling were the remaining *pravaši* and the Progressives.

On March 10 and 11, 1908, less than a month after the elections and a day preceding the sitting of the new Sabor, the executive committee of the Coalition met to discuss its strategy for the coming weeks. The executive committee, which had been elected on March 4,[28] made all policy decisions for the Coalition and therefore included members of each party in proportion to its total membership in the Coalition; also included were Supilo, Nikolić, and Rojć. Nikolić and Rojć were not affiliated with any party, but were on the committee because of their previous experience and political connections. At the meeting of March 10, Supilo, as the acknowledged leader of the organization, spoke first. He contended that, given the Coalition's showing in the elections, it should take advantage of the nation's potential and lead an "uncompromising battle not only against the regime of the moment . . . but against the dualistic Nagodba system as such." He proposed a new national movement, similar to that of 1903, but with the opposition parties (including the *frankovci*, he insisted) at its head. In other words, he saw no gain in negotiating with any factor in the monarchy. "The goal of our policy had to be to free Croatia, emancipate Croatia, to uplift Croatia in the national spirit of *narodno jedinstvo* and make it an attraction point for the South Slavs of the monarchy." He proposed that the Coalition begin by electing a new delegation to the Hungarian Parliament and then refuse their mandates to the Croatian delegation en masse—thereby commencing their battle "on the basis of nonelection to Pest."[29]

The remaining members of the committee refused to support Supilo's proposal. Their refusal probably reflected a generous dose of concern about placing themselves at the head of what might turn out to be an open revolt. Certainly that is what the National Movement of 1903 had been. More than that, however, it illustrated their fear of alienating the powers-that-be in Budapest and Vienna. The behavior of the Independents and Nikolić/Kulmer group indicated that those factions wished to maintain such ties. Supilo was gradually losing his hold on the Coalition in any case. In late 1907, in preparation for the elections, the Independents had already forced him to abandon his mandate in Glina, a town in Banija thickly populated with Serbs.[30] Although Supilo saw this as highly suspect (he had, he believed, served the idea of *narodno jedinstvo* quite well in this Serbian district), the fact remains that Supilo could have been elected in many districts in Croatia by 1907, such was his popularity. Independent candidates could not say the same, so the turnover in Glina made some sense. Supilo, however, believed that the Independents were shunting him aside and betraying their stated belief in *narodno jedinstvo*. It became a source of agitation in the Coalition in any case. There would be more convincing evidence of perfidy on the part of the Independents. Supilo had certainly become more militant than they wished.

Nikolić had never had any fondness for Supilo. Nikolić, it will be remembered, had entered the Coalition through the back door when it was in need of figures appropriate for its government in 1906. Nikolić had made himself available, but was something of an anomaly in the government. He had served Khuen-Héderváry as *veliki župan* until 1905, when he had a falling out with Tomašić. His presumed opposition to the National party after that point recommended him for a government position. However, he had little faith in the Hungarian opposition of Kossuth and Andrassy with whom the Coalition was allied. It was only when the Coalition entered into opposition against the opposition government of Wekerle in Hungary that Nikolić began to play an active role in the Coalition. During the obstruction of the Hungarian Parliament he also probably began to work closely with the Independents, Dušan Popović in particular. Finally, Nikolić did not like or trust Supilo, although he believed that Supilo was incorruptible.[31] Supilo was at once too idealistic, too arrogant, and too headstrong for Nikolić.[32]

Supilo's main fault was his independence: he tended to create the policy of the Coalition on his own, and in so doing, not only confused his allies in the organization, he alienated them. Zagorac described Supilo as "an intolerably autocratic leader . . . anyone who differed from him was at once either a fool or an agent of Austria or Hungary."[33] Even Supilo's most ardent admirers realized that he had autocratic tendencies.[34] Given the attenuated relations between Supilo and the other members, it was to be expected that they would pursue their own courses after they rejected his March proposal. The Independents focused their attention on dealing with the Wekerle government, whereas Nikolić and Kulmer looked to Vienna for salvation from the Rauch regime. Both the Independents and Nikolić/Kulmer were resorting to traditional orientations: Serbs in Croatia had become accustomed to viewing Budapest as an ally, while Nikolić and Kulmer had matured politically as imperial politicians, with connections in Vienna and Budapest. Nikolić's circle of friends included Archduke Leopold Salvator and General Rade Gerba, the commander of the Habsburg military detachment in Zagreb, the Thirteenth Corps.[35] Gerba was known to be sympathetic towards Serbs in Croatia, trusting in their loyalty to the emperor and opposing the measures taken by Rauch.[36] Aehrenthal knew of Nikolić and considered him an able and loyal politician, but did not appreciate his connections with the treasonous Coalition.[37] Nikolić met with Aehrenthal twice, and the minister actually considered making him ban in Rauch's place—Aehrenthal found the idea of giving Croatia a Serbian ban an intriguing one.[38] This, of course, depended on Nikolić leaving the Coalition, which he appeared to Aehrenthal willing to do. Aehrenthal decided not to replace Rauch, which rendered Nikolić's hopes moot. Nikolić was probably not willing to leave the Coalition in any case.[39]

The Independents cast about for any way of removing Rauch, who they still believed was operating on his own initiative. The most effective way would be to compromise in some way with Wekerle, who, as Hungarian minister-president, had the initial say in who occupied the position of ban in Croatia. Unfortunately, Wekerle was implicated in the anti-Serbian measures undertaken by Rauch in Croatia, so such overtures were destined to fail. Besides meeting with Wekerle themselves on at least one occasion before the elections,[40] the Independents supported the attempts of Zagorac to negotiate the removal of Rauch in May 1908.[41] Zagorac's motives were different—he hoped to see Rauch removed so as to facilitate the reunification of all the *pravaši*, because several of their factions would not hear of working with Rauch. According to Supilo, the Serbian Independents wished only to be rid of Rauch and to be close enough to the seat of power to have some control over the outcome of any electoral reform undertaken in Croatia.

The vanity of Nikolić's and the Independents' attempts to compromise with the Hungarian and/or Austrian governments notwithstanding, the departures from unified Coalition policy, as defined in the executive committee, eventually destroyed the organization as it had been until 1907. Supilo, who would leave it in very late 1909, claimed that his proposal of open political rebellion was in the best interests of Croatia. Unfortunately, his approach was not shared by any other member of the executive committee, which did fairly represent the Coalition as a whole. Supilo blamed the Serbian Independents for the failure of his attempts to sway the Coalition to his policy. The *pravaši* and Progressives, he thought, would have accepted his proposal had the Independents been less vehemently opposed. The Independents clearly did not wish to go Supilo's route, yet it is hard to believe that, given Supilo's powers of persuasion, the remainder of the Coalition could have been held back by the Independents; the opposition of the *pravaši* and Progressives was genuine. Supilo, by his own account, lost his leadership of the Coalition at the point when the executive committee refused to follow his advice and begin hard opposition to the dualist organization of the monarchy.[42] In truth, the Coalition lost in Supilo its only visionary; the rest were mere politicians. The attempts of the various principals to negotiate an end to the Rauch regime were in vain, because the actors did not realize the seriousness of the Rauch government. Rauch was not acting independently: he had the sanction not only of Wekerle but of Aehrenthal. When arrests of members of the Serbian Independent party began on August 7, and later when the annexation of Bosnia and Hercegovina was declared on October 6, the situation clarified considerably.

The Coalition and the Annexation of Bosnia and Hercegovina

By early October 1908, all Croatia knew that the monarchy would annex Bosnia and Hercegovina in the very near future.[43] The annexation, which was announced on October 6, revealed a fundamental contradiction within the Coalition.[44] Throughout the nineteenth century, but most heatedly in the latter half of that century, the most contentious question in Croato-Serbian relations was the national character of the provinces of Bosnia and Hercegovina. Bosnia had, and has, a mixed confessional and national character. Orthodox Serbs, Muslims, and Catholic Croats lived there; their populations were mixed to a degree that did not allow for a clean division of the territory into national components. Bosnia could never successfully be partitioned to the satisfaction of any nation. Croats believed that Bosnia was a Croatian patrimony by historical right; Serbs tended to claim that all South Slavs in the territories were Orthodox Christian apostates. Until 1878, Bosnia and Hercegovina were part of the Ottoman Empire. That year, Austria-Hungary began a thirty-year occupation of the provinces. After 1878, many Croats hoped that Austria would annex the territories and include them in a Croatian state within the monarchy. In 1908, Austria-Hungary annexed the territories, but did not unite them with Croatia. Most Serbs, on the other hand, still considered Bosnia a Serbian land and looked to its inclusion in an expanded Serbian state. The question proved the most intractable problem of all for those Croats and Serbs who professed to be Yugoslavs; regardless of their Yugoslavism, each wished that Bosnia would become a part of their own territory within Yugoslavia.

The politics of the new generation of Serbian and Croatian political leaders reflected this tension. Some of the articles in *The National Idea* had addressed the question of the future of Bosnia and Hercegovina, which had induced conflict between Croats and Serbs in the 1870s and 1880s. In that volume, Pribićević expressed fear of Hungarian actions intending to bring Bosnia and Hercegovina into its orbit, that is, into Croatia, thus controlling the region "on whose fate depends also the fate of our [Croato-Serbian] nation."[45] He subtly accused Croats who had wished for the incorporation of Bosnia into Croatia of supporting attempts of the monarchy to gain a foothold in the Slavic south, the Balkan peninsula. "It is necessary not to lose from view that this question is most fateful for us, because when it is decided, the question of the focus of our [Croato-Serbian] national position will be decided, and with it the question of our national future."[46] Pribićević thus emphasized that the focus of South Slavic aspirations must be Serbia, because the Habsburg monarchy would have impure motives for gathering South Slavs within its borders. "We must also come to the conviction that it is in fact absurd that some desire to fight for things Serbian in a camp which is decorated with the flag of the Hungarian state idea."[47] Lorković approved of Franjo Rački's stated belief that Croatia could and should be the leader of South Slavs within the monarchy, including Bosnia, while Serbia would take the forward position outside the monarchy.[48]

In Bosnia, Austria-Hungary supported the activity of the Croatian archbishop of Sarajevo, Josip Stadler, who emphasized the Croatian character of the region and led attempts to "Croatize" *(pohrvaćivati)* and catholicize its Muslim population. Serbs claimed that this gave the (to their minds) false impression that Bosnia was a Croatian land and asserted that Croats assisted German expansionism by so behaving. Croats did in fact desire Bosnia's incorporation into Croatia. The question touched on a more meaningful problem: where would the cultural and political center of the South Slavs be located, Zagreb or Belgrade? Were Croatia to gain Bosnia, Zagreb would become the center of the largest South Slavic political unit; were Serbia to incorporate Bosnia, Belgrade would become that center. All understood that the Bosnian question was one of prestige more than one of historical or ethnic justice, as both Croats and Serbs often claimed it to be. The *frankovci* wanted Bosnia in Croatia in order to strengthen a Croatian unit in the Habsburg monarchy; "Yugoslav"-oriented Croats wanted the center of a future Yugoslav state to be Zagreb; "Yugoslav" Serbs wished that center to be Belgrade; Serbian exclusivists believed Bosnia was a Serbian land and would strengthen Serbia immeasurably. The Bosnian problem involved power and orientation, not how many Croats or how many Serbs there were.

When the annexation came, attitudes within the Croato-Serbian Coalition varied. Many members of the Croatian Party of Right welcomed it. Trialism occupied a central place in the program of the Party of Right of 1894. The party considered the annexation a prelude to a reorganization of the monarchy by which Croatia, Bosnia, and Dalmatia would form a third component alongside Austria and Hungary. The Progressives, who had matured in the Starčević tradition, also welcomed the annexation, and for similar reasons. Specifically, the Croats in the Coalition hoped that Croatia would be the center of any future South Slav state. "This could be the beginning of . . . our future," Vatroslav Jagić wrote Djuro Šurmin on October 8. "But now I am terribly frightened that there will be new friction between Croats and Serbs."[49] Šurmin confirmed Jagić's fear of renewed antagonism with the Serbs in the Coalition.[50]

The Croats in the Coalition did not display their enthusiasm for the annexation publicly. Supilo, for one, did not favor recognition or approval of the annexation. He reasoned that the Coalition could not approve the annexation because there was no mention of Bosnia being united to Croatia. Supilo believed that there were two possibilities in the aftermath of the annexation: either the monarchy would be reorganized trialistically, which he would favor, or dualism would be strengthened, which he would not favor.[51] Furthermore, as the majority in the Sabor, the Coalition should have the opportunity to comment on the annexation in the Sabor itself; so the Sabor should be seated.[52] Whereas Supilo would have welcomed the annexation had Croats and Serbs been consulted (in Bosnia as well as in Croatia), he could not accept the way in which it was handled.[53] Since the Sabor was not seated nor its members consulted, the Coalition would not recognize the annexation.

Nonrecognition suited the Serbs in the Coalition, because most Serbs in the monarchy wished to see Bosnia attached to Serbia and hoped that Serbia would become the center of any future South Slav state. Both the Independents and the Radicals included in their party programs the demand that Bosnia be relinquished by Austria. This demand was justified by the phrase "the East to the Eastern peoples," or "the Balkans to the Balkan peoples," which had also become a slogan used by the Serbian government after 1903. Thus the Serbian Independent and Radical parties condemned the annexation. The reactions of the two parties were dissimilar, however. They responded within the limits that their circumstances allowed: the Independents reservedly, the Radicals with great enthusiasm.

The Independents could not simply state that Bosnia was a Serbian land and that it should belong to the Kingdom of Serbia. That was out of the question for a constitutional party in Austria-Hungary. Instead, they opposed the annexation because, they claimed, it "was carried out against the precedent of the Berlin agreement. . . . [and] the people of Bosnia and Hercegovina were not consulted."[54] The most that the Independents could say was that they opposed the annexation on democratic grounds, which, after all, were the grounds on which they based their activity within the Coalition in the first place. Nobody was deluded into thinking that the Independents did not oppose the annexation on national grounds as well, in spite of their limited public opposition. On October 19, Nikolić attempted to convince the Independents and the Coalition to recognize the annexation, but all present refused. Supilo believed that Nikolić wished to see the Coalition behave more acceptably to the Austrian government in order to facilitate a compromise of some sort in which he would gain a high position in the Croatian government.[55] At another point, Nikolić attempted to convince the Independents to support a trialist organization of the monarchy (for the same reasons), but the issue was never put to the test, and the tension to which Šurmin alluded remained tangible throughout this period and beyond.[56]

The Radicals were free to openly condemn the annexation, in part because they enjoyed some latitude thanks to their relationship with Rauch, in part because they did not belong to the Croato-Serbian Coalition (and thus did not have to compromise their view that Bosnia was a Serbian land), and in part because in Hungary many political parties opposed the annexation as threatening the dualist basis of the monarchy. The Radicals considered the annexation one of the negative consequences of the idea of *narodno jedin-*

stvo, which, they held, enabled Austria to use the idea of Croato-Serbian oneness as an excuse to ignore the Serbian character of the annexed lands.[57] Thus, the Radicals' logic went, Austria could claim that since Croats and Serbs were one nation, Bosnia must be a Croato-Serbian land and not merely a Serbian one. Needless to say, Aehrenthal used no such justification in annexing Bosnia and Hercegovina. The Radical argument served only as another condemnation of the Independents and their cooperation with Croats. The Radicals' argument would be renewed at the time of the trials, when Rauch's prosecution of the supposed traitors hinged on his contention that Serbs did not exist in Croatia—another fruit of the Independents' labors, in the eyes of Tomić's Radicals.

The Trials of 1909

The Rauch regime appeared laughable to contemporary observers, and today we can be excused for failing to understand how such a buffoon could have been effective in any role. But in 1909 all Rauch's capriciousness found an exceedingly serious outlet, in a treason trial known to posterity as the Zagreb high treason trial. What is more, Rauch was shown to be but the tip of the absurd iceberg: a second trial, now known as the Friedjung-*Reichspost* libel trial, demonstrated that the authorities in Vienna, all the way up to Foreign Minister Aehrenthal, were capable of autocratic flights of fancy in the hopes of bringing the Croato-Serbian Coalition to heel. The arrests of 1908 and the two trials in 1909, the first in Zagreb and the second in Vienna, resulted from the attempt of Wekerle and Aehrenthal to create a functioning dualist government for Croatia. The Zagreb high treason trial lasted from March 3 to October 25, 1909.[58] In it, fifty-three Serbs, most of them supporters of the Serbian Independent party, were tried for high treason. In the Friedjung-*Reichspost* libel trial, which took place in December 1909,[59] the fifty-two Coalition representatives in the Sabor sued Heinrich Friedjung, an Austrian historian, and the editor of *Reichspost* after they accused the Coalition as a whole (and several members in particular) of being in the pay and under the influence of the Serbian government.

The Zagreb trial followed months of preparation by Rauch and his government, with the tacit consent of Aehrenthal and Wekerle. Before October 1908, the arrests and eventual trial had been intended by Wekerle and Rauch only as a device to destroy the Coalition. After the annexation, Aehrenthal's need to produce a Serbian conspiracy in Croatia gave the proceedings an added goal: they would prove the existence of a conspiracy among the Serbs of Croatia and Bosnia to overthrow Austro-Hungarian governance of the South Slav lands of the Habsburg monarchy. Rauch, who had been entrusted with the task of executing this scheme, did so enthusiastically. In fact, he expanded his mandate somewhat. Aehrenthal's hope was to justify the annexation without causing a massive upheaval in Croatian politics. But Rauch's personal ambitions left their imprint on the events following his assumption of the banate in January 1908.

Rauch had become ban with the consent of Aehrenthal and Wekerle and the unacknowledged support of the *frankovci*. Early in his banate, Rauch could not count on the open support of the *frankovci* because he (or any ban) represented Hungarian hegemony in Croatia. Frank's support for Rauch was nonetheless an open secret in Croatia. After the annexation, the *frankovci* openly joined Rauch in his attacks on the Serbian Independents. Rauch portrayed himself as the "most Croatian ban," because, in fact, he was the first since Mažuranić who was not a Hungarian client. He attempted to use his orders from Aehrenthal to create an obedient Croatian government party of *pravaši* and *frankovci* and to carve for himself a strong position in Croatia based on his Croatianness. Aehrenthal and Wekerle had no desire to see Rauch extend himself—they knew that he was not a good politician and that he was inept and corrupt.[60] However, he was personally ambitious and often overzealous. As late as September 1909, he approached Aehrenthal with a plan to extend to Croatia complete autonomy, but with no legal rights for Serbs. Aehrenthal told Rauch not to take his plan any further, that the emperor would not be open to it.[61] Although Rauch had a mandate to portray the Serbian Independents as traitors, Aehrenthal did not imagine complete disenfranchisement.

The first blatant manifestation of a contrived campaign to discredit Serbs in Croatia was the pamphlet *Finale*, by Djordje Nastić, which appeared in August 1908.[62] Among other things, Nastić accused Valerijan, Adam, and Milan Pribićević (three brothers of Svetozar; Milan was an officer in the Serbian army) of taking part in the meetings of Slovenski Jug, an organization in Belgrade that Nastić portrayed as a Yugoslav revolutionary body. The three Pribićevićes and Srdjan Budisavljević were also accused of fomenting revolution in southern Austria-Hungary in order to unite the South Slav lands of the monarchy with Serbia under King Petar of Serbia. Ironically, one document that Nastic cited was a revolutionary statute written by Milan Pribićević that called for a republic to be formed of all the South Slav lands, so the internal logic of *Finale* was questioned from the beginning. This document was the only one that Nastić cited that proved to be authentic, but its call for a republic seemed in contradiction to the monarchical goals of the "traitors," as alleged by Nastić. Supilo noted that such a document, written by an obvious romantic and visionary, was clearly not to be taken seriously. Ante Radić compared Pribićević's statute with the thinking of Strossmayer and Gaj, who had envisioned a unified state of similar organization and dimensions.[63]

Rauch's government arrested Adam and Valerijan Pribićević on August 7 and 9, 1908, respectively.[64] In the months that followed, fifty-two more Serbs, mostly Independents, were arrested. The arrested were not notable figures in the Independent party, which gives one pause. Surely, it was assumed at the time, if three Pribićevićes and Budisavljević were involved in treasonous activity, then Svetozar Pribićević was too. And Rauch had already implicated Medaković, the president of the Independent party. There were two reasons why the leaders of the Independent party were not arrested. First, they all enjoyed parliamentary immunity, which meant that the Hungarian government would have to extradite them. This the Hungarians would not do, for it would set a precedent for Austrian mixing in Hungarian affairs. Second, Aehrenthal did not want to exacerbate the situation beyond his control; his only desire was to demonstrate that a Serbian conspiracy existed in order to justify a war with Serbia, should one be forced on him by Serbian intransigence. Should it become necessary to arrest the party members who enjoyed immunity, he would attempt to have them extradited, but not until it was absolutely necessary.

Nastić was known as an Austrian agent months before: *Srbobran* revealed his connections with the Austrian intelligence service in June, in connection with events in Montenegro. Nastić had been the main witness at a trial following an attempt on the life of Prince Nikola of Montenegro in which the Serbian government was implicated. Following this trial, *Srbobran* published correspondence between Nastić and a Captain Forner of the Austrian military intelligence service. The correspondence made clear that Nastić was on the Austrian payroll.[65] His pamphlet appeared in August; days later, the arrests of Serbs commenced, indicating that Rauch intended to utilize Nastić's testimony in spite of the fact that he was already revealed as a spy.[66] As the publication of *Finale* neared, Rauch began a public campaign against the Serbian Independents. In late July, he traveled around Lika, hoping thereby to incite demonstrations against him by the Serbian population of the region. His hopes went unfulfilled, however, as the towns through which he traveled greeted him with silence at the urging of the Independents. Croats in Karlovac, however, demonstrated against him, which should have given him pause. Rauch and the members of his government now began to refer to Serbs and Croats as Orthodox and Catholic Croats, to emphasize his contention that there were no Serbs in Croatia, which would become a central point of the prosecution in the treason trial.[67] In a similar vein, he decreed the illegality of the Cyrillic script in the bureaucracy and for students in Serbian communal schools in November 1908.[68]

The hundred-page indictment of the fifty-three Serbs still under arrest (one died in jail), which appeared on January 12, 1909,[69] was written by Slavko Aranicki (Rauch's department head for justice), Milan Accurti, the Zagreb public prosecutor, and Iso Kršnjavi, a *frankovac*. The involvement of Kršnjavi, a private citizen, in the framing of the indictment caused a scandal when it was revealed by Mile Starčević of the Starčević Party of Right in April 1910. One would have hoped that Accurti, the public prosecutor, could have written the indictment himself. Kršnjavi's involvement revealed that the trial was more political than criminal, a common belief in any case.[70] For the *frankovci*, until now on the margins of Croatian politics, the Rauch regime offered the opportunity to cut loose. The indictment included all the arguments that Josip Frank had been using for a decade in his attempts to portray Serbs as traitors to the Croatian state idea: the Serbian name was unheard of until recently; the Serbian Orthodox church had always been the Greek-Eastern church; Cyrillic had not been used by those Greek-Easterners until recently; when a special name was used for this population, it was called Vlach, not Serb. As the indictment stated, those of the Greek-Eastern faith had until recently "lived with others in the most sincere harmony and purest love."[71] A possible reason for this harmony and love was that these people had lived in Croatia forever: the Greek-Eastern population "did not come from Serbia and is not of Serbian origin, but is in good part autochthonous Croatian population from time immemorial, since it accepted Christianity."[72] Belgrade was the source of the new notion that these are Serbs, which thus became part of a Great Serbian conspiracy. Citations from Serbian schoolbooks, maps, and newspapers were used to illustrate the fact that the Serbian state stood behind the conspiracy. For the formulators of the indictment, *Srbobran* was the pathway into Croatia for Great Serbian propaganda.[73] Other Serbian institutions in Croatia also collaborated with the Serbian government: *Privrednik*, for instance.

The indictment combined the accusations of Nastić with the testimony of other witnesses to implicate the arrested Serbs in preparations for an uprising of Serbs in Bosnia and Croatia to support the Serbian army in a war to liberate Serbs in the monarchy. The prosecution concentrated on the question of the guilt of Valerijan and Adam Pribićević. Most of the other defendants were accused of being enmeshed in the revolutionary activities led by the two Pribićevićes. The witnesses, like the Pribićevićes and the majority of the remaining defendants, were from Serbian-populated regions dominated by the Independents: Lika, Kordun, Banija, and western Slavonia. The charges against the Pribićevićes centered on their activities in Vrginmost, the town in Banija in which both worked as correspondents for *Srpsko kolo*, the Independent newspaper for peasant readers. There they also had founded a Serbian club called Srpski soko (the Serbian falcon). As writers in *Srpsko kolo* and as founders of Srpski soko, they were accused of "preparing the Serbian nation for general revolution."[74] Additionally, they were accused of attending meetings of Slovenski Jug in Belgrade for the purpose of linking their revolution in Croatia with the Serbian government.

Much of the trial was spent in arguing whether genuine Serbs lived in Croatia at all.[75] The prosecution claimed not. This tendentious line of reasoning was used in order to justify the conclusion that anyone who claimed to be a Serb was making a political statement that was by definition treasonous: Serbs lived only in the Kingdom of Serbia, and correspondingly, only Croats lived in Croatia. This clearly harkened back to the *pravaš* concept of the Croatian political nation. The logic of the prosecution led it (willingly) to question the validity of a *Serbian* Orthodox church, and thereby the legitimacy of Serbian religious schools, which were both "in the service of Great Serbian propaganda."[76] The prosecution also saw the use of Cyrillic as treasonous, as was flying the flag of the Serbian Orthodox church, which in fact was quite similar to the flag of the Kingdom of Serbia.[77] In spite of the crude nature of the point, those on trial in Zagreb were forced to defend the fact that they considered themselves to be Serbs. They also had to explain how it could be that they were both Serbs and members of a collective Croato-Serbian nation, which they accomplished using the familiar phrases.[78] Given that Rauch's only support in Croatia came from the *frankovci* and that he wanted to create an autonomous Croatia based only on the existence of the Croatian political nation, the focus of the prosecution on the fiction of Serbs in Croatia is not surprising.

The regime had a weak case at best, as was clearly shown by the arguments of the main defense lawyer, Hinko Hinković.[79] Of 273 witnesses, 218 were *frankovci* and 105 were either in jail or accused of crimes ranging from fraud to murder. Thus the prosecution used as witnesses those most likely to testify against Serbs or for the authorities. Of 158 Serbian witnesses brought by the defense, 98 were refused the right to testify.[80] Those who did testify were allowed to only after six months of the trial had passed.[81] The prosecution witnesses themselves proved often to be illiterate and, under cross-examination, unable to substantiate their testimony. One observer characterized the methods and abuses of the prosecution and the court as entirely corrupt, manipulative, and devoted only to jailing members of the Serbian Independent party and disproving the existence of Serbs in Croatia.[82]

The outcome of the trial was predetermined. On October 5, 1909, after seven months of testimony, thirty-one of the accused were found guilty and sentenced to terms ranging from twelve years hard labor to months of the same.[83] Adam and Valerijan Pribićević received the harshest sentences of twelve years, but Accurti had asked for the death sentence for them and three others.[84] In spite of the sentences, it was clear to all that the trial had been purely political and that the accused had not truly been convicted of any crimes—or, at least, the prosecution had not demonstrated the guilt of the accused. In spite of that, Adam Pribićević has written that he and two others were indeed guilty of the charges. He, Valerijan, and Jovan Oreščanin had taken part in a Slovenski Jug meeting in Belgrade that was also attended by Nastić. The Slovenski Jug that they were members of was, according to Pribićević, a disorganized faction of the cultural club of the same name. The other fifty-one arrestees in Zagreb were, according to Pribićević, innocent.[85]

Few in Croatia believed that the Zagreb high treason trial addressed treasonous behavior—it was a political trial. But given orders to implicate Serbian Independents in treasonous activities in Croatia, Rauch proceeded to build his own political future on an alliance with the *frankovci*. Together they invigorated old hatreds to produce an affair that everyone in Croatia knew was a manipulation of the facts and the law. Although many would have liked to see the Serbian Independents and the Coalition removed from Croatian politics, most Croatian politicians by now recognized that Rauch was a corrupt pawn of Austria-Hungary and therefore of greater danger to them than was the Coalition. The Croatian Party of Right did not leave the Coalition, but the group around Mile Starčević did leave the *frankovci*, for fear of Rauch, and later cooperated with the Coalition. Thus Rauch's "*pravaš* bloc" did not materialize. Others, including the Croatian People's Peasant party of the Radić brothers, also recognized that Rauch endangered Croatian autonomy more than the Coalition offended their political sensibilities.[86] The Zagreb trial and even the Rauch banate thus marked a period of manipulation in Croatian political development insofar as Croatian attitudes toward Serbs were concerned. Whereas they did reflect the time-honored practice of divide and rule in Austro-Hungarian administration of Croatia, they did not represent a revival of supposed latent Croatian tendencies to eliminate Serbs in Croatia. Instead the trial was the product of imperial policy in Croatia and the personal ambitions of Rauch.

The timing of the trial provided evidence of a Great Serbian conspiracy at the time when such evidence was most necessary: when the threat of war with Serbia over the annexation was greatest. Soon after the trial began in March 1909, Aehrenthal sponsored the publication in *Neue Freie Presse* of Vienna of further evidence of such a conspiracy. On March 25, Heinrich Friedjung, a prominent Austrian historian, published an article in that newspaper in which Supilo and other unnamed members of the Coalition were accused of maintaining connections with the Serbian government. Friedjung further charged an unnamed Serbian Independent with meeting Miroslav Spalajković, the head of the Serbian Ministry of Foreign Affairs, in Zemun to receive money from the government of Serbia. Still other members of the Coalition were accused of offering their services to Todor Petković, the Serbian consul in Budapest.[87] Although Friedjung did not name the traitors, six articles written in October and November 1908 by Friedrich Funder in *Reichspost* (which he owned) had made the same charges and named Supilo, Pribićević, Potočnjak, and Edo Lukinić of the Coalition as the principals.[88]

The Coalition responded with a telegram challenging Friedjung to produce his evidence, which the historian refused because his evidence would bear on the Zagreb trial.[89] Spalajković himself suggested that a panel of international experts be appointed to analyze the evidence, but Friedjung also refused that suggestion.[90] The Coalition therefore undertook three suits against

Friedjung and *Reichspost*. One, by Supilo, Pribićević, and Lukinić against *Reichspost*, had been readied by December 1908.[91] Two others, one by the fifty-two elected representatives of the Coalition against Friedjung, and another by Supilo against a specific charge by Friedjung (Supilo was charged by Friedjung with having urged Nikola Pašić to spend his vacation in Crikvenica, on the coast of Croatia south of Rijeka, in order to facilitate their conspiratorial discussions), were prepared by December 1909. The three were combined because the same evidence bore on their proceedings.[92]

The Friedjung trial was much more dramatic than the Zagreb trial, which took place in a European backwater (or so it was often described) and dealt with events far from the consciousness of the average European. The Friedjung trial took place in Vienna; it involved an eminent historian and a renowned newspaper, both of which were presumed innocent as a matter of course; and finally, it introduced high drama, in which the Coalition plaintiffs in fact had to prove their innocence of charges leveled against them in the press (the early portions of the trial were devoted to Friedjung's attempts to convince the jury that they were indeed traitors to Austria). The plaintiffs accomplished their defense so convincingly that the Austrian foreign policy establishment suffered an enormous blow to its prestige. It only heightened the drama that there were dozens of reporters and observers from around Europe on the scene.

The critical issue was the authenticity of the documents that Friedjung and Funder provided as evidence for their assertions. They proved to be demonstrable forgeries, thanks mostly to the testimony of witnesses from Serbia, including Spalajković, who were under threat of arrest should their testimony not provide conclusive evidence that the charges leveled by Friedjung and Funder were untrue.[93] Nonetheless, Spalajković and others came to Vienna and were able to reveal inconsistencies in the documents that even a hostile court could not ignore. Božidar Marković, a key witness whose presence at meetings of the Slovenski Jug was critical to Friedjung's case, was able to prove that he was in Berlin at the time of a meeting in which he was alleged to have been a principal participant. Spalajković demonstrated ably that documents supposedly from the Serbian foreign office bore no resemblance to the real thing: they were written by someone not fluent in Serbian, they were in the wrong form, and they spoke anachronistically of events in Serbia.

Supilo, unlike the collective Coalition or the other two individual plaintiffs, did not escape the trial unscathed, as testimony indicated that he had taken bribes from one Leopold Chlumecky, a functionary in the Austrian diplomatic service, before the formation of the Coalition. Although he was able to show that Chlumecky's evidence was not reliable, doubts regarding Supilo remained that even his Coalition partners shared to a degree.[94] The *frankovci* had long been the source of rumors that Supilo was on Belgrade's payroll and that the Coalition in general was a treasonous organization.[95] Most of the accusations concerned Supilo, who was correctly perceived by Vienna as the guiding force of the Coalition. Frank was working on behalf of Vienna when he sponsored rumors of Supilo's treasonous activity.

The Friedjung trial proved to be a fiasco for Aehrenthal and the monarchy's foreign policy establishment, for it was utterly clear that the foreign ministry had provided the historian and Funder with the documentary evidence for their assertions. Thus, the unavoidable conclusion that the documents were forgeries only made Aehrenthal, and through him Vienna, appear incompetent. Far from achieving their goal of marginalizing the Coalition and chastening Serbia along the way, they heightened the already prevalent impression that the monarchy was no longer capable of maintaining the pretense of being a great power. It was all the more upsetting to the equilibrium of Habsburg foreign and internal policy that the charges were undoubtedly true. Funder, for one, was certain that a conspiracy did exist and that the Coalition was essentially a treasonous body in spite of the fictitious nature of the documents that he provided in the trial.[96] Friedjung was of the same opinion.[97] And by all means they could have demonstrated connections between the Serbian government and the Coalition, as well as other Serbs in Croatia and Hungary. Milovan Milovanović, the Serbian minister of foreign affairs, feared that some connection between the ministry and Supilo, Pribićević, and Medaković might have been discovered by the Austrians, although their correspondence was carried on without written record.[98] He made absolutely sure that Spalajković could not reveal any secrets in Vienna before allowing him to testify.[99] The government of Serbia had supported several newspapers in Bosnia. Hinković had been given money by Serbia, filtered through the Paris embassy, for his work in the Zagreb trial. Connections with various Bosnian groups had been maintained through Emil Gavrila, a lawyer with the Serbian consulate in Budapest.[100] And finally, we have seen that the Serbian government was involved in the formation of the Coalition and had been enmeshed with the Hungarian opposition from 1904 to 1907.

The question also arises, however, of what constituted treason. Ante Radić noted that until 1903, Serbs in Croatia had enjoyed the patronage of the governors of Croatia because, in part, the Obrenović dynasty was allied with Austria-Hungary. Therefore their connections with Serbia had been ignored.[101] Teodor Pejačević, the former ban of Croatia, drew attention to the fact that various Magyars accused of conspiring with the Serbian government were now members of the Hungarian government (a reference to Kossuth and his role in the cooperation of the Hungarian opposition with Serbia in 1904–1907).[102] Gavrila, whose role was perhaps the most treasonous according to the standards of the Zagreb and Friedjung trials, was a Radical, which leads one to wonder whether the decades of cooperation between the Radical party in Hungary and the Radical party in Serbia did not make that party treasonous. The inconsistencies point simply to the fact that this was a political trial just as the Zagreb trial had been.

The annexation era was a watershed for the Coalition and the Serbian Independent party. The Coalition was rewarded for its militant antidualism with great popularity that ultimately bestowed upon it moral authority that no other party in Croatia could match. The Independents themselves emerged from the two trials unscathed. In spite of the essential accuracy of the charges against them, they were able to transform the indictments into a condemnation of Austro-Hungarian policy in Croatia and foreign policy in general. It appeared that a regime such as Rauch's could never be renewed in Croatia. The Coalition could expect to dictate a solution to the deadlock that it faced in Budapest, where the railroad pragmatic had assumed symbolic priority in a long list of grievances that Croatia could present to Hungary. The New Course, the policy of antidualism in cooperation with the independence coalition in Hungary, was dead. But the Croato-Serbian Coalition remained, and it appeared to be in a stronger position than ever.

So it appeared, but in fact the Coalition weakened internally as it gained prestige. Internal dissent had been demonstrated publicly and privately. Supilo proved to be the only member of the Coalition who resolutely addressed the crisis in Croatia and responded according to the logic of the Coalition's previous public militance. The remaining members of the organization responded to Rauch by seeking a way to outmaneuver him. Some, like Nikolić and Kulmer, attempted to achieve the original goals that led them to participate in the Coalition: governmental positions in Croatia that would allow them to advance as imperial politicians. The Serbian Independents tried to negotiate their way out of their difficulties in Croatia. They no doubt feared that the accusations against them could be proved. Although Rauch appeared to be an asinine figure, the fact that the Independents wished privately to avoid a showdown with him reflected their knowledge that his accusations were substantially true, even if his methods were obtuse. The militant stand taken by the Independents in the trials was a product of their inability to strike a bargain with Wekerle and/or Aehrenthal and their knowledge that they could, at least, defend themselves against the specific charges that were leveled at them.

The Independent party did succeed in its goal of eliminating the Radicals from Croatian politics. This was partly due to the fortuitous alliance of Rauch and the Radicals. The Radicals were compelled by the logic of their position in Hungarian politics and their concentration on the Church Congress. Nonetheless, for a Serbian party to support Rauch would signal its demise in Croatia. The Independents also superseded the Radicals in Croatia because they again proved able to merge their individualistic Serbian conceptions with the interests of Croatia. In other words, their opposition to Rauch had two elements: they reacted to his persecution of Serbs, but also to his capricious example as an exponent of dualism and therefore as arbitrary ruler of Croatia. Once again, the Radicals' support of Rauch illustrated their disinterest in the fate of Croatia.

Conclusion

Thanks to the writings of British observers like R. W. Seton-Watson and Henry Wickham Steed, the trials of 1909 are usually treated as circuslike events, ridiculous and revealing of the corroded foundations of Habsburg power in central and southeastern Europe. But it is important to note that they were attacks on the Serbs of Croatia and their culture, attacks which disputed national and ethnic political definitions and which drew attention to the always present threat that Habsburg-style barter politics could pose to Serbian survival in the monarchy. The trials constituted a warning that took some time to sink in. In some ways that warning was purely traditional in the Habsburg context: behave, remain loyal to the emperor, or be persecuted. In another sense, the warning told Serbs that no matter how convincing their support for Croatian statehood, no matter how sincere the relationship of

Serbian and Croatian political parties in Croatia, no matter how firm they all were in support of constitutional government in Croatia, they would never be able to counteract the center, Vienna, the empire. Thus, for Serbs the message said, in essence, not to fool themselves that they could survive without imperial favor in Croatia. Serbian existence was far too tenuous; there were always dangers (Frankists, for instance) that the empire could activate to make it even more tenuous.

That cautionary message took the next three years to fully germinate. In the meantime, the Coalition and its Serbian Independents gloated over their successful humiliation of the Austrian, Hungarian, and Croatian leaders who sponsored the trials: Aehrenthal, Wekerle, Rauch. Serbs (and Croats, in fact) had committed treason, they had worked hand in glove with the Serbian government, and they had gotten away with it. The Coalition had seemingly proved the importance of teamwork, cooperation, brotherly love, as it collectively fought the battle of its individual members. But that was more illusion than reality; the message of fear that the trials imparted to the Serbs of the Coalition worked corrosively on them. They would never forsake the Coalition itself, but they would betray its mission, its faith in the power of *narodno jedinstvo*. By 1914, the Serbian Independents would make of the Coalition something akin to the old National party under Khuen-Héderváry: collaborationist magyarones. They would reject the civic politics of the founders of the Coalition in favor of Habsburg tradition: the politics of barter.

5

THE COLLAPSE OF
THE CIVIC OPTION IN
SERBIAN POLITICS,
1910–1914

Power

ONE MIGHT CHARACTERIZE the difference between the Croato-Serbian Coalition in 1907 and the Coalition of 1910 as analogous to the difference between two personalities: Frano Supilo and Svetozar Pribićević, the organization's leaders in the pre- and post-trial eras. Thus Miroslav Krleža, the great Croatian writer, wrote in 1924: "After the ruin of the Friedjung trial, when Supilo was accused of being Chlumecky's confidant, when he handed over his resignation as a functionary of the coalition, when one of the leading Serb Independents announced that it was fine that that guy was ruined, because with him they would never come to power—after that, Pribićević truly did make it to the top of magyarone power and stay there all the way to October 29, 1918. That path was completely and diametrically contrary to Supilo's conceptions as a fighter for Croatian independence."[1] Others, including Supilo himself, whose memoir of the period, *Politics in Croatia*, is harshly, unsparingly critical of Pribićević, also attribute to the leader of the

Independents a shameless desire for power. And many, especially in light of his postwar behavior as a minister in successive governments in the Kingdom of Serbs, Croats, and Slovenes, also sense in his work a profound Serbian nationalism (which is a different sort of reservation altogether).[2] And just as Pribićević is condemned, Supilo has often been treated as a magnificent but tragic figure, both personally (he died in exile in England in 1917) and for Croatia, for whom his work was an unfulfilled promise.

The verdict of Croatian observers like Krleža is not off the mark. However, there is more logic and consistency to Svetozar Pribićević's work than crass opportunism and Great Serbian nationalism. The Serbian Independents struggled to find a combination by which three things could be achieved: Croatian statehood could be defended, Serbs in Croatia could be protected from assimilation, and they, of course, could come to power. They did not succeed in balancing the three: Croatian statehood (along with the Independents' constitutionalist mission) was the loser by 1914. When the Independents implicitly jettisoned Croatian statehood from their program, Pribićević's critics were proved right. Nonetheless, the explanation for the Independents' apostasy is more complex and more illuminating than those critics would have us believe.

With the trials over, the Serbian Independent party and the Croato-Serbian Coalition began to enjoy, for the first time, true power in Croatian politics. Admittedly, the 1906 elections had made the Coalition a force to be reckoned with. But the Coalition met the attempts of the most powerful forces in the monarchy to destroy it in 1909 and conquered. The Coalition could call the shots for the time being. Events moved rapidly as the Friedjung trial drew to a close. On December 22, 1909, Friedjung capitulated, his evidence admittedly forged. Soon after, the Wekerle government fell, causing ripples through the power structure of Hungary and Croatia. Wekerle was replaced as minister-president of Hungary by Khuen-Héderváry. In turn, Rauch was replaced by Tomašić, Khuen-Héderváry's old protégé. Khuen-Héderváry could not have missed the sense of déjà vu. As in 1883, he was charged with pacifying Croatia and creating a new government party. This time, he and Tomašić believed that the Croato-Serbian Coalition, without Supilo, who would shortly leave, could be bought off and would play the role of the old National party. The Serbian Independents eventually emerged as leaders of this moderate Coalition. Did they realize that they were assuming the roles played by the old National party magyarones?

By January 15, 1910, Tomašić (speaking for Khuen-Hédervary and the Hungarian government) and the Coalition concluded an agreement. The Hungarian government resolved to remove Rauch and his cabinet, and the Coalition swore to support the new government of Tomašić, who in turn agreed to establish constitutional government in Croatia and broaden the right to vote.[3] The Coalition had to scramble to present the agreement with its old archfoe in a positive light. In private conversations, members of the Coalition recognized the improbability of an alliance with Khuen-Hédervary, the personification of the system against which the organization was formed in 1905 to fight. But one member of the Serbian Independent party explained that "no matter who is ban of Croatia, no matter what sort of Hungarian ministry there is, they cannot be worse than Rauch and the former Wekerle cabinet."[4] He also noted practical aspects of the agreement: Rauch had replaced bureaucrats loyal to the Coalition; with him gone, "many of our civil servants will be returned to service." And "a constitutional regime will be brought back and an electoral law will be formulated." "All of that," he added, "is a victory for our party and for our land." Finally, perhaps protesting too much, this representative noted that the Coalition "did not abandon a single point of [its] program. On the contrary, we emphasized its most celebrated point, [opposition to] the railroad legislation. The government was offered to us and we turned it down as long as the question of the railroad legislation is not solved." The irony of a Coalition alliance with Khuen-Hédervary was not lost on the remainder of the Croatian opposition, consisting of Supilo, the Peasant party of Stjepan and Antun Radić, the *frankovci*, and other *pravaši*. The Radićes viewed the Coalition's alliance with Tomašić with revulsion. "All faith in our intelligentsia must be rooted out among the people; with the turnabout of the Coalition . . . the intelligentsia has lost all of its value." From their populist perspective, Antun and Stjepan Radić recognized the descent of the *omladina* of Pribićević and Lorković into the politics of collaboration.[5]

The pact with Khuen-Hédervary and Tomašić completed a transformation in the character of the Coalition. Through 1909, it had maintained its militant persona; one suspects that it did so in spite of its collective desire to be in power rather than in opposition in Croatia. The fact that it remained aggressive so long was unquestionably a tribute to the forceful personality of Frano Supilo, who responded violently to the alliance between the Coalition and Tomašić. The Croatian delegation had not merely capitulated before the minister-president, he said; it had laid down its arms without a solution to the language question on Croatian railroads (in spite of the Coalition's assertions). Furthermore, even though it was the largest party in the Sabor, "it agreed that the government be enthroned from those very elements who are the factual, direct, guilty parties for all of the evil that Croatia suffers . . . from elements against whom the Croato-Serbian Coalition was in fact organized!" Finally, Supilo noted that the Coalition had given in to Khuen-Hédervary for something that would have been surrendered without a fight: "Rauch's head."[6]

For Supilo, the situation was bitter. For four years, he had led the Coalition, making the best of its limited strength to oppose Croatia's foreign governors and to craft a true opposition party. However, in the end, the predominance of politicians willing to barter the Coalition's reputation in order to be near power (and these were not just Pribićević's Serbian Independents) grew too strong. He left the Coalition in January 1910. The Coalition may have asked him to leave, or he may have gone voluntarily.[7] In a letter of February 5, Supilo wrote Tuškan that he had left the Coalition in the national interest and to make it easier for the Coalition to follow the will of the majority and work with Tomašić.[8] For their part, Austrian authorities certainly did not want Supilo around.[9] His instincts had warned him as early as 1906 that this day would come—he could sense that the Coalition was more pliant than he was. In 1910, he spurned (or was abandoned by) the collaborative Coalition, his integrity and his unremitting patriotism forcing him to leave his own creation. With his exit, all historians agree that the Coalition lost its ablest politician.[10] But more than that—the Coalition lost its only member with any leadership qualities who truly believed in the original battle in which the Coalition was engaged: to win for Croatia ever more independence from Hungary.

In January 1911, a year after Supilo's departure, Djuro Šurmin noted that "the truth is that the Coalition does not have a true leadership."[11] A collective leadership was developing. Circumstantial evidence suggests that Svetozar Pribićević may have carried the most weight. The foremost demands of the Serbian members of the Coalition were the removal of Rauch and his lieutenants and a return to the pre-1908 situation regarding Serbian desiderata (*srpske stvari*, which refers consistently to the status of the Serbian church, Cyrillic alphabet, flag, and Serbian employees in the Croatian bureaucracy);

Administrative Divisions of Croatia in 1910. *Meggan Laxalt*

these were all included in the agreement between the Coalition and Tomašić. In fact, they were not critical factors in Croatia's autonomy from Hungary; they were not critical factors to any of the Croatian members of the Coalition; they only mattered to the Independents, who still as always staked much of their popularity on their ability to sustain a thriving Serbian community in Croatia. Given the centrality of *srpske stvari* in the deal with Tomašić, the Independents must have had a guiding voice in the Coalition.

Many Croats believed that Serbs controlled rather than merely influenced politics in Croatia; but that was a fear with a long pedigree in Croatia, an outgrowth of the influence of the old Serbian Club. Pribićević himself apparently was heard to say that because of the trials, "all of Europe takes us into account."[12] It was not that the Serbs necessarily merited such status or influence; rather, the outcome of the Zagreb and Friedjung trials, which were obviously designed to disqualify the Serbian Independent party from political life in Croatia, demonstrated such ineptitude in Vienna, Budapest, and Zagreb that the Independents could count on some sensitivity to claims of maltreatment by authorities. They had moral authority in the Coalition and in Croatia in general, and they knew that anyone would think twice before "persecuting" them. The Croatian members of the Coalition had their own goals, goals which were less easily quantified. For Croats, the survival of the Coalition was an end in itself. It represented a response to the failure of previous strategies based on elimination of Serbs and irreconcilable opposition to both Hungary and Austria. The Coalition had accomplished the near-impossible: it had drawn Serbs out of abject collaboration. The Coalition's *pravaši* and Progressives knew that the continued existence of the organization depended on the Serbs remaining. They were willing to let the Independents play a leading role in the Coalition, if it kept them happy.

Pribićević's mentors after Supilo's departure were a loose-knit group of ex-magyarones, including Vladimir Nikolić. There were several vintage (pre-1903) Serbian Independents involved, but this group would be best characterized as unionists: those old-fashioned Serbs (and Croats) who believed that Croatia was better off as a component of the Lands of the Crown of St. Stephen, or Hungary. The Coalition had coopted many of them in 1905, when their collaborationism or their rivalry with Tomašić and Khuen-Hédérváry led them to the powerful new organization in Croatian politics. This faction behaved as magyarones had—pleasing their Hungarian and Austrian governors in exchange for personal favors and the hope of one day ascending to the top of the Croatian hierarchy, the banate. According to many observers, in late 1909 Nikolić had sought from Aehrenthal a higher position in the Croatian government, such as a vice-banate or the position of ban itself, before Tomašić was appointed. He even lobbied to become vice-ban under Tomašić in early 1911.[13] Kulmer and Rojc shared Nikolić's passion for political advancement, and all were ex-members of the National party that Tomašić was now attempting to revive.

The tension this created between these unionists and the nationalist Progressives and many younger Independents would strain the Coalition, but because it remained the most viable political movement in Croatia, convinced nationalists remained in the Coalition in spite of its conservative turn. Some Independents, for the most part younger ones, were true believers in the Yugoslav mission—Srdjan Budisavljević, for instance. Many Croatian Progressives, including Večeslav Vilder and Djuro Šurmin, also fit into this group. Supilo believed that the Progressives were in his camp even after he left the Coalition. Šurmin described the Progressives and several *pravaši* as *naša garda* (our guard) in conversation with Supilo, who thought that his "guard" might eventually be able to turn the Coalition in his direction once again.[14] Unfortunately, the Croats in the Coalition who were the most idealistic Yugoslavs were also apparently the least capable politicians. They were unwilling to break with the Serbian Independents, with whom they had been allied for five years and who they believed were the strongest politicians in the Coalition. Josip Smodlaka noted the tension: the cooperation of Pribicević and Ivan Lorković made the Coalition the strong organization that it was, but they were entirely different personalities. As "Pribićević imposed himself more, Lorković retired ever more into himself."[15] Those Croats who proved unable to challenge Pribićević's leadership perhaps unwillingly lent him their credibility.

Predictably, the alliance between the Coalition and Tomašić bore little fruit. Tomašić's task was to tame the Coalition; the leading elements of the Coalition wished to govern while appearing to be *untamed*. The combination could not work. The charade lasted some time, however. One way for the Coalition to maintain power while appearing oppositional was to insist that Tomašić keep a promise: the passing of a new electoral law. The new law brought the number of voters in Croatia from 2 percent to 8.5 percent of the population (or from 49,000 to 220,000 voters), thus bringing the Croatian franchise to the level of the Hungarian.[16] Nothing was done to change Khuen-Héderváry's electoral gerrymandering, however. The fact that only the number of voters was changed provoked bitter debate and charges that the Coalition was a Serbian organization. "If the Coalition," wrote Antun Radić, "does not want to remain the same old magyarone *četa* (detachment) of sell-outs and bullies, it will discontinue the current Khuen-Héderváry division of districts and widen the right to vote. If it does not, it will not dare show itself to the people." And although it concerned more than Serbs, Radić wrote, "if Serbs have the slightest bit of honor . . . they must themselves demand the repeal of this disgrace which Khuen-Héderváry set aside for them. Here we will see whether the Pribićevićes and the Banjanins are different Serbs than were the Gjurkovićes and the Gjurgjevićes."[17] The Serbian Independents did respond to the criticisms, because to be called a magyarone was not acceptable for a Yugoslav organization in Croatia in 1910. *Srbobran* claimed, predictably, that there was no injustice in the current electoral districting. According to its reckoning, Serbs, as 25 percent of the population of Croatia, could expect twenty-two of the eighty-eight districts to be of Serbian majority. *Srbobran* counted only nineteen with such a majority. Others figured differently. Vladimir Frank, who took over leadership of the *frankovci* from his ill father in 1909, counted thirty-four districts controlled by Serbs and twelve in which Serbs could win elections with the help of the government and other nationalities.[18]

The shallowness of the Coalition's relationship with Tomašić was revealed when he rejected its second demand, that Rauch's appointees be removed from their positions in the bureaucracy of Croatia. Tomašić quickly switched strategies, now trying to create some new, loyal party from among the members of the Coalition. He failed here too, although several *pravaši* did leave the Coalition to form the so-called Osijek Group. On August 22, 1910, the remaining *pravaši* and the Progressive party announced their plans to fuse to create the new Croatian United Independent party, which with the Serbian Independent party would comprise the Croato-Serbian Coalition. The official fusion took place on October 13, 1910.[19]

In the October elections, the Coalition won only thirty-five of eighty-eight possible seats. This was far from an absolute majority and signaled a half-success for Tomašić, who could count sixteen representatives for his side. However, the Coalition achieved two moral victories. First, two defendants from the Zagreb trial were elected for the Serbian Independent party, and second, Aranicki lost in both of the districts in which he ran. However, the Serbian Independents also saw the editor of *Srbobran* (one of Pribićević's original colleagues) Jovan Banjanin, lose his election in the Udbina district.[20] The results were clearly inconclusive. In spring 1911, the political situation in Zagreb became chaotic.[21] Tomašić postponed the Sabor after the session of March 16 because of its refusal to vote Croatia a budget for the year.[22] From that point onward, the Coalition entered into hard opposition, which rendered the ban's position untenable. The summer of 1911 was dominated by the maneuverings of Tomašić and the Osijek Group to form a new government party. By mid-October 1911, *Srbobran* and *Hrvatski pokret* (the newly renamed newspaper of the Croatian Independent party) were being heavily censored by the Tomašic government. In early November, Ivan Lorković, the leader of the Croatian Independents, was arrested. The situation appeared similar to that of the early days of the Rauch regime and was all the more interesting because elections for a new Sabor were to occur in late December. These elections were preceded by an alliance of the Coalition, the Starčević Party of Right (Mile Starčević's splinter party), and the Peasant party, which meant that Tomašić and his new party, the Party of National Progress,[23] would have to elect a clear majority in the Sabor to be able to govern. In spite of intense government pressure at the polls, the ban failed.[24]

The failure of Tomašić's attempt to split the Coalition is only somewhat mysterious. Why, for instance, did the Croats not form a government party without the Serbs? The answer: the *pravaši* and the Progressives were not interested in merely achieving power—the implications of *narodno jedinstvo* led them to insist on remaining in coalition with the Independents. Without the Serbs in the Coalition, the organization would have lost much of its rhetorical substance and factual support.[25] Second, why did Tomašić decide to eliminate the Serbian Independents from his government party? After all, Serbs had provided valuable support for an earlier incarnation of this regime, under Khuen-Héderváry from 1883 to 1903. But times had changed. For one, the monarchy no longer viewed Serbia as its client—it was now an enemy. Also, in spite of the fact that Pribićević and his party colleagues had succeeded in the Zagreb and Friedjung trials, Aehrenthal and others in power in Vienna were convinced that they were guilty. Similarly, were the Serbian Independent party to become more powerful in Croatia, it would probably, in the eyes of Vienna and Budapest, have an unwelcome echo in Hungary and Bosnia. The Serbian consul in Budapest claimed that "Vienna will not hear of Pribićević and his retinue; Pest in fact abhors the Serbo-Croatian Coalition and both fear the effects that the strengthening and progress of the Serbian element in Croatia and Slavonia will no doubt have on the Serbian population in Hungary and in the annexed provinces [Bosnia and Hercegovina]."[26] In the end, in spite of initial attempts to buy off the Independents, Tomašić, just like Rauch, had to try to eliminate the Serbian Independents from the Coalition; unlike Rauch, Tomašić did not utilize overt persecution. The Independents, who realized more than ever that they could not be marginalized if they wished to defend the Serbian half of the nation, refused to be set aside.

The outcome of the deadlock was determined from above, by the Hungarian government: on January 21, 1912, Tomašić was replaced by Slavko Cuvaj. Cuvaj had been mayor of Zagreb under Rauch, and had run in the 1911 elections and been beaten handily by the Coalition candidate.[27] He intended from the beginning to censor the Croatian press and ignore the Sabor (without either suspending it or calling new elections).[28] If the situation did not become clear and favorable for the government, that is, if the Coalition did not come to heel, Cuvaj would be named the emperor's "commissar" and be given full authority in Croatia.[29] Cuvaj arranged for the Sabor to be suspended on January 28, before it had even met, and the commissariat was declared on April 3, 1912.[30] If there were talks with the Coalition, they did not lead to a fruitful relationship. Even Tomašić's old support from within the Coalition, the Osijek Group, opposed Cuvaj vociferously in his meeting with the Croatian delegation to Budapest, because Cuvaj had suspended the Sabor.[31] All things considered, Cuvaj's position was politically untenable, even if he did have imperial authority. No party in Croatia could abide the suspension of the Sabor, and all remembered Cuvaj as Rauch's appointee in Zagreb. The Croatian opposition as a whole viewed the commissariat as a Hungarian attempt to further restrict Croatia's autonomy. Certainly they were right. But the full meaning of the commissariat cannot be understood without reference to its companion measure, the suspension of Serbian Orthodox church autonomy in the metropolitanate of Srijemski Karlovci.

Serb Versus Serb

After 1910, the Serbian Independent party could be satisfied that it had successfully outdueled the Radicals in Croatia. The Radical party had withdrawn from the Coalition because it could not expect to control the Church Congress as a member and because the Coalition's insistence on Croato-Serbian *narodno jedinstvo* was repugnant to them. The leaders of the party were ideologues of Serbian exclusivity and thus commanded the attention of Serbs in the Habsburg monarchy who feared the disappearance of cultural boundaries between Serbs and Croats. That old wariness of reciprocal (and thus assimilationist) national identities, which first showed its face in Illyrianist times, had not faded. By their withdrawal from the most popular South Slavic political organization in the Habsburg monarchy, the Radicals branded themselves as retrograde and corrupt; their continued support for Wekerle and their passivity toward Rauch placed them firmly in the wrong camp. The Radical party therefore entered 1910 with severely reduced prospects in Croatian politics. It had two representatives in the Croatian Sabor of 1910, holdovers from that elected in 1908, Mladen Lisavac and Jovan Radivojević-Vačić. In 1910, their thankless task had been to defend the Radical party against the charge that it had supported Rauch in 1908 and 1909.[32]

Changed political fortunes hardened the ideological conflict between the two Serbian parties. Tomić and the Radicals reiterated their belief that religious and cultural freedom preceded political freedom: "We see that nations everywhere first won for themselves religious rights and then political rights. Because where religious rights are not recognized, political rights will not be recognized."[33] As always, for Tomić, only the privileges granted by Emperor Leopold to the Serbian Orthodox church in the late seventeenth century could challenge the ideas of Croatian and Hungarian state right successfully, because the privileges were granted by the empire itself. Pribićević still as always believed that Tomić's view was archaic. "The Serbian Radical party has . . . traditions, which have their roots in those times when the legal position of the Serbian nation in the monarchy rested on the emperor's privileges and patents."[34] Pribićević based his entire political philosophy on the validity of political participation, in the belief that political modernity demanded a new conception of citizenship and individual rights. For Pribićević, the question of the survival of the Serbian nation in the Habsburg monarchy was inexorably linked with the idea of constitutionalism and Yugoslavism: only in political harmony with Croats could Serbs in Croatia gain for themselves the liberty necessary for survival. For Tomić, any sort of unity of Serbs and Croats would inevitably come at the expense of the strength and individuality of both nations. For that reason, Tomić treated the Croatian nation not merely as different but as an enemy of the Serbian.

The position of the Radicals on the importance of Serbian individualism was unambiguous: the Independents betrayed Serbdom merely by acknowledging the existence of the *pravaši* in Croatia, because in so doing they granted Croat "Serb-haters" a modicum of legitimacy; Pribićević and the Independents thereby denied the "spiritual community" that was Serbdom. "[Being Serbian] concerns a unified feeling, conception, a unified desire and unified will," which the Independents betrayed.[35] Tomić feared that when Serbs demonstrated their brotherhood with Croats, they had to sacrifice their own identity in order to maintain the fiction. Thus, although the Zadar Resolution had demanded legal guarantees for Serbian cultural attributes, none had been forthcoming, and all that came of it was that "Serbianism" became treason when Serbs opposed the powers in the monarchy, as in Croatia in 1908.[36] Better to work with Austria-Hungary, as the Radicals proposed. Practically, Tomić saw the Church Congress as the only savior of the Serbian nation in the monarchy.

Serbia's Role in the Struggle for Primacy in Croatia and Hungary

The Independents gained a critical ally in their struggle with the Radicals when influential members of the power structure in Serbia perceptibly and publicly began to support the work of the Independents over that of Tomić's Radicals. The Zagreb and Friedjung trials linked the Serbian government to the Croato-Serbian Coalition, purportedly in a treasonous relationship. But until 1910, it was the Radical party in Hungary, older and more established than the Independents, which had links of friendship and practice with the Radical party in Serbia. The Serbian government also supported the work of the Coalition in Croatia, especially during its early years from 1905 to 1907. Then in 1907, when the Coalition had broken with the Hungarian opposition, the Radicals and Independents were both encouraged to leave the Coalition by the Pašić government, which wished to remain on good terms with Wekerle. After 1909, however, the Serbian government began to differentiate between the work of the Radicals and that of the Independents, who worked in different states and thus had different roles to play in the calculations of Serbia's rulers.

Serbia's four major political parties, the Radicals, Independent Radicals, Progressives, and Nationals, did not differ by their national ideologies and programs for the expansion of Serbia. Their party programs all envisioned the unification of all Serbs into one Serbian kingdom.[37] Generally, Serbian policy throughout the late nineteenth century was to favor the strengthening of the Serbian community of the Habsburg monarchy by embellishing the autonomy that it enjoyed in cultural and religious affairs. Any cooperation with Croats was undertaken to that end—not as an ideological prerequisite of a supranational philosophy such as Yugoslavism. From 1903 to 1914, the Serbian government was dominated by Nikola Pašić's Radical party. Were the policy of Serbia toward Croatia to have an ideological basis, it would be that provided by the Radicals. And in Pašić's scheme, there was no consideration given to the idea of Yugoslavism, or to Croats, Slovenes, or Bulgarians, all of whom were generally considered at least to be related to Serbs.[38] However, after the Zagreb and Friedjung trials, leading government figures in Serbia began to appear more Yugoslav than ever before. Whereas historically the Radical party in Serbia had publicly favored the actions and interests of the Serbian Radical party in the Habsburg monarchy, after the trials, newspapers of the Radical party in Serbia began to distance themselves from the Radicals of Tomić and Krasojević. Pašić's lieutenant, Stojan Protić, led the attack on the Radicals of Hungary in his writings in *Samouprava* (Self-government), the Belgrade newspaper of the governing Radical party in Serbia.

Polemics filled the pages of *Srbobran*, *Zastava*, *Srpski glasnik*, and *Samouprava* through 1911 on the subject of the validity of *narodno jedinstvo*, with the newspapers of the Radicals in Hungary failing to measure up; their insistence on Croato-Serbian separateness proved to Serbs in Croatia and Serbia that they were irredeemably traditional.[39] This very public struggle seemed to illustrate that Protić (and implicitly the governing Radical party in Serbia) had become firm believers in the *narodno jedinstvo* of Croats and Serbs and also strong supporters of the Serbian Independent party. But such was not the case: a dual policy, part Croatian, part Hungarian, persisted in the approach of the government in Serbia. The Serbian government undoubtedly reasoned that a policy that guaranteed the maintenance of Serbian separateness while also assuring a close relationship with Croats could only be beneficial in the long run. However, the favor shown the Independents by Protić would be matched occasionally by the favor shown the Radicals and their approach to the maintenance of *srpstvo* in Hungary, which demonstrated not that the Serbian government was now superficially "Yugoslav," but that it always considered the survival of Serbs and their culture the priority.

The Independents Spread Their Wings

The Independents were emboldened by their public relations successes, and the party made good use of the less savory methods of its rivals when it had usurped their place. For instance, in early 1910, it arranged with Khuen-Héderváry to have the elections for the Serbian National-Church Congress called for May, at the same time as the elections for the Hungarian Parliament. The Radicals, torn between two electoral battles,[40] lost their majority in the Church Congress to the Independents, and they also failed to elect a single representative to the Hungarian Parliament (they had never had more than three).[41] The hostility between the two parties reached a tragicomic culmination when Djordje Krasojević challenged Svetozar Pribićević to a duel in the midst of a session of the Church Congress.[42] The duel was never fought.

Pribićević and his cohort now intensified their efforts to establish the strength of their party in southern Hungary, which was far from simple. Croatia and Hungary were unique domains, and the conditions in which Serbs lived were dissimilar. Thus the political situation for Serbs was different in Hungary. Of course, the differences were accentuated by the fact that the Independents and Radicals offered unique visions for the maintenance of the individuality of the Serbian nation and Serbian culture in Austria-Hungary. The Independents, by virtue of their role in the Coalition, had the upper hand, so they focused on eliminating the influence of the "Serbian *frankovci*," the Radicals of the southern Hungary and Srijem. Although the Independents could comfortably count on the Radicals to demonstrate their ineptitude in Croatian politics, they nevertheless went out of their way to thoroughly destroy the influence of the Radical party in Croatia and Hungary. They were able to use questions of personality, policy, and ideology to attack the Radicals. They transparently accepted unreconstructed Radicals into their ranks: the Independents did not care about the politics of these outcasts, as long as they disavowed Jaša Tomić. Radivojević-Vačić, in fact, noted that Pribićević had approached him and pronounced him a "ready-made Independent" if he would renounce Jaša Tomić.[43] Other Radicals were known to have joined the Independent party out of simple dislike of Tomić. The Independents had never shied away from prospective new members, regardless of their politics.[44]

Logically, given their desire to eliminate the Radicals from the political stage in Hungary, the Independents devoted the majority of their attention to fostering entirely new parties in southern Hungary. The result was a messy proliferation of new organizations that represented scarcely more than the families and friends of their leaders. From 1907 to 1910, the Independents cultivated the Serbian Democratic party, led by the brothers Vasa and Milutin Jakšić, the first a lawyer and the organizer of the party, the second a historian of the Serbian church and the party's theorist.[45] The Democrats appeared in late 1906; in April 1907, they launched their party newspaper, *Srpski glas* (Serbian Voice), in Velika Kikinda, southern Hungary. They observed that Serbian parties in Hungary had relied too much on the supposed validity of the privileges. Instead, the Democrats proposed that Serbs could only assure their continued existence in a free and democratic Hungary. Initially, the Jakšićes ascribed the personalization of Serbian politics to Jaša Tomić, the greatest "political cynic and speculator" on the whole Balkan peninsula, according to Milutin.[46] Their disgust with Tomić and their rejection of policy based on the privileges at first made them natural allies of Pribićević and the Independents. Gradually, however, the Democrats were drawn into the personal battles of Tomić and Pribićević, whom they came to see as equally negative forces. Although the Democrats' foremost desire was to remain free of both larger rivals, the Independents had a more proprietary interest. When *Srbobran* once referred to the Democrats as the "Serbian Democratic (Independent) party in Hungary," Democratic resentment of Pribićević boiled over.[47] Lest the party be confused as a mirror image of the Independents, one should note that the Jakšić brothers despised the inability of strong politicians like Tomić and Pribićević to overcome their mutual loathing. Alas, even the Democrats were disunified: one observer once ironically described the Democratic party as "purely Serbian" if only because of its many factions.[48]

Other more pertinent factors divided the Independents from the Democrats. The Democrats, for instance, supported the Hungarian opposition coalition of Kossuth and Gyula Justh because of its attempts to wrest independence for Hungary from Austria. The Independents could not seriously support such a policy after mid-1907, when the railroad pragmatic was introduced by Kossuth. Later, when the Independents were openly allied with Khuen-Héderváry and Tomašić, the Democrats allied with Oscar Jaszi, whose Democratic party in Hungary envisioned universal suffrage as the guarantor of freedom for the nationalities of Hungary (which was clearly a position that the Independents, were they ideologically consistent, would have supported).[49] The Democrats had no stated position on the *narodno jedinstvo* of Serbs and Croats, although Milutin Jakšić professed to dislike Tomić because the latter viewed "Magyars as natural allies of Serbs against Croats."[50] So, while the Independents supported and even nurtured the Democrats, this support was based mainly on the Democrats' opposition to Tomić. The Independents and Democrats were forced to an open break in early 1910, when the latter refused to support Khuen-Héderváry and the government he formed at that time.[51]

After 1910, the Independents attempted to create their own organization in Hungary. Several Democrats split off from the original party to form a tenuous organization known as the Serbian Independent party in Hungary. The Independents in Croatia also sporadically nurtured a small group of dissident Radicals in Hungary who produced the newspaper *Srpstvo* (Serbdom) and then formed the Serbian National party and supported the Hungarian governments of Khuen-Héderváry and István Tisza.[52] The attraction of the *Srpstvo* group for the Independents was its opposition to Tomić's Radicals and support of Khuen-Héderváry and Tisza.[53] Neither of these latter groups helped the Independents dominate the confused Serbian political situation in Hungary.

This uncertain situation for the Serbs of Austria-Hungary and Serbia ended decisively with the declaration of the commissariat in April 1912 and the suspension of Serbian church autonomy on July 11, 1912 by Emperor Franz Josef, at the behest of László Lukács, then minister-president of Hungary. So in addition to the end of civil government in Croatia, the various decrees that comprised the contemporary political and legal basis for Serbian church autonomy were suspended; these included laws of 1871, 1875, and 1908, which regulated the existence of the eparchate, the school committee, elections to the Church Congress, and the administration of the funds of the metropolitanate.[54] The suspension of these decrees and laws left intact only the law which preceded and was superseded by them, that of 1868, which placed control of the Serbian Orthodox church in the hands of the upper clergy, which by 1912 had developed a dependency on the Hungarian government, and especially on the now-defunct Liberal party of István Tisza. Thus the Hungarian government suspended the autonomous decrees in order to be able to eliminate the highly politicized Church Congress from active political life in the monarchy.[55] Given these events, which were directed at the Serbian Independents first and foremost, the Serbian population of Croatia and Hungary once again seemed threatened with (at least) political marginalization.

Serbdom Threatened, Unionism Embraced

The era following the dual blows of the commissariat and the suspension of church autonomy was marked by the two Balkan Wars and the continued decline in Austro-Serbian relations, which eventually led to the outbreak of the First World War. Serbia's Balkan Wars, which lasted from October 1912 to August 1913, were attempts to settle its relations with its southern neighbors. Thus the First Balkan War saw Serbia, Greece, Bulgaria, and Montenegro attack the Ottoman Empire, with the intention of driving the Ottomans from Europe and dividing the abandoned territory among them. The Second Balkan War was a fight over the spoils, as the Serbs and Greeks were joined by the Ottoman Empire and Romania in a war against Bulgaria. The wars caused an upsurge in pro-Serbian feeling among Croats that is nearly impossible to describe adequately. A new nationalistic *omladina* grew in strength with each Serbian victory. The Serbs of the Croato-Serbian Coalition shared the enthusiasm of the rest of the Southern Slav population of the monarchy and beyond—but they had no desire to become the objects of the sort of attention that was paid them during the previous time of troubles, in 1908 and 1909 during the annexation crisis. Thus the Independents had to walk a very thin line between expressing their enthusiasm for Serbia and protecting themselves from persecution in Croatia and Hungary. The commissariat and the suspension of church autonomy would, then, have demanded the most diplomatic of responses from the Coalition and its Serbs; with the addition of the Balkan Wars and the attraction for Serbia that was their result, the Coalition was forced into a particularly delicate position.

Renewed Assault on Croatia and Its Serbs

The declaration of the commissariat in Croatia and the suspension of Serbian Orthodox church autonomy in the metropolitanate unquestionably comprised dual prongs in a policy aimed at lessening the influence of the Serbian Independent party in Croatia and Hungary. There were powerful voices in Vienna and Budapest that wished to abandon the attempt to force the Coalition into subservience; the pendulum had swung again, and those who supported eliminating the troublesome Serbs from political life had again begun to be heard in the monarchy's capitals. In Croatia, the commissariat revealed the exhaustion of authorities in the monarchy with attempts to govern with the seemingly ungovernable Coalition; the Serbs within it led the unruly faction. By suspending church autonomy, Hungarian authorities hoped to stifle the ability of the Independents to utilize the monetary resources of their church. The immediate effect of the commissariat on the Coalition was simply that it limited the organization's public function. Newspapers were subjected to preventive censorship, and the permit fees for their publishers were raised to an unbearable level.[56] The Sabor, of course, did not meet, and since there was no possibility that it would, there was no electoral agitation. There is evidence, however, that even this new assault on Croatia's independence found some members of the Coalition, probably led by Nikolić and seconded by Pribićević, willing to compromise.[57] The first (and only) public statement by the Coalition after the declaration of the commissariat emphasized that the Coalition could still be counted on to undertake positive work for Croatia.[58] Others found the response to be tepid at best, sincere unionism at worst.[59] The only strong public opposition to the commissariat was led by the *omladina* (of which the Coalition's members no longer formed a part).[60]

The period of the commissariat (which lasted until late 1913) proved to be rather barren for the Coalition. For Croatia, however, these two years were energetic, dangerous, and invigorating. The Balkan Wars divided the period, and their effect on the Yugoslav movement was considerable, as youth of all the South Slav nations flocked to the Serbian side, whether physically or morally, justifiedly or not. However, the Coalition no longer reflected the desires of the South Slavic youth. That role had been usurped by a younger generation that was being guided by, among others, Supilo, and which adhered to a far more radical vision of Yugoslavism than the Coalition, as it turned out, could bear, given its recently achieved status as the establishment party in Croatia. The Coalition had little to do with or to say about the rash of assassinations attempted or completed that plagued the governors of the Habsburg monarchy's South Slavic provinces. Within a week of the announcement of the commissariat, Luka Jukić, a youthful Croat, attempted to assassinate Commissar Cuvaj.[61] The Coalition distanced itself from him and other such would-be assassins as Stjepan Dojčić, who wounded newly appointed Commissar Ivan Skerlecz on August 18, 1913. Dojčić, who had no connections with the Coalition, was nonetheless rebuked by it for his action. The leaders of the Coalition hoped their condemnation of Dojčić would facilitate their possible negotiations with the new commissar.[62] For the most part the organization tried to maintain its contact with the authorities in Budapest and Vienna.

But the Coalition had to contend with this growing, angry *omladina* in Croatia and Bosnia. Following Serbia's success in the Balkan wars, this group, or more specifically, Mlada Hrvatska, Nacionalistička omladina, and Mlada Bosna (Young Croatia, Nationalistic Youth, Young Bosnia), came to view Serbia as the natural liberator of South Slavs on the Balkan peninsula.[63] By and large the clarion call of these groups was a truly integrationalist *narodno jedinstvo*. Leaders like the not-so-young Milan Marjanović propagated the idea that Serbia somehow embodied the soul of South Slavdom; Croats should look to the example of Belgrade instead of Zagreb, a weak, tired city.[64] Marjanović himself was a veteran of the National Movement of 1903; from 1912 to 1913 he lived in Belgrade at the urgings of an unenlightened Cuvaj, who had banished him from Croatia, working for the Serbian press bureau and writing *Savremena hrvatska* (Contemporary Croatia), a primer on Croatian history for the Serbian public.[65] In late 1913, upon the reestablishment of constitutional government in Croatia, Marjanović returned to Zagreb and started a newspaper entitled *Narodno jedinstvo*. Marjanovic represented something of a bridge between the establishment Coalition and the more revolutionary youth being nurtured by Supilo and Ivan Meštrović at the same time. All regarded the Coalition as a somewhat jaded but nonetheless valuable representative of Yugoslav desires, of *narodno jedinstvo*. Whereas the Coalition accepted the odium of compromise as a political necessity in Croatia, the *omladina* would be the radical alternative.[66]

The creation of the commissariat struck a blow at the entire Coalition, but the suspension of church autonomy was directed primarily at the Independents. The monarchy could not tolerate the existence of an autonomous Serbian political body within its boundaries, especially during a time of worsening relations with Serbia and looming suspicions of a "Great Serbian" conspiracy. The Serbian Orthodox church in Bosnia, for instance, was hoping to gain autonomy, which the monarchy did not wish to grant; therefore, the autonomy enjoyed in the metropolitanate of Srijemski Karlovci was taken away. Jovan Jovanović, then the minister of foreign affairs in Serbia, contended that the monarchy had never "trusted" Serbs in the south of Hungary;[67] presumably, he believed that the monarchy had come to view the Church Congress as a threat to its southern border. However, the Church Congress had not suddenly grown more powerful. The immediate occasion for the suspension was that the Hungarian government feared that the Church Congress, which commanded funds amounting to forty million crowns, would become a source of capital in the hands of the Coalition and the Independent party, which had only recently gained control of the Congress.[68] Thus the suspension of autonomy accompanied the imposition of the commissariat in Croatia as a measure to control the Croato-Serbian Coalition.[69]

The response of the Independents, Radicals, and the Serbian government to the suspension of autonomy was instructive. The Independents claimed to believe, according to Dušan Peleš, that "Serbs in fact lost nothing by this Magyar violence, because in fact they had nothing to lose."[70] Serbian church autonomy, Peleš believed, was powerless because "neither the Congress nor the Congress committee [executive committee] could execute the most insignificant decision without the approval of the Hungarian government."

Peleš strongly believed that the suspension was part of the "Magyar chauvinistic program" and was designed to restrict the access of the Serbian Independent party to the funds of the metropolitanate. Pribićević added that
the question depended on the behavior of the Independents in Croatia. He
thought "that the Magyars would in a pretty short time be forced to negotiate with the Serbs and that they [Magyars] would be driven to do that by conditions in Croatia, where a solution depends only on Serbs, or that is the
Serbo-Croatian Coalition." In the past, Pribićević noted, Serbs had viewed
the "Karlovci [Church] Congress as the true Serbian parliament," whereas
they "had lost interest in the Zagreb and Pest parliaments, which they viewed
as foreign political bodies." Pribićević used as an example the 1897 elections
for the Croatian Sabor and the Church Congress in which Serbs voted overwhelmingly for magyarones in Croatia but oppositionalists for the Church
Congress. This, he noted, was because of the passivity of Serbs regarding
these foreign parliaments (the Sabor and the Hungarian Parliament) and
their active interest in their own, Serbian, legislative body (the Church Congress).[71] But now the Independents had "developed the interest [of Serbs] in
the Zagreb Sabor, in which lasting success of Serbs was guaranteed in political questions in Croatia." On the other hand, disinterest now reigned in
southern Hungary as it had in Croatia before the Independents changed
things. Pribićević suggested that "in the first place, it is necessary to develop
agitation among Serbs here [in southern Hungary] for interest in the Pest
Parliament, and the fruit of that agitation would be the strengthening of Serbian mandates [there]." In that way, autonomy would be returned if the
Magyars were not forced to negotiate with the Independents beforehand.

So the Independents did not view the suspension of church autonomy to
be a crushing blow to Serbian nationhood, nor did they imagine its return as
a prerequisite for the further growth and development of the Serbian nation.
Instead, the suspension was the product of the passivity of Serbs in southern
Hungary and the inability of the Serbian parties there to "interest" their
constituents in political life in the monarchy. Peleš and Pribićević did not
even speculate on the amount of time it would take to see the return of autonomy. The important thing for them was that it would be returned either
through the work of the Independents in Croatia (it depended on how firm
the opposition of the Coalition was to the commissariat), or, should the
Magyars fail to be forced to negotiate, with the strengthening of the Serbian
element in the Hungarian Parliament, which depended on the success of the
Independents in Hungary.

The Radicals, on the other hand, viewed the loss of autonomy as a sincere loss for the Serbian nation in the monarchy. They did not propose to reorient Serbian politics in southern Hungary toward the parliament in Budapest: they thought that the best way to regain autonomy (which was an end in itself) was to concentrate their work on the local level, in church districts *(crkvene opštine)*, that is, the districts into which the metropolitanate was divided and which had voted for the members of the Church Congress. These districts would remain intact in the new conditions, but would now elect only lesser church committees *(crkveni odbori)*. The Radicals proposed working in these districts to convince all "better elements" to refuse to sit on these committees. Thus, "one day nearly all of the church committees would fall into the hands of problematic elements [unqualified people]," which would force the clerical leaders of the church (the *jerarhija*, the body that governed the church under the law of 1868) to demand the return of autonomy or the imposition of a full commissariat in southern Hungary. Either autonomy would be returned or Europe would once again see that the monarchy could not govern itself.[72] According to Stevan Mihailović, an emissary of the Serbian government who investigated the causes of and possible solutions to the autonomy crisis, the Radicals suggested the possibility of uniting with the Independents in order to fight to regain autonomy; however, the Independents feared that if they worked with the Radicals, the latter party would attempt to regain its lost strength in the Church Congress. For their part, the Radicals feared that the Independents would rather wait for negotiations with the government and possible concessions.[73]

Regardless of the complex scenario, the Radicals clearly saw the strengthening of the Serbian Orthodox church and its administrative structure as the vital element in opposition to the suspension of autonomy. They sought to strengthen the legislative power of Serbs in the Serbian Orthodox church and at the grass roots level, whereas the Independents wished to see Serbian strength improved in the legislative bodies of the state. The point, belabored perhaps, bears repeating: the Radicals viewed the crux of *srpstvo* in the religion and culture of the Serbian nation; the Independents viewed it in Serbian political strength. Thus, the Radicals relied on the privileges granted to the Serbian Church by emperors past, while the Independents concentrated on increasing the political and cultural freedoms of Serbs through contemporary legislative means.

Some months later, the ultimate logic of the Radicals' approach was laid out by Jovan Jovanović, who shared their position and, as minister of foreign affairs in Serbia, represented "official" Serbian policy. Jovanović wrote that, at the time of the creation of the Serbian National-Church Congress, "the ideal of *srpstvo* in Austria-Hungary was not church autonomy but national, practically territorial, autonomy. In the moment of its realization, it had to come into conflict with other nations and territorial autonomies. There was no Serbian territorial autonomy, nor can there be, because that can only be at the expense of Croatia and Hungary."[74] But, he said, the Serbs of Hungary continued to openly desire "national" or even territorial autonomy in Hungary, thus challenging the very foundations of the Habsburg monarchy, which "appeared not from the linking of nations but of territories; the pragmatic sanction was not a pact of nations but of kingdoms and lands." Therefore the monarchy had to suspend this autonomy, which implied the right of a nation to territorial autonomy. As an afterthought, Jovanović added that it was this desire for Serbian national-territorial autonomy that "could explain the antagonism between Croats and Serbs."

The suspension of church autonomy in July was quickly followed by the outbreak of the First Balkan War, which of course dominated the attention of Serbian diplomacy. However, the Serbian government did consider its position regarding the autonomy crisis. The government tended to favor the actions supported by the Radicals, which involved strengthening the church districts' opposition to the suspension. Insofar as the Independent and Radical parties were concerned, the Serbian emissary Mihailović suggested that the government strongly urge the Independents to collaborate with the Radicals. The Radical plan suited the government because only it offered "the best opportunity to awaken the sleeping national feeling of Serbs there." This position rested on the belief of Mihailović that, of Serbian "plutocrats," intellectuals, and peasants, only "peasants still have not submitted to Magyar culture and only they are nearer Belgrade than Pest."[75] Mihailović might have added that the Independent attitude would have drawn Serbs even closer to Budapest. The Independents, he did note, were "little informed on the question of autonomy, and they cannot immediately and easily orient themselves." However, the Independents refused to buckle under the pressure of the Serbian government. Valerijan Pribićević first informed Jovanović (through an unknown intermediary) that the Independents "have no great interest in this battle, since there are not many monasteries there [in Croatia and Slavonia], and those they have are poor. It is [still] possible that they will enter the struggle." Mihailović was right, for on August 9, Jovanović wrote that Pribićević "reported that he thinks that the Independents will be for battle."[76]

The Serbian government had one other reason for supporting the Radical initiative regarding the loss of church autonomy. Publicly, as was described above, the Serbian government had taken to supporting the Independent party over the Radical party, mostly for the position the latter adopted regarding *narodno jedinstvo*. "This is also a suitable occasion," wrote Mihailović, "to draw nearer to the Radicals, who have been estranged by [our] demonstrative switching of fronts and the help [we have given] the Independents." Thus, he wrote, "Serbia must carry out one policy in Zagreb but another in Novi Sad," due to differing legal and political situations in Croatia and Hungary.[77] In other words, because the Croato-Serbian Coalition and the Serbian Independent party were so popular in Croatia, the Serbian government, insofar as it was possible, gave public support to the work of that organization. Because the Radicals had proved completely incapable of working within the framework of the Coalition and its ideology, the Serbian government had disowned it in that context. However, in Novi Sad, the Radicals did not have to contend with the question of Croato-Serbian oneness, and there Serbia's governors saw them as the most effective instrument of Serbian national policy, as envisioned by Belgrade.

Unionism

By the end of the Second Balkan War in the summer of 1913, the Kingdom of Serbia had become quite a magical place in the minds of much of the Croatian and Serbian *omladina* in the monarchy. The government of the monarchy had come to realize that it must attempt to govern the South Slavs in a way that would keep them from embracing revolutionary means of unification. Cuvaj did not prove successful, even as dictator-in-residence. His government, whose goal had been to keep Croatia as quiet as possible while Hungary addressed its internal affairs, had failed in its task. Cuvaj was viewed as an impediment to the pacification of Croatia. From late December 1912, Cuvaj removed to Budapest and a bureaucrat named Karl Unkelhäuser was assigned to administer Croatia in his absence. Cuvaj spent his last few months as commissar in Budapest because Vienna did not want a Hungarian governing Croatia in a time of upheaval. Besides, his life was in danger in Croatia.[78]

In the fall of 1913, Cuvaj was replaced as commissar by Ivan Skerlecz, a Magyar baron who was István Tisza's representative. Tisza and Emperor

Franz Josef assumed that the Coalition would negotiate with Skerlecz an agreement by which constitutional government would be reestablished in Croatia. Hungary also had to be concerned with the renewal of the financial Nagodba with Croatia, which was on the agenda in 1913 (the previous renewal in 1903 had led to the National Movement of that year, something that the Magyars did not want to relive). Negotiations commenced upon Skerlecz's arrival as commissar. The Coalition entrusted its executive committee to negotiate the agreement that was worked out by December 1913. There were dissidents within the Coalition, but the executive committee of the Coalition had by now usurped all functions of negotiation and conclusion of policy and agreement. As early as May 27, 1913, the executive committee implied its willingness to consider negotiations with Skerlecz, who had only then entered Tomašić's Party of National Progress.[79] The committee justified its willingness to negotiate with Skerlecz by noting his conciliatory nature and his personal mission from Tisza and the emperor. However, Cuvaj had had the same authority to negotiate with any and all Croatian parties. But according to Jovan Banjanin (a hostile witness by this time), the executive committee had been slowly overwhelmed by an "intrusive clique which organized itself as a self-named leadership of the Coalition. It [the Coalition] became a weapon in the hands of that clique which collected around a pair of unscrupulous [members of the committee]."[80] This group had taken over the direction of the Coalition and determined to negotiate with Skerlecz. The thesis that the Coalition came to be dominated by a faction that willingly led the organization from its original Croato-Serbian nationalist orientation to a unionist one implies that there were politicians in this opposition party who were willing to "sell out" to the Hungarians. Nikolić (the president of the executive committee) and Pribićević led the committee,[81] of which a majority were ex-magyarones, so the executive committee was dominated by unionists. After nine years of trying to establish themselves as a governing party in Croatia, they were more than willing at this point to listen to Tisza, through Skerlecz.

Many of the actively collaborationist Coalition members were Serbs. Although the members of the group cannot be precisely determined, one can be sure that Banjanin referred to Nikolić and Pribićević, and that Popović, Kulmer, Badaj, Medaković, Muačević, Mažuranić, and Peleš of the executive committee were also members. There is evidence that others on the committee, including Djuro Šurmin and other Croatian Independents, felt pressure from the unionist faction.[82] Ivan Lorković, in spite of assertions that he was uncomfortable in the presence of Pribićević and the other less idealistic members of the Coalition, was known to press a pristine Croatian nationalist to step aside to allow a candidate more amenable to the Hungarian government to run in his place.[83] Of the above who were surely members, only Kulmer and Badaj were Croats. Another Croat unionist, Rojc, was head of the Coalition's election committee, which implied considerable influence for him.[84]

Publicly the Coalition demanded of Tisza that the Hungarian government withdraw the railroad pragmatic and initiate discussions on the use of Croatian in the Hungarian Parliament. As late as September 1913, *Srbobran* insisted that the Coalition would not negotiate with Skerlecz if those conditions were not met and that there was no such thing as a "Pribićević-Nikolić" course that would lead to Croatia's subjugation to Hungary. When the Coalition's opponents accused it of striving only for power in Croatia, *Srbobran* facilely responded that power would be a sacrifice that the Coalition would make if it helped create a democratic Croatia.[85] Weeks later, Banjanin resigned from active participation in the Serbian Independent party and the Coalition and therefore quit as editor of *Srbobran*. He was motivated by his disgust at the negotiations with Skerlecz, and it was rumored that Skerlecz demanded his removal. (Pribićević later wrote that he fired Banjanin because Banjanin was too good at creating news to discredit the opponents of the Independents. Banjanin was probably therefore hindering negotiations with Tisza with his biting journalism.) To such accusations, Pribićević responded that if Skerlecz had wanted to remove someone, he would have gone after Pribićević. The implication was that Pribićević was the one who truly opposed negotiation with Skerlecz.[86] The public myth that the Coalition was firm in opposition to the Magyars was maintained, and Pribićević's public militance supported the myth. The Coalition still extracted as much benefit as possible from its aggressive reputation earned between 1907 and 1909.

During the time in question, the executive committee did negotiate with Skerlecz. Publicly, the Coalition presented Skerlecz as its supplicant.[87] However, soon after Skerlecz's arrival in Zagreb, the Coalition began taking part in general negotiations between the new commissar and all the parties of Croatia.[88] By October 10, the commissar entered into exclusive negotiations with the Coalition, as represented by Nikolić, Popović, and Medaković.[89] The Coalition demanded that the railroad legislation be rescinded and that it "receive some *veliki župan* positions." On November 17, Nikolić, Medaković, Badaj, and Mažuranić of the Coalition met with Tisza personally in Budapest. In this conference, the Coalition demanded again that the pragmatic be rescinded and that approaching elections to the Sabor be completely free of government pressure. Tisza agreed to those demands, but deferred on questions relating to personnel, which were revived after the elections.[90]

The agreement with Skerlecz and Tisza was concluded on November 18. By the time it was presented to the Coalition on December 2, both the Hungarian government and the executive committee had approved a finished product. The Coalition as a whole apparently submitted to the will of the committee.[91] On December 6, 1913, the Coalition announced its candidates for the Sabor elections, which were held on December 15–17.[92] The Coalition gained forty-seven seats, and the Party of National Progress (Skerlecz's party) won twelve, giving the government fifty-nine out of eighty-eight seats. The Coalition insisted that it was not going to act as a unionist majority for the ban. Although it claimed that one of the victories of its agreement with Tisza was free elections, it had nonetheless bound itself to Skerlecz.

The Coalition had used obtuse methods to maintain secrecy about the negotiations and to justify the agreement that was reached. Jovan Banjanin's resignation critiques the agreement from the point of view of one of the dissidents who had disagreed with the Coalition's methods after the resignation of Supilo. According to Banjanin, Vienna had to return constitutional government to Croatia or risk assassination of every commissar who arrived in Zagreb. The Coalition held the key to any majority in the Sabor, which had to meet in order to extend the financial Nagodba, which, in its own way, constituted a pillar of dualism in the monarchy. As Banjanin noted in his resignation, the Hungarian government needed to negotiate, not the Coalition. The agreement with Skerlecz gained for the Coalition that which it could have enjoyed two years before—the ban's patronage in return for collaboration with the Hungarians.[93] Although the Coalition insisted that its agreement had not bound it to support the government of Skerlecz in any way, Skerlecz and Tisza immediately publicized the fact that the Coalition, along with old unionists, would provide their majority in the Sabor.[94] The Coalition itself claimed that the two successes of its negotiations were the removal of the commissariat (Skerlecz was named ban on November 27, 1913) and renewed negotiation regarding the railroad pragmatic.[95] Yet it was not without irony that Banjanin noted that if the removal of the commissariat was a concession, then the Magyars could humble Croatia every five years with that sort of gift.[96]

As far as the railroad pragmatic was concerned, Banjanin concentrates his critique on the fact that it need not have been a subject of bargain. According to him, Tisza had already decided to abandon the pragmatic, since it was clear that no pacification of Croatia could proceed without such action. Thus, once again, according to Banjanin, the Coalition had gained as a concession and claimed as a victory that which would have been handed to it otherwise. Furthermore, the Coalition had relied on the pragmatic to rally public opinion against any enemy, but probably did not really consider it of vital importance. For a true victory, the Coalition would have to have convinced Tisza that the Magyar language had no place in Croatia and that the Croatian delegation could speak Croatian in Budapest, issues that were the crux of the problem for the Coalition in 1907. The amended railroad laws did not affect the mass of employees working on the railroads or other services. In Croatia in 1910, 73 percent of administrators and 40 percent of other workers were Hungarian, and the new arrangement would not change that proportion.[97]

Thus the two victories of the Coalition were chimeras. The original focus of the Coalition's work—the union of Dalmatia and the banate, financial independence of the Croatian land, and language violations in general in Croatia—went untouched. In fact, the main reason that Tisza needed to stabilize a constitutional Croatia was that the renewal of the financial Nagodba approached. The Coalition agreed to vote for its renewal without complaint. The agreement with Tisza was the complete capitulation that Supilo had foreseen, but approximately four years later than he had indicated, for the agreement with Tomašić and Khuen-Héderváry had clearly not been an abject collapse before authority. Had it been so, the militance with which the Coalition greeted Tomašić's behavior in 1910 would not have appeared. In fact, the same people were behind the agreements of 1910 and 1913, but they had not earlier had the support which they mustered by 1913. After the announcement of the commissariat and the limp response of the Coalition in 1912 (which was formulated, according to Banjanin, by Nikolić and Pribićević), "the true inspiration of the declaration [Nikolić], the soul of the clique, said after he returned to Zagreb that he wanted to end the stupidity which [the Coalition] had undertaken the past two years, and the second conceited leader [Pribićević], whom [Nikolić] already had in his hands, quaking with fear of the commissariat, said that he would never more be pushed to the left."[98] The commissariat, in the end, forced those who did not favor the Nikolić line to submit. Nikolić, as the moving spirit of this group, had beaten the necessity of accommodation with Budapest into the rest of the Coalition, which had then not yet conceded the virtues of such a policy.

After the elections, the Coalition continued to negotiate with Skerlecz for positions in his new government. Dušan Popović was offered several times the position of vice-ban. He turned it down, reportedly to avoid conflict with Nikolić, who sought the position. In March 1914, the Coalition requested of Skerlecz that Nikolić be appointed, but required of Nikolić that he step formally into the Serbian Independent party.[99] Later, in April, the Coalition added Badaj and Mažuranić to its list of candidates for government positions, Badaj as head of justice and Mažuranić as director of a newly organized economic division.[100] The Coalition assumed a hostile attitude toward Skerlecz during its attempt to gain seats in the government.[101] Skerlecz proved unwilling to fill his government with Coalition personages; the Coalition demanded that it receive the vice-banate. Apparently, some radical members of the Coalition (including Srdjan Budisavljević and Ivan Ribar) demanded that the Coalition receive all four seats in the government and that Skerlecz join the Coalition.[102] Ultimately, Skerlecz used the candidature of Valerijan Pribićević, an "ex-traitor," as an excuse to deny the Coalition its government seats.[103]

The Threatened Community: The Serbian Logic Behind the Capitulation to Tisza

The theory put forth by a bitter Banjanin, which holds that a clique within the executive committee perverted the will of the Coalition as a whole, works to an extent, but ignores the tendencies of the Coalition from 1910 forward. The organization was filled with people who aspired to be intimately involved in the government of Croatia. For such people, opposition was not an appropriate course of action. Thus, the evolution of the politics of the Coalition from 1910 can be seen as a steady pull toward compromise with the Hungarian government. The Coalition slowly lost from view the possibility that it could achieve power in order to fulfill its original destiny: to preside over the gradual achievement of Croatia's independence from Hungary. The desire for power was not lost, however. The presence of unionists of long-standing makes this tendency logical and clear. People like Banjanin, Srdjan

Budisavljević, Lorković, and Šurmin disagreed with the tendency to desire power at any cost, and during the war (if not before, as in Banjanin's case), they would lead a small exodus from the Coalition.

Yet the Coalition had made its reputation as an aggressive opposition party. The motives of Nikolić, Kulmer, Badaj and other ex-magyarone unionists are perfectly clear. But what about the Serbian Independents? Historians have long blamed the behavior of the Coalition after 1910 on Pribićević and his party. They were in the service of Belgrade, or they were simply a new incarnation of the old "Khuen Serbs."[104] Those are two separate accusations, often confused. To some degree, both are accurate, and indicate that there was a logic to the pact with Tisza that, unlike the above account, could be designated a "Serbian" explanation. There were reasons why the Serbian Independents desired the pact that were separate from the reasons of the unionists in the Coalition (a faction to which some of the Independents belonged). They included the fact that Tisza promised to restore the suspended autonomy of the Serbian Orthodox church; that many Independents perceived an imminent revival of a Rauch-style regime in Croatia; and that the Independents received word that the Serbian government would look favorably on such an agreement. Each of these points will be considered in turn.

As part of the deal to act as Tisza's compliant majority in Croatia, the Independents were, by late 1913, negotiating with the Hungarian minister-president for the restoration of autonomy as part of the pact that the Coalition and the minister-president were concluding. Knowing as early as the summer of 1912 that they would eventually negotiate with the Hungarian government for the removal of the commissariat in Croatia, the Independents refused to adhere to the Radical plan for the return of autonomy, because that plan involved antagonizing the Hungarian government to the point of a second commissariat (this one in Hungary) if need be. The Independents hoped not only to avoid a commissariat in Hungary, they wished to help abolish the one in Croatia; furthermore, they could not afford to antagonize the Hungarian government any more than they already had. Sometime in 1913, Dušan Popović was assured by Tisza that the latter would restore the autonomy of the Serbian Orthodox church.[105] The Independents accepted Tisza's word in the matter, assuming that it would be dealt with at some point in the future. However, when the Independents and the Coalition began negotiations with the minister-president, the question of church autonomy was left out. The Independents still felt certain that Tisza would make good his promise. To push the process along, the address of the Coalition as the Sabor majority in March 1914 demanded that the autonomy of the Serbian Orthodox church be restored.[106] Pribićević and Popović compared the suspension of autonomy with the commissariat in Croatia, allowing that with the end of the latter, the time had come to do away with the former.[107]

By early April, the bishop of the Pakrac bishopric, Miron Nikolić, had gained the assent of Tisza to the restoration of autonomy under the previous conditions.[108] On June 11, Medaković, Pribićević, Peleš, and Popović met with Tisza to discuss autonomy;[109] a day later, Serbian Consul Milanković in Budapest reported that Tisza had invited any other Serbian parties that wished to cooperate with the Independents to meet and discuss the details.[110] The Independents had maintained their predominant role in church affairs and had gained the assent of Tisza to the restoration of autonomy on their terms. As they had promised in 1912, the Independents brought back autonomy as a result of their Croatian political strategy. But the Independents had not wrung this concession from the Hungarian government because of their intransigent insistence on constitutionalism in Croatia—they had bought it with collaboration.

The second reason why the Independents desired an agreement with Tisza was that the situation in Croatia in 1913 resembled that of 1908: voices were heard saying that Croatia should not tolerate the existence of people who called themselves Serbs. Rauch and Kršnjavi, the *frankovac* leader, were given hearings in Budapest, and the prospect of a new Rauch regime gave serious pause to the leaders of the Independent party.[111] Popović heard in Vienna in the spring of 1913 that "all was prepared, on the suggestion of Khuen-Héderváry and Tomašić, for the former state prosecutor from the treason trial, Accurti, to be named vice-ban, and for a purely Croatian, anti-Serbian, course to be inaugurated in Croatia." Popović had then met with Tisza to ascertain the accuracy of the rumors. When Tisza assured Popović that Skerlecz was not tied to anyone but Tisza, Popović became convinced "that it would be a mistake for the Coalition to refuse [to negotiate with] the new imperial commissar [Skerlecz]."[112] Popović later reported that

the Balkan wars showed that Austria would not be peaceful and that it would seek a fight with Serbia. Thus it was necessary to protect the Serbs of Croatia from exile, destruction, and material collapse. In such a situation the question was posed: will the Coalition make an agreement with Tisza, or will the Party of Right come to power, or will the unionists who carry out the will of Pest and of Vienna against Serbs? Given such alternatives, it was necessary in the first place, in the interests of Serbs, to make an agreement with Tisza. That was the real motive of the opportunistic policy of the Coalition toward Tisza.[113]

Even after the Coalition had assumed its position as the unionist Sabor majority in early 1914, fears that Vienna was preparing to persecute Serbs in Croatia remained. Both Popović and Kulmer heard of and warned about such possibilities.[114] Whether or not we believe that fear was justified, it would seem that it did motivate the Independents to seek an alliance with Tisza.

Finally, according to Adam Pribićević, Svetozar Pribićević sent him to Belgrade in the middle of September 1913, in the midst of negotiations with Tisza, to ascertain whether Nikola Pašić and his government would approve of the approaching alliance with Tisza.[115] Pašić and another Radical, Ljuba Jovanović, approved wholeheartedly because Serbia, they asserted, needed time to regroup after the Balkan Wars. Thus, were the Coalition to maintain friendly relations with the Hungarian and Austrian governments, war would be less likely. According to one version of Adam Pribićević's account, "it is very doubtful that [Svetozar Pribićević] would have concluded this pact without the support of Serbia."[116] Another writer, one Slavko Ćirić, relates a similar story: Pašić relayed a message through Valerijan Pribićević calling for the Coalition to remain in good relations with Tisza in early 1914.[117] Pašić gave similar advice to Ivan Meštrović, a leader of the *omladina* in Croatia, in 1913, noting that "[the *omladina*] is excitable, as are all youth, and that it was necessary to calm and console it, and that it be patient." "Tell them," Pašić told Meštrović, "not to go overboard and create difficulties for Serbia. We need a few years of peace."[118] Thus the sympathies expressed to Adam Pribićević were general and self-evident. Serbia clearly did not want any Serbian or Croatian group in the monarchy to inflame Austro-Serbian relations.

Conclusion

The Serbian Independents retreated in 1913–1914 to the politics of collective defense. Having scaled the peak in Croatian politics, they found that the only way to guarantee the continued safety of their community was to cut a deal with Budapest. Sadly, the civic model, to their minds, had not served to integrate and protect the Serbs of Croatia. Quite the opposite: the trials of 1909, the commissariat and suspension of church autonomy of 1912, and the threat of a renewed Rauch regime in 1913–1914 convinced them that as the most powerful single party in Croatia (if not by numbers, then certainly in fact), their best option was to strike a bargain with Tisza. They did so as war threatened the monarchy. When Bosnian Serbs assassinated the Archduke Franz Ferdinand on June 28, 1914, circumstances radically changed for the Independents and the Coalition: now they once again represented the threat of the Serbian enemy. No longer was the resumption of Serbian Orthodox church autonomy a pressing issue; no longer did it matter that the Coalition and Ban Skerlecz could work together.

The verdicts on the work of the Independents and the role of Svetozar Pribićević in Croatia between 1910 and 1914 are not uniform. Serbian historians, insofar as they have concerned themselves with the Serbs of Croatia, believe that, had there been no agreement, attacks on Serbs in Croatia and Bosnia following the assassination of the archduke might well have wiped out Croatia's Serbs. In the words of a Serbian historian who is devoted to the notion that Croats have always, whether openly or secretly, harbored a desire to destroy Serbs, "it turned out that the agreement which the Coalition concluded with Count Tisza in 1913 was a farsighted, wise, and salutary political move for Serbs in Croatia and Slavonia. For if, by some chance, unionists and *frankovci* had been in power during the war, as in the years of the Pavao Rauch government and the Zagreb anti-Serbian high treason trial, it is hard to believe that Serbs could have saved themselves from exile, material ruin, and physical destruction."[119] On the other hand, we have already heard the verdict of two Croatian writers, Miroslav Krleža and August Cesarec, who voice the common condemnation of Pribićević that he was nothing but a political opportunist, without beliefs or convictions, excepting perhaps an abject devotion to Serbia.

One could argue that by being in power, the Independents were fulfilling their mission on their own terms—that they were in fact assuring the safety of the Serbian nation by legislative action, perhaps even constitutionally. However, that argument would not be satisfactory. The Independent party, in leading the Croato-Serbian Coalition into a collaborative arrangement with Tisza, compromised its constitutional principles, rooted as they had been in support for the idea of the Croatian political nation comprised of citizens of a variety of faiths and cultures. In dealing with Tisza, the Independent party most resembled the Serbian Club of the earlier Khuen-Héderváry era, not a modern constitutional party governed by the principle of natural law and the citizenship of the individual.

6

CONCLUSION

The Failure of the Civic Idea Among Croatia's Serbs

A Brief History of Croatia's Serbs, 1914–1996

WITH THE EVENTS in Sarajevo and the outbreak of war in 1914, Serbian politicians in Croatia could look the future in the face: they had assumed that the day would come when Austria-Hungary would be threatened by collapse, and it was possible that it had arrived. So, for the Independents and Radicals alike, a new phase had opened. The Coalition, and especially its Serbian Independents, suffered the abuse of the *frankovci* and others who loudly accused them of being in league with assassins. Many Serbian Independents were interned during the first two years of the war. But almost all of the important Serbian Radicals suffered harsher treatment, remaining in jail until 1917 or 1918.[1] Pribićević spent time under house arrest in Budapest —he could thank Tisza for relatively lenient treatment. Nonetheless, the Croato-Serbian Coalition, with the Serbian Independent party, remained the active Sabor majority throughout the war, and the Coalition provided many of the members of the Narodno vijeće (National Committee) which negotiated the union of Croatia and Serbia with the Serbian government and the

Yugoslav Committee at the end of the war. On December 1, 1918, the Kingdom of Serbs, Croats, and Slovenes was proclaimed in Belgrade by Prince-Regent Aleksandar Karadjordjević. Svetozar Pribićević's career took off at that point. As for Jaša Tomić, his career as a leader in politics was over. Croatia, the land that defined Pribićević's career and much of Tomić's as well, also endured a radical transformation from crownland of the Habsburgs to marginalized territory in the Karadjordjević state.

Today, the Serbian communities described in this book no longer exist. There are of course still Serbs in Croatia—but the thriving communities that grew up as parts of the Military Frontier, in Lika, Banija, western Slavonia, and Srijem are simply no longer there.[2] They disappeared in war, in August 1995 when the Croatian government of Franjo Tudjman undertook an offensive (designated "Oluja" [Storm] by the Croatian military) to liberate lands that it viewed as parts of Croatia, but which were populated by Serbs who had declared themselves independent of the new (1991) Croatian state. In the process, nearly all of those Serbs fled or were killed. The broad perspective shows us that this is one more migration in a several-hundred-year history of migrations on the Balkan peninsula, most if not all of them the by-products of war. But each is unique, and this one is too, very much a part of the twentieth-century history of the lands we are discussing, a product of the hopes, fears, and disappointments of the two Yugoslavias. This book is the story of the beginning of the end of the Serbian communities of Croatia. The offensive of 1995 was the final determining act in their twentieth-century saga.

It is not hard to briefly describe what became of Croatia and its Serbs between 1918 and 1995. With the formation of the Kingdom of Serbs, Croats, and Slovenes, Croatia was lost in a new multinational state. Its statehood, circumscribed in Austria-Hungary, was long gone in the first Yugoslavia, thanks in part to the efforts of Svetozar Pribićević as minister of the interior in the immediate postwar period. Many of Croatia's leading cultural and political figures were thoroughly unconvinced that Croatia belonged in this sort of state. In fact, union with Serbia in 1918 was brought about by but a fraction of Croatia's political parties, and those who opposed it were vocal. Some would be quite powerful: Stjepan Radić, for instance, went from being a marginal but charismatic politician before 1918 to the soul of Croatia, thanks to universal suffrage and his powerful defense of Croatian individuality. In spite of his power and his magnetism, he was inept as a statesman and ultimately must be viewed as a political failure. But the strength of Croatian resentment of Serbia and the Yugoslav state that was formed in 1918 was profound.

Until 1929, this Yugoslavia was a parliamentary democracy, dominated by the Serbian Radical party of Nikola Pašić. But in 1928, in the Skupština, Stjepan Radić was murdered by a Montenegrin deputy, Puniša Račić. That event prompted King Aleksandar Karadjordjević to proclaim a dictatorship, which governed a state whose parliamentary system had nurtured little but chaos. In 1934, the king himself was assassinated in Marseilles by an assassin working for the Croatian and Macedonian terrorist organizations (the Ustaša and IMRO, respectively). Until 1939, the Croatian question remained unresolved and presented an open threat to the integrity of the state. In August 1939, a short-term solution to the Croatian situation was found with the so-called Sporazum, negotiated by Radić's heir as leader of the Croatian Peasant party, Vladko Maček, by which the Banovina of Croatia was formed. Croatia gained autonomy within boundaries that included parts of Bosnia and Hercegovina and nearly all of the Serbian-populated districts of the pre-war Croatian crownland. The formation of an autonomous Croatian unit effectively opened a "Serbian question," since so many Orthodox Serbs were included within its borders and they, unlike the Croats, received no concessions or guarantees. The parallel with Croatia's secession from Yugoslavia in 1991 is obvious. In the case of the 1939 agreement, the Second World War intervened to render it a moot point.

The Nazi puppet Independent State of Croatia, formed in April 1941, was not the legal or spiritual heir of the Banovina of Croatia, although Maček did publicly request that Croats respect the new government. For the Serbs of Croatia and Bosnia, the Independent State of Croatia was an unmitigated nightmare. Allegedly utilizing a formula by which one-third of Croatia's Orthodox Serbs would be converted to Catholicism, one-third would be forced to emigrate, and one-third would be killed, the Ustaša made a sincere and barbarous attempt to create of Croatia and Bosnia a land free of Orthodox Serbs. While the number of Serbs killed in order to ethnically purify the state is debated violently (estimates range from the absurd extremes of 10,000 to 700,000 victims of the Ustaša death camps alone), the ultimate truth is unavoidable: a Croatian state, with the tacit or open knowledge of its citizens of Croatian nationality, attempted to wipe out its Serbs. The Ustaša genocide is the event that conditions all Serbian considerations of Serbian history in Croatia, as is understandable.

Croatia's history since 1945 is one of continuing desire for statehood—

whether independence or within the context of confederation with the other republics of communist Yugoslavia. The Croatian Maspok (mass movement), which ended in 1971, evidenced this desire. The experience of Croatia's Serbs in the second Yugoslavia was one of growing fear that if Croatia's statehood were expressed in any way other than via its membership in a unified Yugoslavia, their population would be endangered. The fear they faced was that the genocide of 1941–1945 could be repeated. In 1991, when Croatia seceded from Yugoslavia, the Serbs of Croatia responded with an armed uprising (which, in truth, had begun a year earlier, as it became clear that Croatia under Franjo Tudjman was heading for independence).[3] The result of that endeavor was abject failure. In August 1995, the Croatian army drove virtually all of Croatia's Serbs from the state.

Understanding 1903–1914

The Serbian community of Croatia has been ignored until recently in Croatian and Serbian historiography. In 1989, for the first time, the historical professions of Croatia and Serbia created small institutes which produced collections of articles on the Serbs of Croatia.[4] That fact undoubtedly reflected the growing interest, especially in Serbia, in the various Serbian populations outside of Serbia proper: in Kosovo, in Croatia, and less so in Bosnia. That interest in turn was prompted by the growing conviction that Serbian history in general has been a tale of victimization, persecution, and even genocide. That conviction, of course, grows not out of the experience of Serbs in Croatia before the Second World War, but out of the wartime attempt of the Ustaša of the Independent State of Croatia to physically eliminate the Serbs on its territory and out of the insoluble problem posed by Kosovo, a territory that is over 90 percent Albanian, yet considered by Serbs to be their own.

Earlier, by the middle 1980s, a few members of the Serbian historical profession began to feed their own obsession with proving that Croats, Catholics, the Catholic church, and/or the Pope had been actively engaged in attempts to eliminate Serbs in Croatia, Serbs in Bosnia, the Serbian state, and various combinations of the three. Some of this historiography is respectable, some of it atrocious. While one historian proposes conspiracy theories regarding the Catholic church's attempts to undermine Serbia and Yugoslavia, another works simply and with more success to demonstrate that Serbian statesmen after the First World War were not fundamentally anti-Croat, and a third suggests absurdly that Croats are inherently genocidal.[5] The fact is that these and other historians have the Second World War to contend with, which makes it very difficult for them to achieve any sort of critical distance. Their work is compromised by their insistence on searching for historical explanations for the Ustaša genocide of Serbs between 1941 and 1945. Unless of course we share Vasilije Krestić's view that the period under discussion in this book provides evidence of an inclination to genocide on the part of Croats, or his and Dragoljub Živojinović's assertion of a Catholic conspiracy to subjugate or eliminate Serbs and Serbia, we must try to examine the period, and Croato-Serbian relations in that period, in a different and more productive light.

For their part, Croatian historians have been wont to portray the Serbian Independent party and its leader, Svetozar Pribićević, as the undertakers of Croatian statehood. Largely as a result of his actions as the first Yugoslavia's interior minister, when he set himself the task of integrating Croatia into a unitary Yugoslavia, these historians have proposed that Croatia's Serbs always inclined to collaboration with Vienna and Budapest, that Pribićević was always a unitarist, was always a slave to the needs of the Serbian state, and was thus little more than a power-mad exponent of Belgrade in Croatia until 1918. Croatian historians, however, have been less interested in the Serbs of their land than have Serbian historians. Insofar as they do concern themselves with Pribićević, his behavior is one example of the brutal treatment that Croatia received at the hands of the Serbian leaders of the new Kingdom of Serbs, Croats, and Slovenes after unification in December 1918 and thus provides one piece to the puzzle of Croatian actions in the Second World War. So between Croatian and Serbian historiography we have a highly imperfect circle: Pribićević, part of the problem in Yugoslavia after 1918, stands as a symbol of why Croats were so disgusted with Yugoslavia by 1941; he thus helps explain, even if only tangentially, the Ustaša genocide. But long before that genocide occurred, he was there in Croatia, defending his Serbs from—genocide, which was purportedly a historical inevitability, given Croatian predispositions. Defending Serbs against a genocide that he caused thirty years in the future, Pribićević, we can safely say, is not well understood. The politics of the Serbs of Croatia are also poorly understood. There has to be a better way to conceive of the Serbs of Croatia and their leaders than through the prisms of Croatian and Serbian historiography to

Svetozar Pribićević, Ante Trumbić, and Josip Smodlaka after the First World War.
From Josip Horvat, Politička povijest Hrvatske *Zagreb: August Cesarec, 1990.*

date: murderer of Croatian statehood, defender of Serbs against imminent genocide. Do these trite constructions have any explanatory force at all?

This study has described the activities of the two Serbian political parties that operated on the territory of Croatia from 1903 to 1914. The Independent and Radical parties chose two different paths to the same goal, which was the protection of the Serbian community of the Habsburg monarchy. The leadership of the Radical party was older than that of the Independent party. It had matured during the 1880s, when Croato-Serbian relations were at their nadir. The Radicals never adhered to any ideology resembling Yugoslavism; they desired a Serbia, nothing more. Jaša Tomić, Djordje Krasojević, and their colleagues began their work when Croats had become so disgusted with Serbian insensitivity toward Croatian culture (ably displayed by the Radicals themselves) that Croats had begun to mimic the intolerance of Serbs. The vicious circle having been created, the Radicals never did free themselves of the prejudices of the 1880s and 1890s. They did not respect the existence of the Croatian state or the Croatian political nation, because they could not and remain consistent: they insisted that much of Croatia was Serbian territory.

Until 1905, therefore, the Radical party ignored the legislative body of the Kingdom of Croatia and Slavonia, the Sabor, in which was invested the legitimacy of the Croatian state and, in the interpretation of the Croatian opposition, the Croatian political nation. The Radicals concentrated their political activity in the Serbian National-Church Congress, which they viewed as the only legitimate legislative body for Serbs in the Habsburg monarchy. By virtue of their interpretation of privileges granted Serbs by Habsburg emperors, the Radicals believed that the Church Congress was not merely the governing body for their church, but the legitimate representative of the Serbian nation in the monarchy. They felt, and indeed insisted, that the Habsburg monarchy should recognize the Serbs as an autonomous political body in Austria-Hungary; the Church Congress, the repository of Serbian nationhood in the monarchy, would then become the recognized legal representative of Serbs in Croatia and Hungary. At some indeterminate time in the future, that body would join the Kingdom of Serbia and Serbs would be united.

The Radical party joined the Croato-Serbian Coalition from late 1905 to the summer of 1907. It did so in the knowledge that the strategy of the New Course implied that those who implemented it were accepting, in substance, Croatian political nationhood. The Radicals left the Coalition when they realized that it did not serve their own limited interests and returned to their earlier emphasis on the Church Congress. They interpreted participation (including that of the Independents) in the Coalition as capitulation to the Croatian state idea, which, they believed, threatened Serbs in Croatia with assimilation. It is also important to note that the Radicals left the Coalition when the Serbian government no longer viewed the work of that organization with favor. The Radical party acted in a practical manner, given its attitude toward the relationship of Croats and Serbs.

Whereas the Radicals matured in an atmosphere of mutual Croato-Serbian intolerance in the 1880s and 1890s, the Independents (in their Pribićević-led years) were the products of a later era. By the late 1890s, when Svetozar Pribićević and Jovan Banjanin made their first public appearances, Croatian and Serbian leaders were becoming distressed at the stagnation of political life in Croatia. Since that stagnation was caused in large part by the inability of the Croatian and Serbian oppositions to cooperate, it was only natural that the response would include that cooperation. The Serbian and Croatian *omladina*s that arose at that time included Pribicevic, Banjanin, and Ivan Lorković; their favored slogan was that Croats and Serbs belonged to one nation and that only their cooperation could make Croatia stronger in relation to Hungary. In the context of this (as yet insignificant) call for the cooperation of Croats and Serbs in Croatia and Dalmatia, the future leaders of the Serbian Independent party were able to sell themselves as Serbs willing to work in the interests of Croatia. In other words, they would behave as civil, or political, Croats. They did not deny their own Serbian nationhood, nor did they deny the validity of Serbian claims to areas that Croatian nationalists also claimed as theirs: Bosnia, for instance. However, in return for the acknowledgement of Serbian existence in Croatia, these Serbs conceded the legality of a Croatian state, agreed to work in and through its legislative body, the Sabor, and agreed to support the New Course, a political strategy designed solely to further the interests of the Croatian state in relation to Hungary. When the strategy of the New Course died in the summer of 1907, the Independents continued to work in the Croato-Serbian Coalition, of which they eventually shared leadership. From that point on, the Coalition entered into opposition to the Hungarian government. The Independent party remained in the Coalition, and thus shared its prominence in the Croatian Sabor, until the end of the Habsburg monarchy in late 1918.

The Independents thus shirked the strategy of the Radical party, which chose to deny the legality of Croatian statehood and to work only through the organs of Serbian church autonomy in the monarchy. The difference between the Radicals and the Independents can be seen in the fact that the Radicals always believed it was more important to dominate the Church Congress while disdaining the Croatian Sabor. The Independents operated in the reverse fashion. The Radicals were on the fringes of Croatian politics and governance, while the Independents were intricately involved in them. The Radicals denied the legitimacy of any Croatian legislative body, only working through the Sabor when it suited their individual or party interests, and even then very reluctantly. The Independents considered the Sabor the critical legislative body in Croatia, even for Serbs; Pribićević and other Independents occasionally expressed the wish that the Church Congress would disappear. And yet both parties believed that their tactics served the best interest of the Serbian nation.

In Yugoslavia the failure of parliamentary democracy was the direct result of ethnic tensions accompanying the formation of the new state. And in the formation of the state, Svetozar Pribićević played a critical role. Svetozar

Pribićević is best known in Yugoslav history as the brains behind the centralism of the first Yugoslav state, the Kingdom of Serbs, Croats, and Slovenes. Croats remember him as the man who wrecked any opportunity for an autonomous Croatia in his role as expert on Croatia for the early cabinets of Pašić's Radicals. Until 1925, he remained a (Pašić) Radical retainer, but thereafter he became one of the party's two most vociferous opponents: the other was Stjepan Radić, Pribićević's most virulent critic in the prewar period. Ironically, with Radić, and then after Radić's assassination in 1928, alone, Pribićević fought for a federal Yugoslavia, the antithesis of the type of state he had fought for through the immediate postwar period. Which Pribićević was the real one? And which one accords best with his prewar activity?

Ivo Banac describes Pribićević as a died-in-the-wool unitarist, a Yugoslav who truly believed in the abiding transformative power of the supranational idea of Yugoslavia. Yet he also acknowledges that Pribićević suffered the schizophrenia of those whose ideals simply cannot overcome their emotional attachments.[6] In the case of Pribićević, as we have seen, his sincere belief in *narodno jedinstvo* competed with his just as sincere fear for the survival of the Serbian community of Croatia and Hungary. Thus he insisted on the identity of Serbs and Croats, but hedged his bets ever more in cooperation with Budapest. In the postwar Yugoslavia, he continued this contradictory approach: he insisted on the validity of unitarist Yugoslavism, while working with Belgrade as a patron for his community outside Croatia. These methods were the last refuge of an energetic politician whose early idealism had petered out by 1913, when he and the prewar Serbian Independent party allowed their fear of an anti-Serbian regime in Croatia to force them to abandon their participationist principles. The fact is, Pribićević the unitarist of 1918–1925 was a Serbian nationalist with a useful, yet merely rhetorical, investment in Yugoslavism. His investment had not always been rhetorical.

Pribićević came to his obstreperous, almost violently defensive position of the early postwar period after twenty years in the vanguard of a grand experiment: an experiment with the politics of civic discourse, politics that rejected abject surrender to the seduction of nationality (unless, of course, we speak of Yugoslav nationality). His generation of Croatian politicians was taught by Masaryk, when not personally, then in spirit. Thus Pribićević and his colleagues rejected historical notions of nationhood, historical claims to political legitimacy, and insisted on the primacy of citizenship. The Serbian

Independents therefore became, for all intents and purposes, political Croats —by agreeing to work in and for Croatia, by placing their civic responsibility before their loyalty to their nation. In so doing, they wiped out twenty years or more of vitriol that had poisoned Croatian politics: Croats insisting that Serbs did not exist in Croatia, Serbs insisting that they would never relinquish their identity. Who cares? said the Independents—we can protect the Serbian community best by working for a constitutional Croatia. And what an uncomfortable notion. In the grand world of politics, one usually separates the politicians with the killer instinct from those with the high ideals, and Pribićević was an aggressive, abrasive politician. And yet he was an idealist. Of course he needed a fight, and he expended all available energy on eradicating the influence of the Serbian Radicals, those Serbian *frankovci*, believers in the barbed-wire fence theory of nationality: don't let anyone else in, they'll steal our souls, turn us into Magyars, Croats, whatever. Alas, it was the nationalist imagery of the Radicals of Jaša Tomić which prevailed. To this day, with rare exceptions, Serbs practice the politics of defense, the politics of insularity. The Pribićević of 1905 is nowhere to be found.

Jaša Tomić was no visionary, he did not found a new political school. His were derivative politics, simplistically applied lessons from the past, out of force of habit, but in very new circumstances. Where corporate politics had worked in the past, when aristocracies ruled and politics were the domain of elites, privileges and patents could assure the survival of any group, at least as well as any other method. When religious and linguistic communities became national communities, those privileges could simply be transferred to the new entities, which were often the same as the old ones, but with new names. Tomić (and for that matter all the states' rights politicians among Czechs, Hungarians, and Croats) relied on the precedent and the continuity. Unfortunately, as older communities became national, their attachment to territory grew apace. And when communities were intermingled, that attachment forced the old politics of privilege into contradictions it could not overcome—how could imperial rescripts, patents, and privileges that applied to people as groups deal with conflicts rooted in definitions of nations' territories? Croatian state's rights could not be accommodated to the Serbian demand that privileges given to Orthodox Christians in the seventeenth century be interpreted as granting territorial autonomy in the nineteenth century. Thus it was that when Tomić argued that the Radicals wished for the transformation of older cultural privileges into territorial ones, his goals were thrust into conflict with those of the *pravaši*. Croatia and Habsburg Serbia would have overlapped. The only solutions were to deny that your neighbor was a Serb (if you were a Starčevićite) or a Croat (if you were an adherent of the Vuk Karadžić school of linguistics), to propose liberal constitutional solutions (the Independents' route), or to appeal to the powers in Budapest and Vienna for modern privileges (the Radicals' approach).

Ethnic and Civic Nationalism in the Croatian Context

This book's subjects speak about the prospects for stateless peoples to become political in the nineteenth century, a century of mass politics in which the image of the unification of Germany seduced nationalists throughout East-Central Europe and the Balkans, without falling into the trap of acting defensively and collectively (as ethnic nationalists). The lesson of the story of the activity of the Serbian Independent party to 1914 is that the ethnic model for political action defeated the civic model. The Serbian Independent party tried to avoid the trap and failed. The straightforward imagery of the nation under siege simply proved too strong. Still, there are a variety of ways to conceive of the Independents' transformation. The easy way is to propose that power corrupts: the Coalition, with the Independents leading the way, became the governing party in 1913–1914 in Croatia because it, the Coalition, was the most popular political alternative. The loyalty of the Coalition was necessary to the stability of the Tisza government, which then offered it the fruits of collaboration. Power thus had corrupted the pristine, Yugoslav, Coalition. That would explain its transformation, but it would cloak a much deeper truth about the process: the Serbian Independents entered into a patron-client relationship with Tisza because they believed that their Serbian community was under threat. Thus, ultimately, their faith in the civic, constitutionalist model of political participation had failed; what remained to them was the tried-and-true politics of barter, the corporate methods of their besieged Serbian forebears, who had concluded agreements with emperors to save their collective skins in a dangerous world of real and perceived enemies. The pact with Tisza was thus the modern analogue to the privileges of the 1690s.

The failure of the Serbs of Croatia to succeed with a civic alternative mirrored one of the major failures of the various governments of the Austrian half of the monarchy after 1867: to overcome the deeply ingrained habit of the imperial politics of patronage that were so much a part of being Habsburg. Francis Joseph was always more comfortable with governments like that of Count Edward Taafe, whose Iron Ring of the 1880s functioned on the basis of exchange: stability for privileges. Thus he kept the loyalty of Czechs, Poles, some Germans, and others who wished to protect their sinecures and their "historic rights" at the expense of finding a liberal, civic model that would alleviate ethnic competitiveness in their lands. The earlier liberal era (and no one could claim that Austria's Liberals had the solution to its nationality problems) was but a period of forced withdrawal for the emperor, for whom ignoring the diets and the hereditary nobility was betrayal of the family tradition and of his own instincts. Thus the monarchy's reputation for a schizophrenic cultural and intellectual life could be extended to its political life, its inability to come to terms with political modernity just as anachronistic and deceptive as its social mores. In such circumstances, the failure of Croatia's Serbs to deemphasize their nationality in favor of their citizenship would seem to be almost natural, and certainly not surprising. Just as in Habsburg cultural and intellectual life dissonance foreshadowed truly novel forms of social, cultural, and artistic inquiry, in politics the failure of the monarchy to modernize was not merely an interesting piece of trivia—it foreshadowed the failure of democracy in the lands of the former monarchy after the First World War, when habits and convictions learned in the haunted house of Habsburg statecraft were transferred to new entities without the tradition, the dynasty, or even the tenuous social stability of the old monarchy. Thus they failed.

The Serbs of the Habsburg monarchy were cursed by demography. Among South Slavs, none but the Serbs were so widely dispersed, intermixed with other peoples who were linguistically so closely related to them. When romantic nationalism invaded the lands of southeastern Europe, those differences could have been accentuated or ameliorated in the name of one or the other national idea: Serbianism, Croatianism, Yugoslavism. A rash of solutions were proposed: Serbs and Croats are different; all are Serbs, or all are Croats; they are Yugoslavs. The first set appealed to many; the second comprised a rhetorical device designed to ignore what did not serve one's interest; the third was utopian. Once the intellectuals among them invested so heavily in the first option by accentuating the differences, it became likely that conflict would ensue. Freud's narcissism of minor differences took over:

if Serbs and Croats were really to be different peoples, then what little separated them had to be enhanced. This strategy was explosive—to enhance the differences among people who lived together would only make of Croatia, Bosnia, Dalmatia, and southern Hungary a battleground of conflicting claims. The only other alternative then was to admit national difference without allowing it to wreak havoc on interethnic relations. In other words, to allow for nationality, but not to allow it to be the foundation of political activity. Then, perhaps, intermixed populations might be able to interact civilly. Thus the approach of the Serbian Independents, the Croatian Progressives, and many others after 1903.

It remains to evaluate the behavior of our protagonists in light of the dichotomy presented in the first chapter. Can we accept the idea that the Serbian Independents attempted a civic solution to the Croato-Serbian national confusion? The answer is yes and no. First, use of the concept of civic nationalism has always presupposed the existence of some sort of fundamental political values associated with the civic identity. It has secondarily proposed that political actors behave according to those values regardless of their cultural (ethnic) identity. Thus French nationalism supposedly incorporates the values of the French revolution into French national identity, allowing anyone to assume that identity as long as they share the value orientation. American national identity is presumably of the same sort—defined by values rather than culture. As an obvious corollary to that rule, political activity in a state whose national identity is civic would never be limited to citizens of a certain culture or ethnic background—instead, it would be limited to citizens who accept the values inherent in nationhood. Civic nationhood is not exclusionary, it is inclusionary. Political action in such a system is based on a constitutional system respecting the rights of the individual, rather than the member of an ethnic group.

How does Croatia, and how do Croatia's various leading political parties after 1903, do on the test of civic nationhood? They fail the test of values, but pass the test of actions. In other words, Croatian political nationhood did not propose any profound and attractive, never mind revolutionary, values on which to found a civic idea. However, the parties in question did propose to act as though there were such an idea, thus proposing constitutional governance without any central values beyond Croatian historical statehood. This was not enough, in any case not enough for the Serbian parties. Whereas the great French and American examples of civic identity emerged in revolutionary conditions, in Croatia political parties that responded favorably to the idea of a Croatian political nation did so in advance of the revolution, should it ever come. The Serbian Independents accepted Croatian political nationhood as a promise, a promise that they believed would eventually bear fruit in a Croatia in which Serbs need not fear for their cultural survival as long as they behaved as citizens of Croatia. But in such conditions, the Serbian acceptance of the Croatian promise was extremely tenuous, and any assumption that Croatian political nationhood was a civic idea and not an assimilationist/ethnic one would have to be proved over and over again. As it turned out, the Serbian Independents and their constituents chose to abandon the project rather quickly, following the trials of 1909, having become convinced that their salvation lay not in the civic idea but in ethnic solidarity.

There have been only two instances when the notion of ethnic community has been rejected as a political foundation in Yugoslav politics, and this book has described one of them (the other was the communist experiment, which was quite different from that described here). Between 1903 and 1914 Serbian leaders quit trying only to unify the ethnic territory of the Serbian people and Croatian leaders relaxed their insistence on rigid respect for the identity of Croatian nation and state—only then and for a short time after 1945. Yet it is clear that those two conditions had to be met for Serbs and Croats to coexist in peace. Unfortunately, those leaders of the two peoples with the moral authority to guide them failed to recognize that fact.

NOTES

1. The Croatian Background

1. I have relied on John V. A. Fine, Jr., *The Early Medieval Balkans: A Critical Survey from the Sixth to the Late Twelfth Century* (Ann Arbor: University of Michigan Press, 1983), 251–91, in my discussion of medieval Croatia.

2. Fine, *Early Medieval Balkans*, 262.

3. Katalin Peter, "The Later Ottoman Period and Royal Hungary, 1606–1711," and Horst Haselsteiner, "Cooperation and Confrontation Between Rulers and the Noble Estates, 1711–1790," in Peter Sugar et al., eds., *A History of Hungary* (Bloomington: Indiana University Press, 1990), 100–08, 142–43, describe the effects of these wars on Hungary.

4. Charles Ingrao, *The Habsburg Monarchy, 1618–1815* (Cambridge: Cambridge University Press, 1994), 214–15.

5. For characterizations of the fluctuating nature of populations and their faiths in the early medieval period, see Fine, *The Early Medieval Balkans*, and *The Late Medieval Balkans: A Critical Survey from the Late Twelfth Century to the Ottoman Conquest* (Ann Arbor: University of Michigan Press, 1987).

6. A good survey of the Serbian Orthodox communities of the Habsburg monarchy is Wayne S. Vucinich, "The Serbs in Austria-Hungary," *Austrian History Yearbook* 3, pt. 2 (1967): 3–47.

7. A recent interesting discussion of the usage of the term Vlach comes from Drago Roksandic, *Srbi u hrvatskoj od 15. stoljeća do naših dana* (Zagreb: Vjesnik, 1991), 15–18.

8. As befits a region of such complexity today, Bosnia's medieval demography is confusing and contentious. The most recent scholarship concludes that Bosnia's population (the population of the medieval Bosnian state, but just as plausibly of the territory of the modern Bosnian state) had no distinct, deeply rooted religious character. Neither Rome nor Constantinople had succeeded in winning the faith of Bosnians except temporarily—as the priest made his way through the village, he could count that village as his own. Bosnia also had its own Bosnian church—one whose character is still debated, although the growing consensus of western historians holds that it was not a Bogumil, heretical, church but a product of Bosnia's isolation, an autonomous church that was a branch of the Roman one. The ephemerality of faith in Bosnia did

not end with the Ottoman conquest, in spite of the addition of the Ottoman administrative structure, which regulated the Orthodox church (which had an official status after the conquest of Constantinople) and allowed the Franciscan order to represent the Roman church in Bosnia. The faith of the people of Bosnia probably remained syncretic, and the addition of Islam to the mix only increased the likelihood that individuals would borrow from the most applicable available orthodoxy in their daily lives. See John V. A. Fine, Jr., *The Bosnian Church: A New Interpretation* (Boulder, Colo: East European Monographs, 1975), and Noel Malcolm, *Bosnia: A Short History* (New York: New York University Press, 1994), 27–42.

9. On the Military Frontier, see Gunther Rothenberg, *The Austrian Military Border in Croatia, 1522–1747* (Urbana: University of Illinois Press, 1960), and *The Military Border in Croatia, 1740–1881* (Chicago: University of Chicago Press, 1966); Jozo Tomasevich, *Peasants, Politics, and Economic Change in Yugoslavia* (Stanford: Stanford University Press, 1955), 74–81; Dragutin Pavličević, ed., *Vojna Krajina: Povijesni pregled, historiografija, rasprave* (Zagreb: Sveučilišna naklada Liber, 1984).

10. Radoslav Grujić, *Apologija srpskoga naroda u Hrvatskoj i Slavoniji i njegovih glavnih obeležja; povodom "Optužnice kr. držav. odvjetnika u Zagrebu od 12. I. 1909 g.* (Novi Sad: Štamparija učiteljskog deoničar. društva "Natošević," 1909), 92–94.

11. Grujić, *Apologija*, 101–03.

12. Ibid., 107.

13. Uskoci (sing. Uskok) were Orthodox Christian migrants from Dalmatia and Montenegro. They achieved reknown as bandits in northern Dalmatia.

14. On Žumberak, see Fedor Moačanin, "Vojna Krajina do Kantonskog uredjenja, 1787," in Pavličević, ed., *Vojna Krajina*, 27–28.

15. Grujić, *Apologija*, 109–111.

16. Moačanin, "Vojna krajina," 40.

17. Grujić, *Apologija*, 116.

18. Ibid., 109; Moačanin, "Vojna krajina," 37–39.

19. Grujić, *Apologija*, 122.

20. Jovan Radonić and Mita Kostić, *Srpske privilegije od 1690 to 1792* (Belgrade: Naučna knjiga, 1954).

21. Moačanin, "Vojna krajina," 37–38.

22. Ibid., 47–50.

23. John R. Lampe and Marvin R. Jackson, *Balkan Economic History, 1550–1950* (Bloomington: Indiana University Press, 1982), 63.

24. Djoko Slijepčević, *Od početka XIX veka do kraja drugog svetskog rata*, v. 2 of *Istorija srpske pravoslavne crkve* (Munich: 1966), 23 ff.; Grujić, *Apologija*, 96 ff.; Moačanin, "Vojna krajina," 42.

25. Roksandić, *Srbi u hrvatskoj*, 36–38.

26. Slijepčević, *Od početka*, 24.

27. Roksandić, *Srbi u hrvatskoj*, 50.

28. Keith Hitchins, *The Rumanian National Movement in Transylvania, 1780–1849* (Cambridge, Mass.: Harvard University Press, 1969), 53.

29. On the Nagodba, see Mirjana Gross and Agneza Szabo, *Prema hrvatskome grad-janskom društvu: Društveni razvoj u civilnoj Hrvatskoj i Slavoniji šezdesetih i sedamdesetih godina 19. stoljeća* (Zagreb: Globus, 1992), 221–38; Hodimir Sirotković and Lujo Mar-getić, *Povijest država i prava naroda SFR Jugoslavije* (Zagreb: Školska knjiga, 1988), 147–56; Josip Šarinić, *Nagodbena hrvatska: Postanak i osnove ustavne organizacije* (Za-greb: Nakladni zavod Matice Hrvatske, 1972).

30. Mirko Valentić, "Hrvatsko-slavonska vojna krajina," in Pavličević, ed., *Vojna krajina*, 83, notes that in Lika *pukovnija* in the 1850s there was an Orthodox majority (51,010 to 25,846; 66 percent); same in Banska I (40,860 to 20,281; 67 percent), and Banska II (33,898 to 19,380; 64 percent), with the other number being combined Catholic/Uniates. Vasilije Krestić, "Srbi u Habsburškoj Monarhiji, 1849–1868," in Vladimir Stojančević, ed., *Istorija srpskog naroda*, v. 5, pt. 2, *Od prvog ustanka do berlin-skog kongresa, 1804–1878* (Belgrade: Srpska književna zadruga, 1981), 136, asserts that the Lika Regiment was 70 percent Serb in 1850s; the Banska I was 67 percent Serb; and the Banska II was 62.2 percent; additionally, he notes that the Petrovaradin Regiment was 63.2 percent Serb.

31. Andrija Radenić, "Srbi u Habsburškoj Monarhiji, 1868–1878," in Vladimir Stojančević, ed., *Istorija srpskog naroda*, v. 5, pt. 2, *Od prvog ustanka do berlinskog kon-gresa, 1804–1878* (Belgrade: Srpska književna zadruga, 1981), 251.

32. Mirko Valentić, *Vojna krajina i pitanje njezina sjedinjenja s hrvatskom 1849–'881* (Zagreb: Sveučilište u Zagrebu, 1981), is the most recent and most thorough study of the Military Frontier in this period. Valentić has been criticized by Krestić for ignor-ing Serbs in his study; see Krestić's "Neprihvatljive ocene o Srbima Vojne krajine," in *Srpsko-hrvatski odnosi i jugoslovenska ideja u drugoj polovini XIX veka* (Belgrade: Nova Knjiga, 1988), 385–410. The process by which the Military Frontier was absorbed by Croatia actually lasted nearly twenty years. The imperial authorization for the incor-poration of the region came in 1869. See also Gross and Szabo, *Prema hrvatskome gradjanskom društvu*, 485–507.

33. Jaroslav Šidak et al., *Povijest hrvatskog naroda 1860–1914* (Zagreb: Školska kn-jiga, 1968), 83.

34. One source for 1900 divided populations by mother tongue and concluded that there were 1,490,672 Croats (61.69 percent) and 610,908 Serbs (25.28 percent) in Croa-tia (Josip Lakatoš, *Narodna statistika* [Osijek: Naklada Radoslava Bačića, 1914], 12). Another source notes that there were 612,604 Orthodox Christians (25.53 percent) in Croatia, which seems to confirm the first figure for speakers of "Serbian" (R. Signjar, ed., *1875–1915 Statistički atlas Kraljevina Hrvatske i Slavonije* [Zagreb: Tisak i litografija Kraljevske i zemaljske tiskare, 1915], 7). Lakatoš states that there were 644,955 Serbs (24.60 percent) in 1910.

35. Radenić, "Srbi u Hrvatskoj i Slavoniji, 1868–1878," 164.

36. Gross and Szabo, *Prema hrvatskome gradjanskom društvu*, 45. Valentić indicates that the figure for nonagricultural population was .007 percent in 1857, but that figure seems amazingly low; in "Hrvatsko-slavonska vojna krajina," 83–84.

37. Gross and Szabo, *Prema hrvatskome gradjanskom društvu*, 44.

38. Charles Jelavich, *South Slav Nationalisms: Textbooks and Yugoslav Union Before 1914* (Columbus: Ohio State University Press, 1990), 53–54.

39. Valentić, "Hrvatsko-slavonska vojna krajina," 89.

40. Gross and Szabo, *Prema hrvatskome gradjanskom društvu*, 413.

41. Mirjana Gross, *Počeci moderne hrvatske: Neoapsolutizam u civilnoj Hrvatskoj i Slavoniji 1850-1860* (Zagreb: Globus, 1985), 299.

42. Ibid., 299.

43. The only description of schooling in the Military Frontier in the nineteenth century that I have found is in Valentić, "Hrvatsko-slavonska vojna krajina," 72–73; he only notes that there were at least 104 schools in the frontier in 1820, with the Karlovac and Slavonian frontiers best served and Banija the worst. By 1870, there were about 549. He offers no religious breakdown. The conditions of schooling were far worse in the frontier than in Civil Croatia/Slavonia: teachers were not respected, well-paid, or well-treated; teachers were often virtually uneducated; and the language of instruction was often German.

44. Valentić, "Hrvatsko-slavonska vojna krajina," 89.

45. Gross, *Počeci*, 298.

46. Ibid., 293; Krestić, "Srbi u Habsburškoj Monarhiji," 138.

47. Krestić, "Srbi u Habsburškoj Monarhiji," 138. Several descriptive reports of conditions in Croatian schools by school administrators and inspectors can be found in Vasilije Krestić, ed., *Gradja o Srbima u Hrvatskoj i Slavoniji (1848–1914)* (Belgrade: Beogradski izdavačko-grafički zavod, 1995), v. 1, 168–87.

48. The best discussion of this legislation can be found in Jelavich, *South Slav Nationalisms*, 41–45, and Gross and Szabo, *Prema hrvatskome gradjanskom društvu*, 402–12; see also Mirjana Gross, "Zakon o osnovnim školama 1874. i srpsko pravoslavno školstvo," *Zbornik radova o povijesti i kulturi srpskog naroda u Socijalističkoj Republici Hrvatskoj* 1 (1988): 75–118; James Krokar, "Liberal Reform in Croatia, 1872–75: The Beginnings of Modern Croatia Under Ban Ivan Mažuranić" (Ph. D. diss., Indiana University, 1980), 117–204; Radenić, "Srbi u Habsburškoj Monarhiji, 1868–1878," 251–53.

49. Antun Cuvaj, *Gradja za povijest školstva Kraljevine Hrvatske i Slavonije od najstarijih vremena do danas* (Zagreb: Naklada Kr. Hrv.-Slav.-Dalm. zem. vlade, odjela za bogoštovlje i nastave, 1911), 1–362.

50. Gross, "Zakon o osnovnim školama," 90; Šidak et al., *Povijest*, 87–88.

51. Krestic, *Gradja*, v. 2, 131.

52. Radenić, "Srbi u Habsburškoj Monarhiji, 1868–1878," 154, 263.

53. Ibid., 264.

54. Lazar Rakić, *Jaša Tomić (1856–1922)* (Novi Sad: Matica Srpska, 1986), 242–46, and *Radikalna stranka u Vojvodini (do početka XX veka)* (Novi Sad: Institut za izučavanje istorije Vojvodine, 1975), 275–79 (hereafter, *Radikalna stranka* I).

55. Mato Artuković, *Ideologija srpsko-hrvatskih sporova (*Srbobran, *1884–1902)* (Zagreb: Naprijed, 1991), 51–52.

56. Rakić, *Radikalna stranka I*, 277.

57. Artuković, *Ideologija srpsko-hrvatskih sporova*, 54–55.

58. Ibid., 55–56.

59. This formulation of the process of nation building among the peoples of Eastern Europe comes from Ernest Gellner, *Nations and Nationalism* (Ithaca: Cornell University Press, 1983); Benedict Anderson, *Imagined Communities: Reflections on the Origin and Spread of Nationalism*, rev. ed. (London: Verso, 1991), makes the same point regarding elites and their role in the transmission of national identity.

60. Anderson, *Imagined Communities*.

61. On the Illyrian movement, see Elinor Murray Despalatović, *Ljudevit Gaj and the Illyrian Movement* (Boulder, Colo.: East European Monographs, 1975); Jaroslav Šidak et al., *Hrvatski narodni preporod-Ilirski pokret* (Zagreb: Školska knjiga, 1988), covers the movement and Croatian history in general during the period.

62. On the language issue, see Ivo Banac, *The National Question in Yugoslavia: Origins, History, Politics* (Ithaca: Cornell University Press, 1984), 77–80.

63. On Vuk Karadžić, see Duncan Wilson, *The Life and Times of Vuk Stefanović Karadžić, 1787–1864* (Oxford: Oxford University Press, 1970), a well-written synthesis of Yugoslav works; it is not scholarly, and it does not treat the language question in Vuk's work in depth. For that subject, the best short English discussion is in Banac, *The National Question*, 80–81. See also Miodrag Popović, *Vuk Stef. Karadžić 1787–1864* (Belgrade: Nolit, 1987), 295–305.

64. Karadžić's article entitled "Srbi svi i svuda," which appeared in 1836, first presented his ideas on the matter; it concluded that all who spoke Stokavian were Serbs. It is available in Mil. S. Filipovic, ed., *Sabrana dela Vuka Karadžica* (Belgrade: Prosveta), v. 17, *Etnografski spisi*, 31–48.

65. Banac, *The National Question*, 80.

66. For a discussion of the historiography of the Načertanije, see Nikša Stančić, "Problem 'Načertanije' Ilije Garašanina u našoj historiografiji," *Historijski zbornik* 21–22 (1968–69): 179–96; see also Banac, *The National Question*, 83–85.

67. Stančić concludes that it was Great Serbian ("Problem 'Načertanije'," 195–96). Banac shares his view (*The National Question*, 83–85). Vasilije Krestić disagrees; he thinks that Garašanin was a Yugoslav. See his *Srpsko-hrvatski odnosi*, 267–92. For other opinions, see Stančić, passim.

68. Two articles by Vasilije Krestić, both published in *Srpsko-hrvatski odnosi*, address attempts by Croats to cooperate with the government of Serbia: "Srbi i revizija hrvatsko-ugarske nagodbe 1873. godine," 159–214, and "Garašanin i Hrvati," 267–92. They do not critically assess the failure of Serbian policy to accommodate itself to Croatian needs.

69. Rade Petrović, *Nacionalno pitanje u Dalmaciji u XIX stoljeću* (Sarajevo: Svjetlost, and Zagreb: Prosvjeta, 1982), 17–18.

70. Justin McCarthy, "Ottoman Bosnia, 1800–1878," in Mark Pinson, ed., *The Muslims of Bosnia-Hercegovina: Their Historic Development from the Middle Ages to the Dissolution of Yugoslavia* (Cambridge, Mass.: Harvard University Press, 1994), 81.

2. Serbs As Political Actors, 1867–1903

1. For the organization of the Croatian government after the Nagodba, see Sirotković, *Povijest država i prava*, 147–53; on the question of the ban's responsibility to the Sabor, see pp. 150 and 152 of the same work.

2. Theoretically, the Croatian Sabor dealt only with Croatian issues, while the Hungarian Parliament dealt with issues affecting the entire Hungarian half of the monarchy including Croatia. The Croatian delegation to the joint government only conferred on issues affecting Croatia. See ibid., 151.

3. On the Croatian national movement of 1883, see Dragutin Pavličević, *Narodni pokret 1883. u Hrvatskoj* (Zagreb: Sveučilišna naklada Liber, 1980).

4. Šidak et al., *Povijest*, 124.

5. They were placed in top administrative positions in the Croatian government; Frano Supilo, *Politika u Hrvatskoj*, edited with an introduction by Vaso Bogdanov (Zagreb: Kultura, 1953), 115. Supilo notes that "while therefore Count Khuen got his Croatian mandates through use of force which became legendary, he received Serbian mandates in Serbian districts not only without any sort of battle, but indeed with the goodwill and enthusiasm of Serbian voters" (114).

6. "Zakon od 14. Maja 1887. O uredjenju posala crkve grčkoistočne i o upotrebi ćirilice" and "Odredbe školskog zakona od 31. Oktobra 1888. Godine o konfesionalnim i srpskim autonomnim školama" in Krestić, *Gradja*, v. 2, 89–90, 131–33.

7. Artuković, *Ideologija srpsko-hrvatskih sporova* is a good study of the Independent party from 1884 to 1902. See also Krestić, *Istorija srpske štampe u Ugarskoj, 1791–1914* (Novi Sad: Matica Srpska, 1980), 238 ff. for a short discussion. The programs of all the Serbian parties in Croatia and Hungary are included in Vasilije Krestić and Radoš Ljušić, eds., *Programi i statuti srpskih političkih stranaka do 1918. godine* (Belgrade: Književne novine, 1991).

8. Supilo, *Politika*, 113–14. Supilo notes that in the five Sabor sittings during Khuen's time in office, there were a total of 460 representatives, of which 354 were government, 106 opposition. Of the government representatives, 224 were Croats, 130 Serbs; of the oppositionalists, 104 were Croats, only 2 Serbian. He demonstrates (convincingly) that if Serbs had been represented in the opposition in the same proportion as their population in Croatia, there would have been a minimum of 34 Serbian oppositionalists.

9. The historian of the Radical party is Lazar Rakić: *Radikalna stranka* I, and *Radikalna stranka u Vojvodini 1902–1919* (Novi Sad: Filozofski fakultet, 1983) (hereafter *Radikalna stranka* II). See also Andrija Radenić, "Borba za politička prava u južnoj Ugarskoj," in Andrej Mitrović, ed. *Istorija srpskog naroda*, v. 6, pt. 1, *Od berlinskog kongresa do ujedinjenja, 1878–1918* (Belgrade: Srpska književna zadruga, 1983), 534–37.

10. Rakić, *Jaša Tomić*.

11. Vasilije Krestić, "Politički, privredni, i kulturni život u Hrvatskoj i Slavoniji," in Andrej Mitrović, ed., *Istorija srpskog naroda*, v. 6, pt. 1, *Od berlinskog kongresa do*

ujedinjenja 1878–1918 (Belgrade: Srpska književna zadruga, 1983), 401.

12. Rakić, *Radikalna stranka* II, 203.

13. "Program Srpske narodne radikalne stranke u kraljevini Hrvatskoj i Slavoniji" (October 3, 1903), in Krestić, *Gradja*, v. 2, 357–69.

14. Rakić, *Radikalna stranka* II, 85.

15. Mirjana Gross, *Povijest pravaške ideologije* (Zagreb: Sveučilište u Zagrebu, Institut za hrvatsku povijest, 1973), is an outstanding monograph on the history of the ideology of the Party of Right and its progeny.

16. Grga Tuškan and Franko Potočnjak were two *domovinaši* who would later be active in the Croato-Serbian Coalition.

17. On the *domovinaši* and the *frankovci*, see Gross, *Povijest pravaške ideologije*, 260–81, 294–321, and Rene Lovrenčić, *Geneza politike 'novog kursa' u Hrvatskoj* (Zagreb: Sveučilište u Zagrebu, Institut za hrvatsku povijest, 1972), 53–88.

18. See especially Lovrenčić, *Geneza*, 40–42.

19. Often, Croats emphasize only the student demonstrations, Serbs only the Frankist anti-Serbian demonstrations. Vasilije Krestić, for instance, forgot to mention the students when speaking of the Frankist excesses in "O genezi genocida nad Srbima," 358, in *Srpsko-hrvatski odnosi;* Bogdan Krizman, one of Croatia's ablest historians of the period, reminded Krestić of this and other lapses in *Hrvatska u prvom svjetskom ratu: Hrvatsko-srpski politički odnosi* (Zagreb: Globus, 1989), 6. The preface (5–12) to the latter recent work is a short, able response to Krestić's provocative article.

20. *Omladina* means youth, but in politics it refers to any group that is young and has a fresh, new political perspective.

21. Jovan Banjanin et al., *Narodna misao* (Zagreb: Dionička tiskara, 1897).

22. Lovrenčić, *Geneza*, 41–45; Gross, *Povijest pravaške ideologije*, 316–18.

23. For a recent biographical sketch of Pribićević, see Bogdan Krizman, "Skica za biografiju Svetozara Pribićevića (1875–1936)," the afterword to Svetozar Pribićević, *Diktatura kralja Aleksandra* (Zagreb: Globus, 1990), 275–300.

24. August Cesarec, "Svetozar Pribićević, posveceno onima koji još u njega vjeruju," in Cesarec, *Eseji i putopisi* (Belgrade: Prosveta, 1964), 117. The article was originally published in 1924 in the Zagreb journal *Književna republika*.

25. Svetozar Pribićević, "Misao vodilja Srba i Hrvata," in Banjanin et al., *Narodna misao,* 49–77. See Vaso Bogdanov, "Hrvatska i srpska prošlost u interpretaciji S. Pribićevića," in *Likovi i pokreti* (Zagreb: Mladost, 1957), 225–35, for a critique of Pribićević's conceptions.

26. Pribićević, "Misao vodilja," 50.

27. Ibid., 55–56.

28. Ibid., 65.

29. Ibid., 76.

30. D. Dimović, "Historijsko državno pravo," in Banjanin et al., *Narodna misao,* 227–33.

31. Ibid., 229, 231, 232.

32. Ibid., 231.

33. Pribićević, "Misao vodilja," 50, 56.

34. Dušan Mangjer, "Zagreb, na uskrs 1897," in Banjanin et al., *Narodna misao*, 3.

35. Pribićević, "Misao vodilja," 73.

36. Ibid., 72; see also Lovrenčić, *Geneza*, 47–48.

37. Pribićević, "Misao vodilja," 73.

38. Ibid., 76.

39. Ibid., 67.

40. Stojanović, "Srbi i Hrvati," *Srpski kniževni glasnik* (Belgrade) 6, no. 1 (August 1902): 1149–59.

41. See Lovrenčić, *Geneza*, 144–48.

42. Regarding this, in 1928, Stojanović wrote Djuro Šurmin, a member of the Croato-Serbian Coalition from 1905 to 1918, that the article was not prompted by Khuen; Nikola Stojanović–Djuro Šurmin (November 19, 1928, Sarajevo), Nacionalna i Svevčilišna Biblioteka, Ostavština Djura Šurmina, 5896b. (Hereafter NSB, ODS, followed by number of document.)

43. *Stenografički zapisnici sabora Kraljevine Hrvatske, Slavonije, i Dalmacije (1901–1906)* (Zagreb: Tisak kraljevske zemaljske tiskare, 1903), v. 2, pt. 2, 40. (Hereafter, *SKH*.).

44. Ibid., 40–41.

45. Ibid., 41, 43.

46. Ibid., 111.

47. Ibid., 70.

48. Ibid., 122, 124 (Derenčin), 25 (Vrbanić).

49. Ibid., 27.

50. Rakić, *Radikalna stranka* I, 177; see also Rakić, *Jaša Tomić*, 157–58; Krestić, "Politički, privredni, i kulturni život," 420–22.

51. Rakić, *Radikalna stranka* II, 178; Rakić, *Jaša Tomić*, 158.

52. Lovrenčić, *Geneza*, 98.

53. Stojanović, "Srbi i Hrvati," 1158–59.

54. Lovrenčić, *Geneza*, 144–46.

55. Stjepan Radić, *Hrvati i Srbi*, in Stjepan Radić, *Politički spisi: Autobiografija/Clanci/Govori/Rasprave*, ed. Zvonomir Kulundžic (Zagreb: Znanje, 1971), 250–74.

56. Ibid., 256.

57. Ibid., 268.

58. "Svetozar Pribićević–Jovanu Pačuu" (Karlovac, September 18, 1902), in Krestić, *Gradja*, 340–41; "Zapisnik sednice Središnjeg odbora Srpske samostalne stranke održane 11. juna 1903" in Krestić, *Gradja*, 351–52.

59. "Letter of S. Pribićević to the heads of the Serbian opposition parties" (July 19, 1933, Paris), in Ljubo Boban, *Svetozar Pribićević u opoziciji 1928–1936* (Zagreb: Sveučilište u Zagrebu, Institut za hrvatsku povijest, 1973), 230.

60. Lovrenčić, *Geneza*, 143–224; Vaso Bogdanov, *Hrvatski narodni pokret 1903/4* (Zagreb: Jugoslavenska akademija znanosti i umjetnosti, 1961).

61. The term *skupština* usually refers to an official assembly of some sort. How-

ever, it can also denote meetings of political parties and their supporters or public rallies, most often designed to garner support for a political program.

62. Lovrenčić, *Geneza*, 164.

63. "Načelnik sreza iz Vrginmosta Ličko-krbavskoj županiji," in Krestić, *Gradja*, v. 2, 382–85; "Zapisnik sednice centralnog odbora Srpske samostalne stranke držane 27. maja 1904.," in ibid., 385–86.

64. Lovrenčić, *Geneza*, 182.

65. *Novi Srbobran* (Zagreb), December 22, 1903; quoted in Bogdanov, *Hrvatski narodni pokret*, 301.

66. *Obzor* (Horizon) was the organ of the Croatian Party of Right at this time; *Novi Srbobran* (Zagreb), August 8, 1903; quoted in Bogdanov, *Hrvatski narodni pokret*, 306.

67. *Novi Srbobran* (Zagreb), January 4, 1904; quoted in Bogdanov, *Hrvatski narodni pokret*, 307.

68. From a meeting of the Independents in Osijek in October 1903; Bogdanov, *Hrvatski narodni pokret*, 307.

69. See Wayne Vucinich, *Serbia Between East and West: The Events of 1903–1908* (Stanford: Stanford University Press, 1954), on these events.

70. Frano Supilo, "Preokret," *Novi List* (Rijeka), August 28, 1903, in Frano Supilo, *Politički spisi: Članci/Govori/Pisma/Memorandumi*, ed. Dragovan Šepić (Zagreb: Znanje, 1970), 260–62.

71. Miroslav Krleža, "Razgovor sa sjenom Frana Supila," in *Knjiga studija i putopisa* (Zagreb: Biblioteka nezavisnih pisaca, 1939), 99. This article first appeared in 1925 in the Croatian journal *Hrvat*.

72. For a recitation of these complaints, see Ante Trumbić, "Govor na sjednici dalmatinskog sabora 7. studenoga 1903. godine," in *Izabrani spisi*, ed. Ivo Petrinović (Split: Književni krug, 1986), 37–57.

73. On this episode, see Ivo Petrinović, *Politička misao Frana Supila* (Split: Književni krug, 1988), 60; Lovrenčić, *Geneza*, 185–225, esp. 192; and Milan Marjanović, *Savremena Hrvatska* (Belgrade: Srpska književna zadruga, 1913), 323–24.

74. Supilo, *Politika*, 132–33.

75. On the genesis of the New Course, see Supilo, *Politika;* Ante Trumbić, "Riječka rezolucija," in *Izabrani spisi*, 156–219; Lovrenčić, *Geneza*, 185–243; Dragovan Šepić, "Političke koncepcije Frana Supila," in Supilo, *Politički spisi*, 26–35.

76. Trumbić, "Govor," 46–54.

77. Frano Supilo–Šima Mazzura (May 17, 1903, Rijeka), in Hamdija Hajdarhodžić et al., eds., "Korespondencija Frana Supila iz perioda 1891–1914," *Arhivski vjesnik 6* (1963): 93 (hereafter, Hajdarhodžić et al., "Korespondencija").

78. Krleža, "Razgovor," 99.

79. Frano Supilo, "Udri, ali čuj," *Novi list* (Rijeka), October 10, 1902, in Supilo, *Politički spisi*, 250–53.

80. Frano Supilo, "Najvažniji dogodjaji na dnevnome redu," *Novi list* (Rijeka), June 23, 1903, in Supilo, *Politički spisi*, 255.

3. The Birth and Short Life of the New Course, 1903–1907

1. Frano Supilo, "Hrvatska i Ugarska," *Novi list* (Rijeka), April 30, 1905, in Supilo, *Politički spisi*, 287–91.

2. Ante Trumbić, "Dalmacija u borbi izmedju Ugarske i Austrije," *Narodni list* (Zadar), March 11, 1905, in Trumbić, *Izabrani spisi*, 65.

3. Frano Supilo–Ante Trumbić (March 16, 1905, Rijeka), in Hajdarhodžić et al., "Korespondencija," 114–15.

4. Frano Supilo, "Madžaronski Jelačići," *Novi list* (Rijeka), March 25, 1905, in Supilo, *Politički spisi*, 286.

5. Ante Trumbić, "Riječka rezolucija," in Trumbić, *Izabrani spisi*, 177.

6. "Pokret," *Pokret* (Zagreb), April 17, 1904, 1.

7. "Starčevićanstvo i mladja generacija," *Pokret* (Zagreb), May 8, 1904, 3.

8. This discussion is drawn from articles entitled "Srpsko pitanje u hrvatskom svijetlu," (I–IX), that appeared in *Pokret* (Zagreb), from July to September 1904.

9. Dimitrije Djordjević, "Pokušaji srpsko-ugarske saradnje i zajedničke akcije 1906. godine," in *Istorija XX veka: Zbornik radova* 2 (1961): 353–82.

10. Frano Supilo–Ante Trumbić (April 4, 1905, Rijeka), in Hajdarhodžić et al., "Korespondencija," 115–16; see also Supilo, *Politika*, 155–59.

11. Frano Supilo–Ante Trumbić (April 27, 1905, Rijeka), in Hajdarhodžić et al., "Korespondencija," 117–18.

12. Dimitrije Djordjević, *Carinski rat Austro-Ugarske i Srbije, 1906–1911* (Belgrade: Istorijski institut, 1962), 570.

13. Jovan M. Jovanović [Inostranac], "Ugarska kriza," *Srpski književni glasnik* 15, no. 10 (May 1905): 791–93.

14. Frano Supilo–Ante Trumbić (June 21, 1905, Rijeka), Hajdarhodžić et al., "Korespondencija," 118–19.

15. Frano Supilo–Pero Čingrija (December 14, 1905, Rijeka), in Hajdarhodžić et al., "Korespondencija," 131–32. The Živkovic in question was Ljubomir, a member of Stojanović's Independent Radical party in Serbia.

16. Trumbić, "Riječka Rezolucija," 192–95. In R. W. Seton-Watson, *The Southern Slav Question and the Habsburg Monarchy* (New York: Howard Fertig, 1969), 393–94, there is an English translation.

17. Bogdan Medaković, Svetozar Pribićević, and four other Independents; Djordje Krasojević, Žarko Miladinović, Jovan Radivojević-Vačić, and Milivoj Babić of the Serbian Radical party; and thirteen members of the Serbian National party in Dalmatia were present. For an English translation, see Seton-Watson, *The Southern Slav Question*, 395–96.

18. *SKH*, 1901–1906, v. 5, pt. 2, 966.

19. "Konferencija predstavnika srpskih stranaka u Zadru," *Novi Srbobran* (Zagreb), October 17, 1905, 1.

20. Andrija Radenić, ed. *Austro-ugarska i Srbija, 1903–1918: Dokumenti iz Bečkih arhiva* (Belgrade: Istorijski institut, 1973–1985), v. 3, 488–89.

21. *SKH*, 1901–1906, v. 5, pt. 2, 924.

22. Ibid., 903.

23. Ibid., 958.

24. Ibid., 959.

25. Ibid., 926.

26. Ibid., 962.

27. "A šta to bi na Reci," *Branik* (Novi Sad), October 7, 1905; quoted in Kosta Mi-lutinović, *Vojvodina i Dalmacija 1790–1914* (Novi Sad: Institut za izučavanje istorije Vojvodine, 1973), 361.

28. "Srpsko-hrvatski sporazum," *Novi Srbobran* (Zagreb), November 15, 1905, 1.

29. "Narode," *Pokret* (Zagreb), December 14, 1905, 1; "Narode," *Novi Srbobran* (Zagreb), December 14, 1905, 1.

30. "Konačni rezultat saborskih izbori," *Novi Srbobran* (Zagreb), May 7, 1906, 1. See also Supilo, *Politika*, 171–72.

31. "Naši delegati i Pejačević," *Novi Srbobran* (Zagreb), May 29, 1906, 1; Djuro Šurmin, the secretary of the executive committee of the Coalition, reported this agreement to Vatroslav Jagić in a letter of May 28, 1906: Djuro Šurmin–Vatroslav Jagić (May 28, 1906, Budapest), Nacionalna i sveučilišna biblioteka, Ostavština Vatroslava Jagića, R4610b (hereafter, NSB, OVJ); Frano Supilo–Pero Čingrija (June 1, 1906, Rijeka), in Hajdarhodžić et al., "Korespondencija," 143.

32. Frano Supilo–Ante Trumbić (June 6, 1906, Budapest), in Hajdarhodžić et al., "Korespondencija," 144–45; "Narodne tekovine—uspjesi koalicije," *Novi Srbobran* (Zagreb), June 2, 1906, 1.

33. "Naši delegati i Pejačević," *Novi Srbobran* (Zagreb), June 29, 1906, 1.

34. Frano Supilo–Pero Čingrija (June 1, 1906, Rijeka), in Hajdarhodžić et al., "Korespondencija," 143.

35. Note of July 4, 1907, in Iso Kršnjavi, *Zapisci iža kulisa hrvatske politike*, ed. Ivan Krtalić (Zagreb: Mladost, 1986), 291.

36. Frano Supilo–Ante Trumbić (June 6, 1906, Budapest), in Hajdarhodžić et al., "Korespondencija," 144–45.

37. Supilo, *Politika*, 128; Josip Horvat, *Supilo: Život jednoga hrvatskoga političara* (Zagreb: Binoza, 1938), 151; Mirjana Gross, *Vladavina hrvatsko-srpske koalicije 1906–1907* (Belgrade: Institut društvenih nauka, Odeljenje za istorijske nauke, 1960), 42.

38. Horvat, *Supilo*, 151.

39. Nikolić, according to Supilo, constantly "provoked crises and friction" within the Coalition; Supilo, *Politika*, 178. He noted at the time that "Nikolić is a little *jugo-nast*, something of the 'old school,' and something of the 'child of Zagreb.'" By "child of Zagreb" I presume he means that Nikolić was involved in the old patronage politics that Supilo saw in Zagreb; Frano Supilo–Ante Trumbic (December 27, 1906, Rijeka), in Hajdarhodžić et al., "Korespondencija," 161.

40. Kršnjavi, *Zapisci*, 461.

41. "Kandidati srpske narodne samostalne stranke za izbore za narodno-crkveni sabor," *Novi Srbobran* (Zagreb), November 21, 1906, 1. On his election to the delegation,

see *SKH*, 1906–1910, v. 1, 61; Arhiv Hrvatske, Ostavština Djura Šurmina, box 1, folder a, number 21 (hereafter: AH, ODS, 1.a.21): meeting of delegation in Budapest of April 29, 1907; 1.a.22: meeting of delegation in Budapest of April 30, 1907; 1.a.24: meeting of delegation in Budapest of May 1, 1907; 1.a.25: meeting of delegation in Budapest of May 1, 1907. See also Supilo, *Politika*, 188–93, in which he describes how Peleš got into the Independent party.

42. "Bude," *Narodno jedinstvo* (Zagreb), March 28, 1914, 4.

43. Frano Supilo–Pero Čingrija (June 1, 1906, Rijeka); Frano Supilo–Ante Trumbić (June 6, 1906, Budapest); and Frano Supilo-Pero Čingrija (September 24, 1906, Rijeka), in Hajdarhodžić et al., "Korespondencija," 143, 144, 153.

44. Supilo, *Politika*, 178.

45. Gross, *Vladavina*, 23.

46. Gross and others have identified the specific interests of various members of the Croato-Serbian Coalition. Supilo, according to Gross, was the only member of the Coalition with no outside financial interests. Rene Lovrenčić analyzed Supilo's economic orientation in two articles: "Ekonomska problematika u Supilovu 'Novom listu' 1903–1905," in *Radovi Filozofskog fakulteta* (Zagreb: Sveučilište u Zagrebu, Odsjek za povijest, 1960), v. 3, and "Ekonomska problematika u Supilovu 'Novom listu' 1906–1914," in *Radovi* (Zagreb: Sveučilište u Zagrebu, Institut za hrvatsku povijest, 1974), v. 6, 129–269. Among Serbs, Medaković and Muačević of the Independent party were landowners and founders of the Serbian Bank; Muačević was also vice-president of the Slavonian Estate Society and owned part of the Osijek Sugar Factory; Popović of the Independent party was a lawyer who worked for the Mitrovica Savings Bank in Srijemska Mitrovica and represented industrialists in Srijem; Pribićević and Banjanin were "known to have ties with the Serbian Bank." Of the Radicals, Krasojević and Miša Mihailović were on the directorates of the National Credit Bank in Srijemski Karlovci, and Miladinović was on the directorate of the Serbian Economic Bank in Ruma; see Andrija Radenić, *Položaj i borba seljaštva u Sremu od kraja XIX veka do 1914* (Belgrade: Naučno delo, 1958), 96, 259.

47. Gross, *Vladavina*, 52–54.

48. "Odgovor 'Zastavi'," *Novi Srbobran* (Zagreb), April 2, 1906, 1.

49. Supilo, *Politika*, 178.

50. These newspapers included *Novi Srbobran*, *Zastava* (of the Radical party), and others, including *Srpsko kolo* (Serbian Circle) of Zagreb, *Sloboda* (Liberty) of Srijemska Mitrovica, *Srbin* (The Serb) of Gospić, and *Srpska misao* (The Serbian Idea) of Srijemski Karlovci (all Independent organs); and *Narodni glasnik* (The National Herald) of Zemun and later *Srpski glasnik* (The Serbian Herald) of Zagreb (both Radical organs).

51. Adam Pribićević, *Moj život* (Windsor, Canada, 1981), 10–12.

52. "Preokret kod hrvatskih Srba," *Sloboda* (Split), October 20, 1906, 1; "Sloboda," *Novi Srbobran* (Zagreb), October 13, 1906, 1.

53. Supilo, *Politika*, 172.

54. "Naša prva reč," *Narodni glasnik* (Zemun), June 20, 1906, 1.

55. "Zapisnik sednice Središnjeg odbora Radikalne stranke" (Srijemski Karlovci, February 2, 1907), in Krestić, *Gradja*, v. 2, 461–62.

56. "Zemunski kandidat," *Narodni glasnik* (Zemun), June 23, 1906, 1; see also "Hrvati u Zemunu," *Pokret* (Zagreb), May 9, 1906, 1, and June 20, 1906, 2 (several articles appeared in *Pokret* at this time with the same title).

57. "Hrvati u Zemunu," *Pokret* (Zagreb), June 20, 1906, 2.

58. "Hrvati u Zemunu," *Pokret* (Zagreb), June 26, 1906, 1; "Pangermani u Srijemu," *Pokret* (Zagreb), August 25, 1906, 1. The Radicals' first response came in "Zemun," *Narodni glasnik* (Zemun), September 19, 1906, 2.

59. "Germansko pitanje u Hrvatskoj," *Narodni glasnik* (Zemun), October 13, 1906, 1.

60. After igniting the German uproar, the Progressives did take part, but only superficially. See three articles entitled "Pangermanism u Srijemu," *Pokret* (Zagreb), August 25, September 7, and September 15, 1906. One Radical response to the situation is "Jovan Magarašević Djordju Krasojevicu" (Čepin, February 28, 1907), in Krestić, *Gradja*, v. 2, 464–65.

61. Lazar Rakić, "Manastirska uredba (1908)," in *Zbornik za istoriju Matica Srpska* (Novi Sad: Matica Srpska, Odeljenje za društvene nauke, 1983), v. 27, 11–15.

62. Rakić, "Manastirska uredba."

63. On Branković, see Slijepčević, *Od početka*, 205–09.

64. See four articles in *Novi Srbobran* (Zagreb) entitled "Kandidati srpske narodne samostalne stranke za izbore za narodno-crkveni sabor," November 21, 23, 24, and December 5, 1906, and "Izabrani poslanici srp. nar. samostalne stranke," December 7, 1906, all p. 1. The elections were held on December 5 and 6, 1906.

65. "Čast samostalaca," *Novi Srbobran* (Zagreb), December 12, 1906, 1.

66. "Poslije eksodusa samostalnih poslanika," *Novi Srbobran* (Zagreb), February 5, 1907, 1.

67. "Jedan ili dva," *Narodni glasnik* (Zemun), February 13, 1907, 1.

68. Šidak et al., *Povijest*, 230; Gross, *Vladavina*, 70; Petrinović, *Politička misao Frana Supila*, 85.

69. AH, ODS, 1.a.22: record of meeting of April 30, 1907 of the executive committee of the Croatian delegation to the Hungarian Parliament.

70. "Jedan ili dva," *Narodni glasnik* (Zemun), February 13, 1907, 1.

71. "Jedan ili dva," *Novi Srbobran* (Zagreb), April 8, 1907, 1.

72. Frano Supilo–Djordje Krasojević (April 4, 1907, Rijeka), in Hajdarhodžić et al., "Korespondencija," 171.

73. Frano Supilo–Pero Čingrija (April 3, 1907, Rijeka), ibid., 170.

74. "Proglas hrvatske delegacije," *Novi Srbobran* (Zagreb), July 1, 1907, 1; "Narode," *Narodni glasnik* (Zemun), July 3, 1907, 1. Part of the declaration is reprinted in Milutinović, *Vojvodina i Dalmacija*, 367.

75. One member of the Radical party, Živko Kostić, expressed general sentiments within the party in a letter to Krasojević in June: "The Radical party will not get popular through battle with the Magyars, just as a lack of solidarity in this battle will not harm it. And besides, what sort of concessions has the Serbian people in Croatia

gained for its stooping? . . . Why finally provoke an ever more personal conflict in Pest? Why experience threats from Wekerle?" ("Živko Kostić Djordju Krasojeviću" [Opatija, July 1, 1907], in Krestić, *Gradja*, v. 2, 469-70).

76. "Smemo li i dalje zajedno?" *Narodni glasnik* (Zemun), August 16, 1907, 1.

77. "Koalicija," *Narodni glasnik* (Zemun), August 19, 1907, 1.

78. AH, ODS, 1.b.21: notes of a meeting of the Croatian delegation in Budapest of August 2, 1907.

79. Gross, *Vladavina*, 206.

80. Frano Supilo–Pero Čingrija (August 19, 1907, Rijeka), in Hajdarhodžić et al., "Korespondencija," 177.

81. Frano Supilo–Pero Čingrija (August 19, 1907, Rijeka), ibid., 177. Mladen Lisavac was one of the two Radicals in the Croatian delegation in Budapest. Krasojević was the other.

82. "Radikalsko izdajstvo," *Novi Srbobran* (Zagreb), August 19, 1907, 1.

83. Supilo, *Politika*, 187.

84. Jaša Tomić, *Reč našoj braći u Srbiji* (Novi Sad: Srpska štamparija dra Svetozara Miletića, 1907), 16–17.

85. Jaša Tomić, *Samostalci iz Hrvatske i Slavonije i Samostalci iz Srbije* (Novi Sad: Srpska štamparija dra Svetozara Miletića, 1907).

4. Interlude: Persecution and Temptation, 1907–1909

1. Mirjana Gross, "Hrvatska uoči aneksije Bosne i Hercegovine," in *Istorija XX veka: Zbornik radova* (Belgrade) 3 (1962): 153–275.

2. Kršnjavi, *Zapisci*, 503–04, 505; Gross, "Hrvatska uoči aneksije," 171.

3. "Objava absolutizma," *Srbobran* (Zagreb), January 23, 1908, 1; Gross, "Hrvatska uoči aneksije," 171.

4. Gross, "Hrvatska uoči aneksije," 175.

5. "Naša riječ," *Narodni glasnik* (Zagreb), October 15, 1907, 1. See also "Uroš Popović Djordju Krasojeviću" (Zagreb, October 19, 1907), "Jovan Radivojević Vačić Djordju Krasojeviću" (Zemun, October 22, 1907), and "Stijepo Kobasica Djordju Krasojeviću" (Zagreb, October 24, 1907), in Krestić, *Gradja*, v. 2, 482–84.

6. "Zašto smo došli u Zagreb?" *Narodni glasnik* (Zagreb), October 15, 1907, 1; "Priznanje kapitulacije," *Srbobran* (Zagreb), April 3, 1908, 1.

7. "Današnji politički položaj II," *Narodni glasnik* (Zagreb), October 17, 1907, 1; "Što je prouzrokovalo današnju ustavnu krizu I," *Narodni glasnik* (Zagreb), October 19, 1907, 1; "Što je prouzrokovalo današnju ustavnu krizu III," *Narodni glasnik* (Zagreb), October 24, 1907, 1; "Što je prouzrokovalo današnju ustavnu krizu IV," *Narodni glasnik* (Zagreb), October 29, 1907, 1.

8. See "Rauh i radikali," *Srbobran* (Zagreb), January 14, 1908, 1; "U Rauhovoj službi," *Srbobran* (Zagreb), January 17, 1908, 1; "Na koljenima pred Wekerlom," *Srbobran* (Zagreb), January 25, 1908, 1; "Srpski radikali-izrodi," *Srbobran* (Zagreb),

January 28, 1908, 1; "Oni su protiv Beča," *Srbobran* (Zagreb), January 29, 1908, 1; and "Pakt sa Rauhom," *Srbobran* (Zagreb), February 1, 1908, 1.

9. "Rauh i radikali," *Srbobran* (Zagreb), January 14, 1908, 1.

10. Kršnjavi, *Zapisci*, 513.

11. *SKH*, 1908–1913, v. 1, 111.

12. Gross, "Hrvatska uoči aneksije," 194.

13. See "Koprcanje," *Novi Srbobran* (Zagreb), September 6, 1907, 1.

14. Radenić, *Položaj i borba*, 310; Rakić, *Radikalna stranka* II, 143.

15. "Krvava klika," *Narodni glasnik* (Zagreb), February 14, 1908, 1.

16. Radenić, *Položaj i borba*, 311.

17. "Pobjeda koalicije," *Srbobran* (Zagreb), February 29, 1908, 1; "Rezultat saborskih izbora dne. 14. februara," *Narodni glasnik* (Zagreb), February 27, 1908, 1; Gross, "Hrvatska uoči aneksije," 183; Supilo, *Politika*, 194–95; "Narodna pobjeda," *Srbobran* (Zagreb), February 29, 1908, 1.

18. *SKH*, 1908–1913, v. 1, 1–21; "Sabor je odgodjen," *Srbobran* (Zagreb), March 14, 1908, 1; Gross, "Hrvatska uoči aneksije," 187.

19. Gross, "Hrvatska uoči aneksije," 183.

20. "Proglas srpsko-hrvatske koalicije," *Srbobran* (Zagreb), March 21, 1908, 1; Supilo, *Politika*, 196–97.

21. "Rauh prijeti srpskom narodu," *Srbobran* (Zagreb), April 3, 1908, 1.

22. "Otvoreno pismo," *Srbobran* (Zagreb), April 10, 1908, 1; Gross, "Hrvatska uoči aneksije," 206–07.

23. "Otvoreno pismo," *Srbobran* (Zagreb), April 10, 1908, 1. On this and other aspects of the open letter and the effect that it had, see Seton-Watson, *Southern Slav Question*, 159–60.

24. "Izjava," *Srbobran* (Zagreb), April 15, 1908, 1; "Zagreb, 10./23. aprila," *Srbobran* (Zagreb), April 23, 1910, 1; "Afera barun Rauh-dr. Medaković završena," *Srbobran* (Zagreb), April 24, 1908, 1; "Afera Rauh-Medaković," *Srbobran* (Zagreb), April 25, 1908, 1. "Vitezovi bez obraza," *Srbobran* (Zagreb), April 28, 1908, 1.

25. "Suspenzija dr-a Manojlovića," *Srbobran* (Zagreb), May 2, 1908, 1; Djuro Šurmin–Vatroslav Jagić (May 2, 1908, Zagreb), NSB, OVJ, R4610b; "Atentat na sveučilište," *Srbobran* (Zagreb), April 28, 1908, 1; Gross, "Hrvatska uoči aneksije," 207. More on this incident can be found in Seton-Watson, *Southern Slav Question*, 160–61; and Kršnjavi, *Zapisci*, 525–26, 533.

26. "U borbi protiv nepravde i nasilja," *Srbobran* (Zagreb), May 4, 1908, 1.

27. "Koalicija i današnji političtki položaj," *Srbobran* (Zagreb), June 17, 1908, 1.

28. "Sjednica srpsko-hrvatske koalicije," *Srbobran* (Zagreb), March 4, 1908, 1.

29. Supilo, *Politika*, 195.

30. Ibid., 188–93.

31. Kršnjavi, *Zapisci*, 493–95.

32. Supilo, according to Kršnjavi, had "played all of his cards in Budapest" (ibid., 495).

33. Seton-Watson, *Southern Slav Question*, 257.

34. R. W. Seton-Watson, a personal friend, acknowledged that Supilo was an auto-crat. See R. W. Seton-Watson, "Frano Supilo: A Southern Slav Patriot," *The New Europe* 4, no. 51 (October 4, 1917).

35. Kršnjavi, *Zapisci*, 600; Gross, "Hrvatska uoči aneksije," 198–200.

36. Gross, "Hrvatska uoči aneksije," 200.

37. AH, ODS, 1.b.28, 1908: notes of Aehrenthal's discussions with Rauch, Josipović, and Nikolić; also, see Gross, "Hrvatska uoči aneksije," 197, 199.

38. Gross, "Hrvatska uoči aneksije," 200; see also 191, 192 of the same work. See also Kršnjavi, *Zapisci*, 510, 531, 600.

39. Kršnjavi, *Zapisci*, 600; instead, he tried to convince higher powers that the Serbs in the Coalition actually favored trialism.

40. Ibid., 512–13.

41. Supilo, *Politika*, 202–03; Gross, "Hrvatska uoči aneksije," 220–21.

42. Supilo, *Politika*, 199.

43. "Aneksije Bosne i Hercegovine i progoni Srba," *Srbobran* (Zagreb), October 2, 1908, 1; "Pitanje aneksije Bosne i Hercegovine," *Srbobran* (Zagreb), October 3, 1908, 1; "Krupni dogodjaji," *Srbobran* (Zagreb), October 6, 1908, 1.

44. Gross, "Hrvatska uoči aneksije," 241–57.

45. Pribićević, "Misao vodilja," 72; see also Lovrenčić, *Geneza*, 47–48.

46. Pribićević, "Misao vodilja," 73.

47. Ibid., 76.

48. Ivan Lorković, "Rački," in Banjanin et al., *Narodna misao*, 201–02.

49. Vatroslav Jagić–Djuro Šurmin (October 8, 1908, Vienna), NSB, ODS, R5896.

50. Djuro Šurmin–Vatroslav Jagić (December 27, 1908, Zagreb), NSB, OVJ, R4610b.

51. See "Trializam," *Novi list* (Rijeka), December 23, 1908, in Supilo, *Politički spisi*, 366–68.

52. Supilo, *Politika*, 212–13.

53. See "Aneksija Bosne i Hercegovine," *Novi list* (Rijeka), October 8, 1908, in Supilo, *Politički spisi*, 358–60.

54. "Aneksije Bosne i Hercegovine," *Srbobran* (Zagreb), October 6, 1908, 1.

55. Supilo, *Politika*, 213–14; "Sjednica koalicije," *Srbobran* (Zagreb), October 20, 1908, 1.

56. On Nikolić, see Kršnjavi, *Zapisci*, 547.

57. Jaša Tomić, *Veleizdajnička parnica u Zagrebu* (Novi Sad: Srpska štamparija dra Sv. Miletića, 1909), 12, and *Gde je srpska politika? i Samouprava napred* (Novi Sad: Srpska štamparija dra Sv. Miletića, 1911), 26.

58. "Rasprava optuženim Srbima," *Srbobran* (Zagreb), March 3, 1909, 1. For the only lengthy discussion of the trial and its character, see Seton-Watson, *Southern Slav Question*, 165–94; see also Srgjan Budisavljević, *Veleizdajnička parnica: Ništovna žaoba proti osudi kr. sudbenog stola u Zagrebu od 5. listopada 1909* (Zagreb, 1911).

59. See Hodimir Sirotković, "Pravni i politički aspekti procesa 'Reichspost'-Friedjung," in *Starine* (Zagreb: Jugoslavenska akademija znanosti i umjetnosti, 1962),

v. 52, 49–180; Seton-Watson, *Southern Slav Question*, 209–328; Šidak et al., *Povijest*, 248–51.

60. Gross, "Hrvatska uoči aneksije," 172.

61. Arhiv Srbije, Ministarstvo inostranih dela-pokloni i otkupi (hereafter, AS, MID-PO), Izveštaj iz Beča, Pov. br. 204, September 30, 1909.

62. "Nastićeve laži," *Srbobran* (Zagreb), August 4, 1908, 1; "Naša stranka i Nastićeva zavjera," *Srbobran* (Zagreb), August 5, 1908, 1.

63. Supilo, *Politika*, 203–05; see also Adam Pribićević, *Moj život*, 15."Nastićeve laži," *Srbobran* (Zagreb), August 4, 1908, 1; Radić, "Što je to sa Srbima," *Dom* (Zagreb), no. 34, 1908, in Antun Radić, *Sabrana djela Dra Antuna Radića*, ed. Vladko Maček and Rudolf Herceg (Zagreb: Seljačka sloga, 1935–1939), v. 10, 196.

64. "Domaće vijesti," *Srbobran* (Zagreb), August 8, 1908, 2; "Zatvaranje Srba," *Srbobran* (Zagreb), August 10, 1908, 2.

65. Gross, "Hrvatska uoči aneksije," 225. See also "Nastićeve laži," *Srbobran* (Zagreb), August 4, 1908, 1. The genesis of *Finale* was revealed by Srdjan Budisavljević of the Coalition in the Sabor in March 1911: see *SKH*, 1910–1915, v. 1, 1100–22.

66. Gross, "Hrvatska uoči aneksije," 230–31.

67. Ibid., 224.

68. "Naredba protiv ćirilice," *Srbobran* (Zagreb), November 4, 1908, 1; Cuvaj, *Gradja*, v. 10, 551–62.

69. "Optužnica kraljevskog državnog odvetnika Milana Akurtija protiv Adama Pribićevića i pedeset i dva Srbina podignuta radi zločina veleizdaje" (January 12, 1909), in Krestić, *Gradja*, v. 2, 507–609 (hereafter "Indictment"); "Optužnica u 'velezdajničkoj' [sic] parnici," *Srbobran* (Zagreb), January 16, 1909, 1; Ante Radić, "Obtužnica proti Srbima radi veleizdajstva," *Dom* (Zagreb), no. 3, 1909, in Radić, *Sabrana djela*, v. 11, 30; Budisavljević, *Ništovna žaoba*, 7–9, 15–17.

70. See *SKH*, 1908–1913, v. 1, 1044–45; "Jedna velika senzacija," *Srbobran* (Zagreb), April 23, 1910, 1; "Skandal Kršnjavi-Akurti," *Srbobran* (Zagreb), April 25, 1910, 1; Šidak et al., *Povijest*, 246.

71. "Indictment," 518.

72. Ibid., 519.

73. Ibid., 523.

74. Budisavljević, *Ništovna žaoba*, 8–9.

75. See Grujić, *Apologija*, and Ljub. Kovačević, *Srbi u Hrvatskoj i veleizdajnička parnica 1909* (Belgrade: Nova Štamparija Davidović, 1909), two responses by Serbian historians to the charges of the prosecution that there were no Serbs in Croatia.

76. Grujić, *Apologija*, 215, 235.

77. Ibid., 191, 259.

78. See Adam Pribićević's remarks in court, quoted by Viktor Novak in his *Antologija Jugoslovenske misli i narodnog jedinstva (1390–1930)* (Belgrade, 1930), 545–46.

79. Budisavljević, *Ništovna žaoba*.

80. Ibid., 16–17.

81. Seton-Watson, *Southern Slav Question*, 184.

82. Ibid., 104–94.

83. "Osuda optuženim Srbima," *Srbobran* (Zagreb), October 5, 1909, 1.

84. "U Rauhovoj službi," *Srbobran* (Zagreb), September 16, 1909, 1.

85. Adam Pribićević, *Moj život*, 14–18. Although only fifty-three Serbs were tried in the Zagreb trial, fifty-four were arrested in total; one died in jail.

86. Radić, "Srbi pod obtužbom," *Dom* (Zagreb), no. 3, 1909, in Radić, *Sabrana djela*, v. 11, 26–29.

87. "Jedna tobožnja senzacija," *Srbobran* (Zagreb), March 26, 1909, 1; Seton-Watson, *Southern Slav Question*, 202–05; Sirotković, "Pravni i politički aspekti," 67–70.

88. "Klevete bečkog 'Rajhsposta'," *Srbobran* (Zagreb), November 5, 1908, 1; Sirotković, "Pravni i politički aspekti," 64; Friedrich Funder, *From Empire to Republic: An Austrian Editor Reviews Momentous Years* (New York: Albert Unger, 1963), 135–36.

89. "Još o tobožnjoj senzaciji," *Srbobran* (Zagreb), March 27, 1909, 1; "Fridjungov odgovor," *Srbobran* (Zagreb), March 29, 1909, 1.

90. "Spalajković Fridjungu," *Srbobran* (Zagreb), April 5, 1909, 1; "Fridjungova afera," *Srbobran* (Zagreb), October 26, 1909, 1.

91. "Tužba protiv 'Reichsposta'," *Srbobran* (Zagreb), December 3, 1908, 1.

92. Sirotković, "Pravni i politički aspekti," 72.

93. Ibid., 129.

94. Ibid., 110.

95. On Frank's attempts to discredit the Coalition, see Supilo, *Politika*, 151–59; Gross, *Vladavina*, 61–66, 141–43; Sirotković, "Pravni i politički aspekti," 53–54.

96. Funder, *From Empire to Republic*, 136.

97. Heinrich Friedjung–R. W. Seton-Watson (January 6, 1910, Vienna), in Hugh Seton-Watson et al., *R. W. Seton-Watson and the Yugoslavs: Correspondence, 1906–1941* (London and Zagreb: British Academy and University of Zagreb, 1976), v. 1, 68.

98. Dimitrije Djordjević, *Milovan Milovanović* (Belgrade: Prosveta, 1962), 154.

99. AS, MID-PO, Izveštaj iz Beča (telegram), December 15, 1909.

100. Djordjević, *Carinski rat*, 569–71.

101. "Srbi pod obtužbom," *Dom* (Zagreb), no. 3, 1909, in Radić, *Sabrana djela*, v. 11, 28.

102. Seton-Watson, *Southern Slav Question*, 274.

5. *The Collapse of the Civic Option in Serbian Politics, 1910–1914*

1. Krleža, "Razgovor," 101.

2. August Cesarec, whose penetratingly hostile article "Svetozar Pribićević, posvećeno onima koji još u njega vjeruju," focuses mostly on his ambition and crass lack of convictions, also notes Pribićević's inability to think in any terms but Serbian. It was first published in *Književna republika* (Zagreb) in 1924.

3. AH, ODS, 1.b.32: document headed "Ovo je bio pakt s drom Nikolom Tomašićem da on kao ban preuzme vladu u Hrvatskoj od Raucha." Supilo, *Politika*, 238. See also Stojan Protić [Jedan novinar], *Hrvatske prilike i narodno jedinstvo Srba i Hrvata* (Belgrade: Štamparije "Dositije Obradović," 1911), 22–31; and Jovan M. Jovanović [Inostranac], "Hrvatska," *Srpski književni glasnik* (Belgrade) 25, pt. 4, (October 1910): 306–07.

4. AS, MID-PO, Izveštaj iz Budimpešte, Pov. br. 1, February 4, 1910.

5. For the response of the Peasant party, see Antun Radić, "Preokret koalicije," *Dom* (Zagreb), no. 6, 1910, in Radić, *Sabrana djela*, v. 11, 183.

6. Frano Supilo, "Kapitulacija," *Novi list* (Rijeka), January 28, 1910, in Supilo, *Politički spisi*, 373, 376.

7. On Supilo's exit from the Coalition, see R. W. Seton-Watson, *The Southern Slav Question*, 300, 303; Sirotković, "Pravni i politički aspekti," 147, 161; Petrinović, *Politička misao Frana Supila*, 131–33; Jaroslav Šidak, "Hrvatsko pitanje u Habsburškoj monarhiji," in *Studije iz hrvatske povijesti XIX stoljeća* (Zagreb: Sveučilište u Zagrebu, Institut za hrvatsku povijest, 1973), 38.

8. Frano Supilo–Grga Tuškan (February 5, 1910, Rijeka), in Hajdarhodžić et al., "Korespondencija," 197.

9. Regarding Khuen's disposition toward Supilo, see AS, MID-PO, Izveštaj iz Budimpešte, Pov. br. 1, February 4, 1910. In this document, the Serbian consul in Budapest writes that "Vienna will not hear of him [Supilo] because there is positive evidence that he received large sums of money from Italian irredentists."

10. See for instance Šidak, "Hrvatsko pitanje," 38; Vaso Bogdanov, "Uloga koalicije i S. Pribićevića do godine 1918.," in *Likovi i pokreti*, 242–43; Seton-Watson, *South Slav Question*, 303; Petrinović, *Politička misao Frana Supila*, 132–33; Sirotković, "Pravni i politički aspekti," 160–61; Šidak et al., *Povijest*, 267.

11. Djuro Šurmin–Vatroslav Jagić (January 29, 1911, Zagreb), NSB, OVJ, R4610.

12. "Savremeni aforizmi," *Srpski glasnik* (Zagreb), March 30, 1912, 3.

13. Kršnjavi, *Zapisci*, 600; Josef Redlich also noted in his diary that Nikolić had been with Josef Baernreither to see Aehrenthal sometime before January 9, 1910. Supilo supposed that Nikolić wished to use Baernreither to negotiate with Aehrenthal and the Archduke Franz Ferdinand (Redlich, *Schicksalsjahre Osterreichs 1908–1919: Das politische Tagebuch Josef Redlichs*, v. 1, *1908–1914*, ed. Fritz Fellner [Graz: Hermann Bohlaus, 1953], 46; Kršnjavi, *Zapisci*, 643–44.

14. Supilo, *Politika*, 239–40.

15. Josip Smodlaka, "Crtice o Ivanu Lorkoviću," 52, in *Zapisi dra Josipa Smodlake*, ed. Marko Kostrenčić (Zagreb: Jugoslav akademija znanosti i umjetnosti, 1972), 52–53.

16. *SKH*, 1908–1913, v. 1, 1200. The law is printed in *SKH*, 1908–1913, v. 2, prilog 20.

17. Antun Radić, "Novi izborni zakon," *Dom* (Zagreb), no. 11, 1910, in Radić, *Sabrana djela*, v. 11, 194. Gjurković and Gjurgjević were well-known Serbian magyarones.

18. *SKH*, 1908–1913, v. 1, 1238.

19. "Odluka srpske samostalne stranke," *Srbobran* (Zagreb), August 23, 1910, 1;

"Nova hrvatska stranka," *Srbobran* (Zagreb), October 13, 1910, 1. Tomašić did entice Pejačević and one faction of *pravaši* from the Coalition: AS, MID-PO, Izveštaj iz Budimpešte, Pov. br. 45, July 30, 1910; Kršnjavi, *Zapisci*, 628, 634. On the Osijek Group, see "Lojalnost gospode oko 'Narodne obrane'," *Srbobran* (Zagreb), August 22, 1910, 1; "Banova izjava," *Srbobran* (Zagreb), August 24, 1910, 1; "Srpska samostalna stranka," *Srbobran* (Zagreb), September 2, 1910, 1.

20. *SKH*, 1910–1915, v. 1, 33–34; "Izbori u Hrvatskoj," *Srbobran* (Zagreb), October 29, 1910, 1; AS, MID-PO, Izveštaj iz Budimpešte, Pov. br. 58, October 31, 1910; "Izbor u Udbinskom kotaru," *Srbobran* (Zagreb), November 2, 1910, 1.

21. AS, MID-PO, Izveštaj iz Budimpešte, Pov. br. 4, January 31, 1911.

22. *SKH*, 1910–1915, v. 1, 1204.

23. "Vladina stranka," *Srpski glasnik* (Zagreb), July 22, 1911, 1.

24. "Godina 1911 kod Srba i Hrvata," *Srbobran* (Zagreb), January 16, 1912, 1; "Dosadašnji rezultat izbora," *Srbobran* (Zagreb), December 20, 1911, 2–3; "Godina 1911 kod Srba i Hrvata," *Srbobran* (Zagreb), January 16, 1912, 1. On the elections, see R. W. Seton-Watson, *Absolutism in Croatia* (London: Constable, 1912).

25. Djuro Šurmin–Vatroslav Jagić (August 27, 1910, Zagreb), NSB, OVJ, R4610b.

26. AS, MID-PO, Izveštaj iz Budimpešte, Pov. br. 50, August 15, 1910.

27. "Tomašić pao—Novi ban," *Srbobran* (Zagreb), January 22, 1911, 1; "Cuvajeva vlada," *Srbobran* (Zagreb), January 23, 1912, 1.

28. Kršnjavi, *Zapisci*, 660.

29. "Cuvaj i Srbi," *Srbobran* (Zagreb), January 26, 1912, 1; AS, MID-PO, Izveštaj iz Budimpešte, Pov. br. 3, January 30, 1912.

30. AS, MID-PO, Izveštaj iz Budimpešte, Pov. br. 3, January 30, 1912; "Proglašenje komesarijata," *Srbobran* (Zagreb), April 4, 1912, 1.

31. AS, MID-PO, Izveštaj iz Budimpešte, Pov. br. 7, February 8, 1912.

32. Radivojević-Vačić in particular took it upon himself to defend the party against charges of Rauchism, largely because Lisavac had been publicly announced as a candidate on Rauch's unionist ticket of 1908; he failed to accomplish his task; *SKH*, 1908–1913, v. 1, 885.

33. Djordje Krasojević and Jaša Tomić, *Rat u srpskoj narodnocrkvenoj avtonomiji* (Novi Sad: Električna štamparija dra Svetozara Miletića, 1914), 7.

34. "Jugoslavensko pitanje (pitanje hrvatsko-srpsko)," *Srbobran* (Zagreb), August 12, 1911, 1.

35. Jaša Tomić, *Kako se zovemo (Srpsko i hrvatsko pitanje)* (Novi Sad: Srpska štamparija dra Svetozara Miletića, 1909), 90.

36. Ibid., 7.

37. Dragoslav Janković, *Srbija i jugoslovensko pitanje 1914–1915. godine* (Belgrade: Institut za savremenu istoriju i NIP eksport-pres, 1973), 28. The introduction to this book is the most concise existing discussion of the development of the Yugoslav national question in Serbia from 1903 to 1914. Other works that consider the subject include Djordje Stanković, *Nikola Pašić i jugoslovensko pitanje* (Belgrade: Beogradski izdavačko-grafički zavod, 1985), which covers only Pašić's conceptions. Although

Stanković concludes that Pašić was a "Yugoslav" by the onset of World War I, his evidence does not support his conclusion.

38. Among Serbian governmental figures after 1903, two, Nikola Pašić and Milovan Milovanović, had stated their views on the relationship of Serbs and Croats and their roles in any future state. Pašić's "Unity of Serbs and Croats" was written in or about 1890 and represents his only general written commentary on the subject of the future relations of the two nations. It was not published at the time. He concluded that Serbia should have the leading role in the formation of a state encompassing the "related" Serbian and Croatian nations (Stanković, *Nikola Pašić*, 77–80). Milovanović produced his piece in 1895. Entitled "Serbs and Croats," it, contrary to Pašić's, was published. Milovanović posited the assumption that Serbs and Croats must work together because of their geographical position and their close ethnic relationship. He allowed no talk of their comprising one nation, however; Milovan Milovanović, "Srbi i Hrvati," *Delo: List za nauku, književnost, i društveni život* (Belgrade) 3 (1895): 354–85.

39. Protić presents a vision of Serbo-Croatian unity seldom seen in Serbs of the Kingdom of Serbia. "The theory of *two nations* cannot today be defended at all, no matter how Tomić tries to demonstrate it scientifically and historically," Protić wrote. Protić claims that "the principle of self-government, a democratic and completely contemporary principle, protects Serbs as well as Croats, and any minority, from equalization and the imposition on the minority of something strange and foreign to it." "The Radicals thus must abandon this theory of two nations. Not only will it not strengthen the position of Serbs in Croatia, it will harm it." Protić's exposition mirrors Pribićević's. This material can be found in Protić, *Hrvatske prilike*, 15, 16, 64–147; "Prilike u Hrvatskoj," *Srbobran* (Zagreb), September 11, 1911, 1; Tomić, *Gde je srpska politika?*

40. "Kandidati srpske narodne samostalne stranke za srpski narodno-crkveni sabor," *Srbobran* (Zagreb), April 22, 1910, 1.

41. Rakić, *Radikalna stranka* II, 119.

42. *Rad srpskog narodnocrkvenog sabora po stenografskim zapisnicima od 2. maja do 15. juna 1911. god.* (Srijemski Karlovci: Naklada srpskog narodnocrkvenog sabora, 1911), May 24, 1911, 20; May 29, 1911, 3–13. See Krestić, *Istorija srpske štampe*, 338–39; Rakić, *Radikalna stranka* II, 37–38. Krestić and Rakić state that Pribićević challenged Krasojević; they are wrong.

43. *Rad srpskog narodnocrkvenog sabora*, May 24, 1911, 26.

44. Dušan Peleš, for instance, had been a magyarone until 1905; he would soon become the independent vice-president of the Church Congress. See *SKH*, 1908–1913, v. 1, 887; *SKH*, v. 1, 1908–1913, 896.

45. There are two short studies of this party, as well as several works that include discussions of it: see Milivoj Rajkov, "'Srpski glas' i kikindski demokrati," *Zbornik za istoriju Matice Srpske* (Novi Sad) 6 (1972): 157–172; and Vasilije Krestić, "Iz istorije demokratskog pokreta Srba u Ugarskoj," *Balcanica* (Belgrade) 8 (1977): 397–411. See also Vasa Stajić, "Milutin Jakšić (1863–1937)," *Godišnjak istoriskog društva u Novom Sadu* (Novi Sad) 12, pt. 1 (1939): 57–62; Rakić, *Radikalna stranka* II, 148–51; Krestić,

Istorija srpske štampe, 344–60; and Arpad Lebl, *Gradjanske partije u Vojvodini 1887–1918* (Novi Sad: Filozofski fakultet u Novom Sadu, Institut za istoriju, 1979), 110–26.

46. Krestić, *Istorija srpske štampe*, 347.

47. "Srpska demokratska stranka u Ugarskoj," *Srbobran* (Zagreb), September 3, 1909.

48. AS, MID-PO, Izveštaj iz Budimpešte, Pov. br. 15, March 14, 1910.

49. AS, MID-PO, Dnevna beleška, August 10, 1912. This file contains two reports: one based on an investigation by Stevan Mihailović, a secretary in the ministry of foreign affairs in Serbia who was sent by Jovanović to investigate. Mihailović's report was filed on August 7, 1912 (hereafter designated report "a"); the other by a Serbian journalist sent to Budapest to inquire into the reasons for the suspension of autonomy, dated August 21, 1912 (hereafter designated report "b"). This citation comes from report "b" of August 21, 1912.

50. Stajić, "Milutin Jakšić," 60.

51. Krestić, *Istorija srpske štampe*, 351–52; Stajić, "Milutin Jakšić," 60.

52. Rakić, *Radikalna stranka* II, 161; Krestić, *Istorija srpske štampe*, 425–31.

53. "Odnošaji Srba u Ugarskoj," *Srbobran* (Zagreb), January 21, 1913, 1.

54. Rakić, *Radikalna stranka* II, 121–22; Jovan M. Jovanović [Inostranac], "Srpska crkva u Ugarskoj," *Srpski književni glasnik* (Belgrade) 29, no. 5 (December 1912): 394.

55. Jovanović, "Srpska crkva u Ugarskoj," 394–95; Rakić, *Radikalna stranka* II, 121–23; see also AS, MID-PO, report "b" to Jovanović, August 21, 1912.

56. "Naredba kr. komesara o štampi," *Srbobran* (Zagreb), April 11, 1912, 1.

57. AH ODS 1.b.158. This is the letter of resignation of Jovan Banjanin from the Serbian Independent party and the Croato-Serbian Coalition, dating from December 1913 or January 1914.

58. "Deklaracija koalicije," *Srbobran* (Zagreb), April 25, 1912, 1.

59. Banjanin's resignation, AH, ODS, 1.b.158.

60. On the *omladina*, see Mirjana Gross, "Nacionalne ideje studentske omladine u Hrvatskoj uoči I svjetskog rata," *Historijski zbornik* 21–22 (1968–1969): 75–140.

61. "Atentat na kraljevskog povjerenika S. pl. Cuvaja," *Srbobran* (Zagreb), April 10, 1912, 1.

62. Banjanin's resignation, AH, ODS, 1.b.158.

63. Gross, "Nacionalne ideje studentske omladine"; Vladimir Dedijer, *Sarajevo 1914* (Belgrade: Prosveta, 1966); Banac, *The National Question in Yugoslavia*, 98–106.

64. See Banac, *The National Question in Yugoslavia*, 101–03; Milan Marjanović, *Narod koji nastaje* (Rijeka: G. Trbojevic, 1913). On Marjanović himself, see Dragovan Šepić, "Jugoslavenski pokret i Milan Marjanović 1901–1919," *Zbornik historijskog instituta Jugoslavenske Akademije* 3 (1960): 531–61.

65. Marjanović, *Savremena Hrvatska*.

66. "Narodna samopomoć," *Narodno jedinstvo* (Zagreb), May 16, 1914, 1.

67. AS, MID-PO, 1912, fascicle N-11, p. 34.

68. The monetary figure, from 1905, comes from Rakić, *Radikalna stranka* I, 201. Jovan Jovanović believed that the funds amounted in 1912 to two hundred million crowns; see AS, MID-PO, 1912, fascicle N-11, p. 34.

69. AS, MID-PO, Dnevna beleška, August 10, 1912.

70. AS, MID-PO, report "b" to Jovanović, August 21, 1912.

71. Ibid.

72. AS, MID-PO, report "a," Mihailović–Jovanović, August 7, 1912.

73. Ibid.

74. Jovanović, "Srpska crkva u Ugarskoj," 394–95.

75. AS, MID-PO, report "a," Mihailović–Jovanović, August 7, 1912.

76. Ibid.

77. Ibid.

78. AS, MID-PO, Izveštaj iz Budimpešte, Pov. br. 27, April 7, 1913; Banjanin's resignation, AH, ODS, 1.b.158; Šidak et al., *Povijest*, 285.

79. Banjanin's resignation, AH, ODS, 1.b.158.

80. Ibid.

81. Ibid.; see also "Položaj u Hrvatskoj," *Srbobran* (Zagreb), September 13, 1913, 1.

82. Šurmin evinced unconvincing support for any policy that would maintain the Coalition as a harmonious Croato-Serbian organization (letter of September 2, 1913 to Jagić; NSB, OVJ, R4610b).

83. Historijski Arhiv-Zagreb, Ostavština Ivana Ribara (hereafter, HAZ, OIR), box 9: manuscript entitled "Koliko snaga zahteva jedan život: Iz biografije dr. I. Ribara," by Pavel Čanji, 130–31. Ribar describes an instance in which Lorković demanded that Ribar allow a German magyarone to be a candidate in Djakovo, Ribar's home district that had nominated Ribar.

84. Milan Rojc–Djuro Šurmin (February 28, 1913, Zagreb), AH, ODS, 32.529.

85. "Položaj u Hrvatskoj," *Srbobran* (Zagreb), September 13, 1913, 1.

86. "Promjena u uredništvu 'Srbobrana'," *Srbobran* (Zagreb), October 8, 1913, 1. See Boban, *Svetozar Pribićević*, 230.

87. "Politički položaj u Hrvatskoj," *Srbobran* (Zagreb), October 29, 1913, 1.

88. AS, MID-PO, Izveštaj iz Budimpešte, Pov. br. 70, July 26, 1913.

89. AS, MID-PO, Izveštaj iz Budimpešte, Pov. br. 100, October 10, 1913.

90. AS, MID-PO, Izveštaj iz Budimpešte, Pov. br. 104, October 23, 1913; AS, MID-PO, Izveštaj iz Budimpešte, Pov. br. 119, November 18, 1913.

91. "Jučerašnji sastanak hrv-srp koalicije," *Srbobran* (Zagreb), December 3, 1913, 1.

92. "Izbornicima!" *Srbobran* (Zagreb), December 6, 1913, 1.

93. Banjanin's resignation, AH, ODS, 1.b.158.

94. Ibid.; see also Kršnjavi, *Zapisci*, 698, in which Tisza is heard to say that he would not deal with the Coalition insofar as it would not cooperate with unionists in the Sabor.

95. On Skerlecz as ban, see *Srbobran* (Zagreb), December 1, 1913, 1.

96. Banjanin's resignation, AH, ODS, 1.b.158.

97. Šidak et al., *Povijest*, 290.

98. Banjanin's resignation, AH, ODS, 1.b.158. I am suggesting that Nikolić and Pribićević are the two in question, in the roles I have assigned them. Banjanin never names them.

99. AS, MID-PO, Izveštaj iz Budimpešte, Pov. br. 22, March 19, 1914.

100. AS, MID-PO, Izveštaj iz Budimpešte, Pov. br. 27, April 2, 1914.

101. "Jučerašnja sjednica i zakljucak narodne zastup. hrv.-srp. koalicije," *Srbobran* (Zagreb), April 22, 1914, 1; "Značenja zaključka hrv.-srp. koalicije, *Srbobran* (Zagreb), April 23, 1914, 1; "Nova koalicijona vlada," *Narodno jedinstvo* (Zagreb), April 4, 1914, 2; "Pitanje vlade," *Narodno jedinstvo* (Zagreb), April 4, 1914, 2.

102. "Jučerašnja sjednica i zaključak zastup. hrv.-srp. koalicije," *Srbobran* (Zagreb), April 22, 1914; "Iz sjednice koalicije," *Narodno jedinstvo* (Zagreb), April 24, 1914, 2.

103. "Ban, Sabor, i narod," *Narodno jedinstvo* (Zagreb), April 18, 1914, 1–4.

104. Supilo, *Politika*, 238–39; Banac, *The National Question in Yugoslavia*, 98; Šidak, "Hrvatsko pitanje," 38; Petrinović, *Politička misao Frana Supila*, 133; Dragovan Šepić, "Političke koncepcije Frana Supila," in Frano Supilo, *Politički spisi: Članci/Govori/Pisma/Memorandumi*, ed. Dragovan Šepić (Zagreb: Znanje, 1970), 50–51, 54.

105. Kosta Milutinović, "Hrvatsko-srpske koalicije," in Andrej Mitrović, ed., *Istorija srpskog naroda*, v. 6, pt. 1, *Od berlinskog kongresa do ujedinjenja 1878–1918* (Belgrade: Srpska književna zadruga, 1983), 491.

106. *SKH*, 1913–1918, v. 2, 223, 434–35; Milutinović, "Hrvatsko-srpska koalicija," 492.

107. *SKH*, 1913–1918, v. 2, 434–35.

108. AS, MID-PO, Izveštaj iz Budimpešte, Pov. br. 33, April 10, 1914.

109. AS, MID-PO, Izveštaj iz Budimpešte, (telegram), June 11, 1914.

110. AS, MID-PO, Izveštaj iz Budimpešte, Pov. br. 59, June 12, 1914.

111. AS, MID-PO, Izveštaj iz Budimpešte, Pov. br.45, May 17, 1913.

112. AS, MID-PO, Izveštaj iz Budimpešte, Pov. br. 71, July 28, 1913.

113. Milutinović, "Hrvatsko-srpska koalicija," 489.

114. AS, MID-PO, Izveštaj iz Budimpešte, Pov. br. 27, April 2, 1914; Izveštaj iz Budimpešte, Pov. br. 29, April 3, 1914; Adam Pribićević, *Moj život*, 133–34.

115. Adam Pribićević, *Moj život*, 31–33; Krizman cites a second version of Pribićević's autobiography, in manuscript form in the Arhiv Jugoslavije, in which the same basic story is told (*Hrvatska u prvom svjetskom ratu*, 45–46).

116. Krizman, *Hrvatska u prvom svjetskom ratu*, 46; this line is in the manuscript version but not in *Moj život*.

117. Slavko Ćirić, "Stvaranje jugoslovenske države," *Letopis Matice Srpske* (Novi Sad) 335 (1933): 53.

118. Ivan Meštrović, *Uspomene na političke ljudi i dogodjaje* (Zagreb: Matica Hrvatska, 1969), 29.

119. Vasilije Krestić, *Istorija srba u Hrvatskoj i Slavoniji, 1848–1914*, 2d. ed. (Belgrade: Politika, 1992), 564.

6. Conclusion: The Failure of the Civic Idea Among Croatia's Serbs

1. On Croatia during the war, see Krizman, *Hrvatska u prvom svjestkom ratu*, passim, and Krizman, *Raspad Austro-Ugarske i stvaranje jugoslavenske države* (Zagreb:

Školska knjiga, 1977), passim; on Tomić and other Radicals, see Rakić, *Jaša Tomić*, 273–81.

2. In truth, as of this writing (May 1996), the Sremsko-Baranska Oblast of the Republika Srpske Krajine, with Vukovar as its destroyed center, still exists as a Serbian entity, but its Serbian population is preparing to leave as a result of the Erdut Agreement, signed in 1995, which hands the region over to Croatia in 1997.

3. I will leave aside assertions regarding a Serbian government conspiracy to provoke the collapse of the Yugoslav and Croatian states and to support the armed Serbian insurgency in Croatia.

4. In Croatia: *Zbornik radova o povijesti i kulturi srpskog naroda u Socialističkoj Republici Hrvatskoj* (Zagreb: 1988), v. 1; in Serbia: *Zbornik o Srbima u Hrvatskoj* (Belgrade: Srpska akademija nauka i umetnosti, 1989–1994), v. 1–3.

5. Dragoljub Živojinović has worked studiously to prove his point that the Catholic church has long conspired to undermine the viability of the Serbian and then the Yugoslav state. Djordje Stanković has written extensively on Pašić's conceptions regarding Croats and Croatia. Vasilije Krestić has spent much of his effort on demonstrating the genocidal inclinations of Croats.

6. Banac, *The National Question*, 171; remarking that Croatia's Serbs traditionally used two methods to account for their separateness: to become Yugoslav, or to cooperate with outsiders, he notes that Pribićević "combined elements of these two rather different avenues."

BIBLIOGRAPHY

Archival Sources (with abbreviations used in the notes)

Historijski Arhiv-Zagreb (HAZ)
    Ivan Ribar Papers (OIR)
Arhiv Hrvatske, Zagreb (AH)
    Djuro Šurmin Papers (ODS)
Arhiv Srbije, Belgrade (AS)
    Ministry of Foreign Affairs, Political Division (MID-PO)
Nacionalna i Sveučilišna Biblioteka, Zagreb (NSB)
    Djuro Šurmin Papers (ODS)
    Vatroslav Jagić Papers (OVJ)

Newspapers

    Dom (Zagreb)
    (Hrvatski) Pokret (Zagreb)
    Narodni glasnik (Zemun and Zagreb)
    Narodno jedinstvo (Zagreb)
    Novi list (Rijeka)
    (Novi) Srbobran (Zagreb)
    Obzor (Zagreb)
    Sloboda (Split)
    Srpski glasnik (Zagreb)

Published Primary Sources

Bogičević, Miloš. *Die auswärtige Politik Serbiens, 1903–1914.* 3 vols. Berlin: Brucken-verlag, 1928–1931.

Cuvaj, Antun. *Gradja za povijest školstva Kraljevina Hrvatske i Slavonije od najstarijih vremena do danas.* 11 vols. Zagreb: Naklada Kr. Hrv.-Slav.-Dalm. zem. vlade, odjela za bogoštovlje i nastave, 1910–1913.

Vojvodić, Mihailo, et al., eds. *Dokumenti o spoljnoj politici Kraljevine Srbije, 1903–1914*. v. 5–7. Belgrade: Srpska akademija nauka i umetnosti, Odeljenje istorijskih nauka, 1981–1986.

Hajdarhodžić, Hamdija, et al., eds. "Korespondencija Frana Supila iz perioda 1891–1914." *Arhivski vjesnik* 6 (1963): 7–229.

Krestić, Vasilije, ed. *Gradja o Srbima u Hrvatskoj i Slavoniji (1848–1914)*. 2 vols. Belgrade: Beogradski izdavačko-grafički zavod, 1995.

Krestić, Vasilije, and Radoš Ljušić, eds. *Programi i statuti srpskih političkih stranaka do 1918. godine*. Belgrade: Književne novine, 1991.

Krizman, Bogdan. *Korespondencija Stjepana Radića*. V. 1, *1885–1918*. Zagreb: Sveučilište u Zagrebu, Institut za hrvatsku povijest, 1972.

Kršnjavi, Iso. *Zapisci iža kulisa hrvatske politike*. 2 vols. Edited by Ivan Krtalić. Zagreb: Mladost, 1986.

Lakatoš, Josip. *Narodna statistika*. Osijek: Naklada Radoslava Bačića, 1914.

Andrija Radenić, ed. *Austro-ugarska i Srbija, 1903–1918: Dokumenti iž Bečkih arhiva*. Belgrade: Istorijski institut, 1973–1985.

Radić, Antun. *Sabrana djela Dra Antuna Radića*. Edited by Vladko Maček and Rudolf Herceg. 19 vols. Zagreb: Seljačka sloga, 1935–1939.

Radic, Stjepan. *Politički spisi: Autobiografija/Članci/Govori/Rasprave*. Edited by Zvonimir Kulundžić. Zagreb: Znanje, 1971.

Rad srpskog narodnocrkvenog sabora po stenografskim zapisnicima od 2. maja do 15. juna 1911. god. Srijemski Karlovci: Naklada srpskog narodnocrkvenog sabora, 1911.

Redlich, Josef. *Schicksalsjahre Osterreichs 1908–1919: Das politische Tagebuch Josef Redlichs*. V. 1, *1908–1914*. Edited by Fritz Fellner. Graz: Hermann Bohlaus, 1953.

Seton-Watson, Hugh et al., eds. *R. W. Seton-Watson and the Yugoslavs: Correspondence, 1906–1941*. 2 vols. London and Zagreb: British Academy and University of Zagreb, 1976.

Signjar, R., ed. *1875–1915 Statistički atlas kraljevina Hrvatske Slavonije*. Zagreb: Tisak i litografije kraljevske i zemaljske tiskare, 1915.

Srbobran: Narodni srpski kalendar 1906. Edited by Svetozar Pribićević and Jovan Banjanin. Zagreb: Srpska štamparija u Zagrebu, 1906.

Statistički godišnjak Kraljevina Hrvatske i Slavonije 1 (1905). Zagreb: Tisak kraljevske tiskare, 1913.

Statistički godišnjak Kraljevina Hrvatske i Slavonije. 2 (1906–1910). Zagreb: Tisak kraljevske tiskare, 1915.

Stenografički zapisnici sabora Kraljevina Hrvatske, Slavonije, i Dalmacije. Zagreb: Tisak kraljevske zemaljske tiskare.

Supilo, Frano. *Politički spisi: Članci/Govori/Pisma/Memorandumi*. Edited by Dragovan Šepić. Zagreb: Znanje, 1970.

Trumbić, Ante. *Izabrani spisi*. Edited by Ivo Petrinović. Split: Književni krug, 1986.

Other Literature

Anderson, Benedict. *Imagined Communities: Reflections on the Origins and Spread of Nationalism*. Rev. ed. London: Verso, 1991.

Artuković, Mato. *Ideologija srpsko-hrvatskih sporova* (Srbobran, 1884–1902). Zagreb: Naprijed, 1991.

Artuković, Mato. "Izdavačka djelatnost Srpske samostalne stranke." *Zbornik o Srbima u Hrvatskoj i Slavoniji* (Belgrade) 1 (1989): 103–15.

Banac, Ivo. *The National Question in Yugoslavia: Origins, History, Politics*. Ithaca: Cornell University Press, 1984.

Banjanin, Jovan et al. *Narodna misao*. Zagreb: Dionička tiskara, 1897.

Behschnitt, Wolf Dietrich. *Nationalismus bei Serben und Kroaten, 1830–1914: Analyse und Typologie der nationalen Ideologie*. Munich: R. Oldenbourg, 1980.

Boban, Ljubo. *Svetozar Pribićević u opoziciji (1928–1936)*. Zagreb: Sveučilište u Zagrebu, Institut za hrvatsku povijest, 1973.

Bogdanov, Vaso. *Historija političkih stranaka u Hrvatskoj od prvih stranačkih grupiranja do 1918*. Zagreb: Novinarstvo izdavačko poduzeće, 1958.

———. *Hrvatski narodni pokret 1903/4*. Zagreb: Jugoslavenska akademija znanosti i umjetnosti, 1961.

———. *Likovi i pokreti*. Zagreb: Mladost, 1957.

———. "O životu i radu Frana Supila." In Frano Supilo, *Politika u Hrvatskoj*, 7–109. Zagreb: Kultura, 1953.

Budisavljević, Srgjan. *Veleizdajnička parnica: Ništovna žaoba proti osudi kr. sudbenog stola u Zagrebu od 5. listopada 1909*. Zagreb, 1911.

Čehak, Kalman. *Političke borbe u Bačkoj i Banatu u vreme vladavine koalicije 1906–1909*. Novi Sad: Filozofski fakultet u Novom Sadu, Institut za istoriju, 1987.

Cesarec, August. "Svetozar Pribićević, posvećeno onima koji još u njega vjeruju." In *Eseji i putopisi*, 109–29. Belgrade: Prosveta, 1964.

Ciliga, Vera. *Slom politike narodne stranke (1865–1880)*. Zagreb: Nakladni zavod Matice Hrvatske, 1970.

Ćirić, Slavko. "Stvaranje jugoslovenske države." *Letopis Matice Srpske* (Novi Sad) 335 (1933): 52–63.

Čubrilović, Vaso. *Istorija političke misli u Srbiji XIX veka*. Belgrade: Prosveta, 1958.

Čubrilović, Vaso, ed. *Jugoslovenski narodi pred prvi svetski rat*. Belgrade: Naučno delo, 1967.

Dedijer, Vladimir. *Sarajevo 1914*. Belgrade: Prosveta, 1966.

Despalatović, Elinor Murray. *Ljudevit Gaj and the Illyrian Movement*. Boulder, Colo.: East European Monographs, 1975.

Djordjević, Dimitrije. *Carinski rat Austro-Ugarske i Srbije, 1906–1911*. Belgrade: Istorijski institut, 1962.

————. *Milovan Milovanović*. Belgrade: Prosveta, 1962.

————. "Pokušaji srpsko-ugarske saradnje i zajedničke akcije 1906. godine." *Istorija XX veka: Zbornik radova* (Belgrade) 2 (1961): 353–82.

————. "The Serbs As an Integrating and Disintegrating Factor." *Austrian History Yearbook* 3, pt. 2 (1967): 48–82.

Fine, John V. A., Jr. *The Early Medieval Balkans: A Critical Survey from the Sixth to the Late Twelfth Century*. 2 vols. Ann Arbor: University of Michigan Press, 1983.

————. *The Late Medieval Balkans: A Critical Survey from the Late Twelfth Century to the Ottoman Conquest*. Ann Arbor: University of Michigan Press, 1987.

Funder, Friedrich. *From Empire to Republic: An Austrian Editor Reviews Momentous Years*. New York: Albert Unger, 1963.

Gačeša, Nikola L. "Srpsko zadrugarstvo u Hrvatskoj i Slavoniji od 1897. do 1918." *Zbornik o Srbima u Hrvatskoj i Slavoniji* (Belgrade) 1 (1989): 133–69.

Gavrilović, Slavko. *Iz istorije srba u Hrvatskoj, Slavoniji, i Ugarskoj (XV–XIX vek)*. Belgrade: Filip Višnjić, 1993.

————. *Srbi u Habsburškoj Monarhiji (1792–1849)*. Novi Sad: Matica Srpska, 1994.

Gavrilović, Slavko, ed. *Srbi u XVIII veku*. V. 4, *Istorija srpskog naroda*. Belgrade: Srpska književna zadruga, 1986).

Gellner, Ernest. *Nations and Nationalism*. Ithaca: Cornell University Press, 1983.

Greenfeld, Liah. *Nationalism: Five Roads to Modernity*. Cambridge: Harvard University Press, 1992.

Gross, Mirjana. "Hrvatska uoči aneksije Bosne i Hercegovine." *Istorija XX veka: Zbornik radova* (Belgrade) 3 (1962): 153–269.

————. "Nacionalne ideje studentske omladine uoči prvog svjetskog rata." *Historijski zbornik* (Zagreb) 21–22 (1968–1969): 75–140.

————. *Počeci moderne hrvatske: Neoapsolutizam u civilnoj Hrvatskoj i Slavoniji 1850–1860*. Zagreb: Globus, 1985.

————. *Povijest pravaške ideologije*. Zagreb: Sveučilište u Zagrebu, Institut za hrvatsku povijest, 1973.

————. *Vladavina hrvatsko-srpske koalicije 1906–1907*. Belgrade: Institut društvenih nauka, Odeljenje za istorijske nauke, 1960.

————. "Zakon o osnovnim školama 1874. i srpsko pravoslavno školstvo." *Zbornik radova o povijesti i kulturi srpskog naroda u Socialističkoj Republici Hrvatskoj* 1 (1988): 75–117.

Gross, Mirjana, ed. *Društveni razvoj u Hrvatskoj (od 16. stoljeća do početka 20. stoljeća)*. Zagreb: Sveučilišna naklada Liber, 1981.

Gross, Mirjana, and Agnesa Szabo. *Prema hrvatskome gradjanskom društvu: Društveni razvoj u civilnoj Hrvatskoj i Slavoniji šezdesetih i sedamdesetih godina 19. stoljeća*. Zagreb: Globus, 1992.

Grujić, Radoslav. *Apologija srpskoga naroda u Hrvatskoj i Slavoniji i njegovih glavnih obeležja; Povodom "Optužnice" kr. držav. odvetnika u Zagrebu od 12. I. 1909 g.* Novi Sad: Štamparija učiteljskog deoničar. društva "Natošević," 1909.

Haelsteiner, Horst. *Die Serben und der Ausgleich: Zur politischen und staatsrechtlichen Stellung der Serben Südungarns in den Jahren 1860–1867.* Vienna: Hermann Böhlaus, 1976.

Horvat, Josip. *Politička povijest Hrvatske.* Zagreb: August Cesarec, 1989.

————. *Supilo: Život jednoga hrvatskoga političara.* Zagreb: Binoza, 1938.

Ibler, Janko. *Hrvatska politika, 1903–1913.* 2 vols. Zagreb: Kraljevska zemaljska tiskara, 1914.

Janković, Dragoslav. *Srbija i jugoslovensko pitanje 1914–1915. godine.* Belgrade: Institut za savremenu istoriju i NIP eksport-pres, 1973.

Jelavich, Charles. "The Croatian Problem in the Habsburg Empire in the Nineteenth Century." In *Austrian History Yearbook* 3, pt. 2 (1967): 83–115.

————. *South Slav Nationalisms: Textbooks and Yugoslav Union Before 1914.* Columbus: Ohio State University Press, 1990.

Jovanović, Jovan M. [Inostranac, pseud.]. "Hrvatska." *Srpski književni glasnik* (Belgrade) 25, pt. 4 (October 1910): 306–07.

————. "Srpska crkva u Ugarskoj." *Srpski književni glasnik* (Belgrade) 29, pt. 5 (December 1912): 394–95.

————. "Ugarska kriza." *Srpski književni glasnik* (Belgrade) 15, pt. 10 (May 1905): 791–93.

Kessler, Wolfgang. *Politik, Kultur, und Gesellschaft in Kroatien und Slawonien in der ersten Hälfte des 19. Jahrhunderts: Historiographie und Grundlagen.* Munich: R. Oldenbourg, 1981.

Kohn, Hans. *The Idea of Nationalism.* New York: Macmillan, 1967.

Kovačević, Ljub. *Srbi u Hrvatskoj i veleizdajnička parnica 1909.* Belgrade: Nova Štamparija Davidović, 1909.

Krasojević, Djordje, and Jaša Tomić. *Rat u srpskoj narodnocrkvenoj avtonomiji.* Novi Sad: Električna štamparija dra Svetozara Miletića, 1914.

Krestić, Vasilije. *Hrvatsko-Ugarske nagodbe 1868. godine.* Belgrade: Srpska akademija nauke i umetnosti, 1969.

————. *Istorija srba u Hrvatskoj i Slavoniji, 1848–1914.* 2d. ed. Belgrade: Politika, 1992.

————. *Istorija srpske štampe u Ugarskoj, 1791–1914.* Novi Sad: Matica Srpska, 1980.

————. "Iz istorije demokratskog pokreta Srba u Ugarskoj." *Balcanica* (Belgrade) 8 (1977): 397–411.

————. "Politički, privredni, i kulturni život u Hrvatskoj i Slavoniji." In *Istorija srpskog naroda.* V. 6, pt. 1, *Od berlinskog kongresa do ujedinjenja 1878–1918,* 375–431. Edited by Andrej Mitrović. Belgrade: Srpska književna zadruga, 1983.

————. "Srbi u Habsburškoj Monarhiji, 1849–1868." In *Istorija srpskog naroda.* V. 5, pt. 2, *Od prvog ustanka do berlinskog kongresa, 1804–1878*. Edited by Vladimir Stojančević. Belgrade: Srpska književna zadruga, 1981.

———. *Srpsko-hrvatski odnosi i jugoslovenska ideja u drugoj polovini XIX veka*. Belgrade: Nova knjiga, 1988.

———. "Zagreb—Političko središte Srba u Austro-Ugarskoj." *Zbornik o Srbima u Hrvatskoj* (Belgrade) 1 (1989): 91–101.

Krestić, Vasilije, ed. *Zbornik o Srbima u Hrvatskoj*. V. 1. Belgrade: Srpska akademija nauka i umetnosti, 1989.

Krizman, Bogdan. "The Croatians in the Habsburg Monarchy in the Nineteenth Century." *Austrian History Yearbook* 3, pt. 2 (1967): 116–58.

———. *Hrvatska u prvom svjetskom ratu: Hrvatsko-srpski politički odnosi*. Zagreb: Globus, 1989.

———. *Raspad Austro-Ugarske i stvaranje jugoslavenske države*. Zagreb: Školska knjiga, 1977.

Krleža, Miroslav. "Razgovor sa sjenom Frana Supila." In *Knjiga studija i putopisa*. Zagreb: Biblioteka nezavisnih pisaca, 1939.

Krokar, James. "Liberal Reform in Croatia, 1872–1875: The Beginnings of Modern Croatia Under Ban Ivan Mažuranić." Ph.D. dissertation, Indiana University, 1980.

Lampe, John R., and Marvin R. Jackson. *Balkan Economic History, 1550–1950: From Imperial Borderlands to Developing Nations*. Bloomington: Indiana University Press, 1982.

Lebl, Arpad. *Gradjanske partije u Vojvodini 1887–1918*. Novi Sad: Filozofski fakultet u Novom Sadu, Institut za istoriju, 1979.

———. "Hrvatsko pitanje kroz prizmu ugarskog parlamenta 1892–1918." *Historijski zbornik* (Zagreb) 17 (1964): 259–301.

———. "Vojvodjanske gradjanske partije u svetlosti zapisnika peštanskog parlamenta." In *Jugoslovenski narodi pred prvi svetski rat*. Edited by Vaso Čubrilović, 417–78. Belgrade: Srpska akademija nauka i umetnosti, 1967.

Lovrenčić, Rene. "Ekonomska problematika u Supilovu 'Novom listu' 1903–1905." *Radovi filozofskog fakulteta* (Zagreb) 3 (1960): 95–122.

———. "Ekonomska problematika u Supilovu 'Novom listu' 1906–1914." *Radovi* (Zagreb) 6 (1974): 129–269.

———. *Geneza politike 'novog kursa' u Hrvatskoj*. Zagreb: Sveučilište u Zagrebu, Institut za hrvatsku povijest, 1972.

Marjanović, Milan. *Hrvatski pokret*. 2 vols. Dubrovnik: Jadran, 1905.

———. *Narod koji nastaje*. Rijeka: G. Trbojević, 1913.

———. *Savremena Hrvatska*. Belgrade: Srpska književna zadruga, 1913.

Matković, Hrvoje. *Svetozar Pribićević: Ideolog, stranački vodja, emigrant*. Zagreb: Hrvatska sveučilišna naklada, 1995.

———. *Svetozar Pribićević i Samostalna demokratska stranka do šestojanuarske diktature*. Zagreb: Sveučilište u Zagrebu, Institut za hrvatsku povijest, 1972.

Meštrović, Ivan. *Uspomene na političke ljude i dogodjaje.* Zagreb: Matica Hrvatska, 1969.

Miller, Nicholas. "R. W. Seton-Watson and Serbia During the Reemergence of Yugoslavism, 1903–1914." *Canadian Review of Studies in Nationalism* 15, no. 1–2 (1988): 59–69.

————. "Two Strategies in Serbian Politics in Croatia and Hungary Before the First World War." *Nationalities Papers* 23, no. 2 (1995): 327–51.

Milovanović, Milovan. "Srbi i Hrvati." *Delo: List za nauku, književnost, i društveni život* (Belgrade) 3 (1895): 354–85.

Milutinović, Kosta. "Hrvatsko-srpska koalicija." In Andrej Mitrović, ed., *Istorija srpskog naroda.* V. 6, pt. 1, *Od berlinskog kongresa do ujedinjenja 1878–1918*, 432–495. Belgrade: Srpska književna zadruga, 1983.

————. "Josip Smodlaka i jugoslavensko pitanki u Habsburškoj Monarhiji." *Rad Jugoslavenske akademije znanosti i umjetnosti* (Zagreb) 359 (1971): 163–287.

————. *Studije iz srpske i hrvatske istoriografije.* Novi Sad: Matica Srpska, 1986.

————. *Vojvodina i Dalmacija 1760–1914.* Novi Sad: Institut za izučavanje istorije Vojvodine, 1973.

Mitrović, Andrej, ed. *Od berlinskog kongresa do ujedinjenja, 1878–1918.* V. 6, *Istorija srpskog naroda.* Belgrade: Srpska književna zadruga, 1983.

Novak, Viktor. *Antologija jugoslovenske misli i narodnog jedinstva (1390–1930).* Belgrade, 1930.

Pavličević, Dragutin. *Narodni pokret 1883. u Hrvatskoj.* Zagreb: Sveučilišna naklada Liber, 1980.

Pavličević, Dragutin, ed. *Vojna Krajina: Povijesni pregled, historiografija, rasprave.* Zagreb: Sveučilišna naklada Liber, 1984.

Petrinović, Ivo. *Ante Trumbić: Politička shvaćanja i djelovanje.* Zagreb: Nakladni zavod Matice Hrvatske, 1986.

————. *Politička misao Frana Supila.* Split: Književni krug, 1988.

Petrović, Rade. *Nacionalno pitanje u Dalmaciji u XIX stoljeću.* Sarajevo: Svjetlost and Prosvjeta, Zagreb, 1982.

Petrovich, Michael. *History of Modern Serbia, 1804–1918.* New York: Harcourt, Brace, Jovanovic, 1976.

Popović, Dušan. *Srbi u Vojvodini.* V. 3, *Od temišvarskog sabora 1790. do blagoveštenskog sabora 1861.* Novi Sad: Matica Srpska, 1963.

Popović, Miodrag. *Vuk Stef. Karadžić 1787–1864.* Belgrade: Nolit, 1987.

Pribićević, Adam. *Moj život.* Windsor, Canada, 1981.

Pribićević, Svetozar. *Diktatura kralja Aleksandra.* Zagreb: Globus, 1990.

Protić, Stojan [Jedan novinar, pseud.]. *Hrvatske prilike i narodno jedinstvo Srba i Hrvata.* Belgrade: Štamparija "Dositije Obradović," 1911.

Radenić, Andrija. "Borba za politička prava u južnoj Ugarskoj," in Andrej Mitrovic, ed., *Istorija srpskog naroda.* V. 6, pt. 1, *Od berlinskog kongresa do ujedinjenja 1878–1918*, 496–554. Belgrade: Srpska književna zadruga, 1983.

————. *Položaj i borba seljaštva u Sremu od kraja XIX veka do 1914*. Belgrade: Naučno delo, 1958.

————. "Srbi u Habsburškoj Monarhiji, 1868–1878." In *Istorija srpskog naroda*. Edited by Vladimir Stojančević. V. 5, pt. 2, *Od prvog ustanka do berlinskog kongresa*, 153–275. Belgrade: Srpska akademija nauka, 1981.

Radonić, Jovan, and Mita Kostić. *Srpske privilegije od 1690 to 1792*. Belgrade: Naučna knjiga, 1954.

Rajkov, Milivoj. "'Srpski glas' i kikindski demokrati." *Zbornik za istoriju Matice Srpske* (Novi Sad) 6 (1972): 157–72.

Rakić, Lazar. *Jaša Tomic (1856–1922)*. Novi Sad: Matica Srpska, 1986.

————. "Manastirska uredba (1908)." In *Zbornik za istoriju* (Novi Sad: Matica Srpska, Odeljenje za društvene nauke, 1983), v. 27, 7–48.

————. *Radikalna stranka u Vojvodini (do početka XX veka)*. Novi Sad: Institut za izučavanje istorije Vojvodine, 1975.

————. *Radikalna stranka u Vojvodini, 1902–1919*. Novi Sad: Filozofski fakultet, 1983.

Ribar, Ivan. *Politički zapisi*. Belgrade: Prosveta, 1948. V. 1.

Roksandić, Drago. *Srbi u hrvatskoj od 15. stoljeća do naših dana*. Zagreb: Vjesnik, 1991.

Rothenberg, Gunther. *The Austrian Military Border in Croatia, 1522–1747*. Urbana: University of Illinois Press, 1960.

————. *The Military Border in Croatia, 1740–1881: A Study of an Imperial Institution*. Chicago: University of Chicago Press, 1966.

Šarinić, Josip. *Nagodbena hrvatska: Postanak i osnove ustavne organizacije*. Zagreb: Nakladni zavod Matice Hrvatske, 1972.

Schödl, Günter. *Kroatische Nationalpolitik und "Jugoslavenstvo": Studien zu nationaler Integration unde regionaler Politik in Kroatien-Dalmatien am Beginn des 20. Jahrhunderts*. Munich: R. Oldenbourg, 1990.

Schwicker, Johan Heinrich. *Istorija unijaćenja srba u vojnoj krajini*. Translated by Nikola Živković. Novi Sad: Arhiv Vojvodine, 1995.

Šepić, Dragovan. "Jugoslavenski pokret i Milan Marjanović 1901–1919." *Zbornik historijskog instituta Jugoslavenske Akademije* (Zagreb) 3 (1960): 531–61.

————. "Političke koncepcije Frana Supila," in Frano Supilo, *Politički spisi: Članci/Govori/Pisma/Memorandumi*, edited by Dragovan Šepić, 7–95. Zagreb: Znanje, 1970.

Seton-Watson, Hugh, and Christopher Seton-Watson. *The Making of a New Europe: R. W. Seton-Watson and the Last Years of Austria-Hungary*. Seattle: University of Washington Press, 1981.

Seton-Watson, Robert William. *Absolutism in Croatia*. London: Constable, 1913.

————. "Frano Supilo: A Southern Slav Patriot." *The New Europe* 4, no. 51 (October 4, 1917): 366–75.

————. *The Southern Slav Question and the Habsburg Monarchy*. New York: Howard Fertig, 1969.

Šidak, Jaroslav, et al. *Povijest hrvatskog naroda 1860–1914*. Zagreb: Školska knjiga, 1968.

————. *Hrvatski narodni preporod-Ilirski pokret*. Zagreb: Školska knjiga, 1988.

————. "Hrvatsko pitanje u Habsburškoj monarhiji." In *Studije iz hrvatske povijesti XIX stoljeća*. Zagreb: Sveučilište u Zagrebu, Institut za hrvatsku povijest, 1973.

Sirotković, Hodimir. "Pravni i politički aspekti procesa 'Reichspost'-Friedjung." In *Starine* 52 (Zagreb, 1962): 49–180.

Sirotković, Hodimir, and Lujo Margetić. *Povijest država i prava naroda SFR Jugoslavije*. Zagreb: Školska knjiga, 1988.

Slijepčević, Djoko. *Od početka XIX veka do kraja drugog svetskog rata*. V. 2 of *Istorija srpske pravoslavne crkve*. Munich, Iskra, 1966.

Smodlaka, Josip. *Zapisi dra Josipa Smodlake*. Edited by Marko Kostrenčić. Zagreb: Jugoslav akademija znanosti i umjetnosti, 1972.

Stajić, Vasa. "Milutin Jakšić (1863–1937)." *Godišnjak istoriskog društva u Novom Sadu* (Novi Sad) 12, pt. 1 (1939): 43–65.

Stančić, Nikša. "Problem 'Načertanije' Ilije Garašanina u našoj historiografiji." *Historijski zbornik* 21–22 (1968–1969): 179–96.

Stanković, Djordje. *Nikola Pašić i Jugoslovensko pitanje*. 2 vols. Belgrade: Beogradski izdavačko-graficki zavod, 1985.

Stojanović, Nikola [N. S., pseud.]. "Srbi i Hrvati." *Srpski književni glasnik* (Belgrade) 6, pt. 1 (August 1, 1902): 1149–59.

Stojančević, ed. *Od prvog ustanka do berlinskog knogresa, 1804–1878*. V. 5, *Istorija srpskog naroda*. Belgrade: Srpska književna zadruga, 1981.

Sugar, Peter, ed. *A History of Hungary*. Bloomington: Indiana University Press, 1990.

Supilo, Frano. *Politika u Hrvatskoj*. Edited with an introduction by Vaso Bogdanov. Zagreb: Kultura, 1953.

Tomasevich, Jozo. *Peasants, Politics, and Economic Change in Yugoslavia*. Stanford: Stanford University Press, 1955.

Tomić, Jaša. *Gde je srpska politika? i Samouprava napred*. Novi Sad: Srpska štamparija dra Sv. Miletića, 1911.

————. *Kako se zovemo (Srpsko i hrvatsko pitanje)*. Novi Sad: Srpska štamparija dra Svetozara Miletića, 1909.

————. *Reč našoj braći u Srbiji*. Novi Sad: Srpska štamparija dra Svetozara Miletića, 1907.

————. *Samostalci iz Hrvatske i Slavonije i Samostalci iz Srbije*. Novi Sad: Srpska štamparija dra Svetozara Miletića, 1907.

————. *Veleizdajnička parnica u Zagrebu*. Novi Sad: Srpska štamparija dra Sv. Miletića, 1909.

Turczynski, Emanuel. "The National Movement in the Greek Orthodox Church in the Habsburg Monarchy." In *Austrian History Yearbook* 3, pt. 3 (1967): 83–128.

Valentić, Mirko. *Vojna krajina i pitanje njezina sjedinjenja s Hrvatskom 1849–1881*. Zagreb: Sveučilište u Zagrebu, 1981.

Vucinich, Wayne. *Serbia Between East and West*. Stanford: Stanford University Press, 1954.

———. "The Serbs in Austria-Hungary." *Austrian History Yearbook* 3, pt. 2 (1967): 3–47.

Wilson, Duncan. *The Life and Times of Vuk Stefanović Karadžić, 1787–1864*. Oxford: Oxford University Press, 1970.

INDEX

Bosnia (1908), 123; on assassination of Aleksandar Obrenović, 66; biography of, 69–71; on collaborationism among Serbian voters, 94; and exit of Radicals from the Croato-Serbian Coalition, 103, 105; and formation of first Croato-Serbian Coalition government (1906), 87–89; and Friedjung trial, 131–33; and implementation of New Course, 75–76, 79, 80–82; leaves Croato-Serbian Coalition, 139–41; and origins of the New Course, 68–71; and Pribićević, compared, 137–38; and Railroad Pragmatic, 101; and Rauch regime in Croatia, 110, 117–21; and youth, 154–55

Šurmin, Djuro, 116, 123, 140, 142, 160, 165

Széll, Kálmán, 68

Taušanović, Kosta, 23

Tisza, István, 69, 75, 80, 152, 159–66

Tisza, Kálmán, 74

Tomašić, Nikola, 88, 138–40, 166; as ban of Croatia, 143–46, 151

Tomić, Jaša, 23, 38–39, 51, 53, 72, 146–47; and demonstrations of 1902, 56; and First World War, 170; in prison, 39; and Radicals' exit from the Croato-Serbian Coalition, 103; on the Rauch regime, 125; on Zadar Resolution, 85–86

Treaty of Karlowitz (1699), 3, 9, 11, 14

Trialism, 59, 123

Trumbić, Ante, 68, 70, 75–76, 82

Tudjman, Franjo, 170, 172

United Croatian and Serbian Youth, 47, 56

Unkelhäuser, Karl, 159

Ustaša, 171

Varaždin Generalcy, 7, 9–11

Vilder, Večeslav, 142

Vlachs, 5

Vrbanić, Fran, 56, 102

Wekerle, Sándor, 100, 104, 109, 138; and Rauch regime in Croatia, 110, 112, 114–15

Young Bosnia, 154

Young Croatia, 154

Yugoslavism, 26, 28, 32, 57–58, 148–49, 154

Zadar Resolution, 83–84, 92, 102

Zagorac, Stjepan, 101, 110, 118

Zagreb high treason trial (1909), 125–31

Zemun, 94–97

Žumberak, 6–7, 10, 14